AMERICAN HISTORY BY ERA

The Civil War:
1850–1895

VOLUME 5

Other titles in the
American History by Era series:

AMERICAN HISTORY BY ERA

The Civil War: 1850–1895

VOLUME 5

Auriana Ojeda, *Book Editor*

Daniel Leone, *President*
Bonnie Szumski, *Publisher*
Scott Barbour, *Managing Editor*

GREENHAVEN
PRESS®

THOMSON

GALE

San Diego • Detroit • New York • San Francisco • Cleveland
New Haven, Conn. • Waterville, Maine • London • Munich

For more information, contact
Greenhaven Press
27500 Drake Rd.
Farmington Hills, MI 48331-3535
Or you can visit our Internet site at http://www.gale.com

Cover inset photo credits (from left): Planet Art; Corel; Digital Stock; Corel; Library of Congress; Library of Congress; Digital Stock; Painet/Garry Rissman

Main cover photo credit: © Hulton/Archive by Getty Images

Dover Publications, 23, 132
Library of Congress, 21, 87, 102, 145, 169, 198, 241
National Archives, 48
North Wind Picture Archives, 16

LIBRARY OF CONGRESS CATALOGING-IN-PUBLICATION DATA
The Civil War : 1850–1895 / by Auriana Ojeda, book editor.
p. cm. — (American history by era; v. 5)
Includes bibliographical references and index.
ISBN 0-7377-1140-X (lib. bdg. : alk. paper) — ISBN 0-7377-1139-6 (pbk. : alk. paper)
1. United States—History—Civil War, 1861–1865—Juvenile literature. 2. United States—History—1849– 1877—Juvenile literature. 3. United States—History—1865–1898—Juvenile literature. [1. United States—History—Civil War, 1861–1865. 2. United States—History—1849–1877. 3. United States—History—1865– 1898.]
I. Title. II. Series.
E468 .O54 2003
973.7—dc21   2001007928

CONTENTS

The social outrage the novel caused contributed to the outbreak of war.

petuosity contributed to the attack on Fort Sumter
and initiated the Civil War.

slavery was not fully abolished until the ratification of the Thirteenth Amendment in 1865.

7. Surrender at Appomattox

Although the war officially ended on May 26, 1865, General Lee's surrender at Appomattox Courthouse in Virginia on April 9 represented the depletion and exhaustion of the Confederate army. The Rebels had proved excellent soldiers, but they were severely outnumbered by the Yankees.

Chapter 3: The Reconstruction Era

1. President Abraham Lincoln's Assassination

The assassination of President Abraham Lincoln shocked a nation that struggled to recover from the ravages of civil war. During his final hours, many former slaves gathered outside the White House and mourned the man who had set them free.

2. The Freedmen's Bureau

The Freedmen's Bureau provided food, clothing, and shelter to black and white Southerners during Reconstruction. Its purpose was to facilitate the transformation from slavery to freedom.

3. The Black Codes

After emancipation, white Southerners feared that the ex-slaves would threaten the white man's domination with unruly carousing and insolence. The Black Codes were sets of laws that regulated blacks' activities, and they were nearly as rigorous as slavery laws.

4. The Fourteenth Amendment

The Fourteenth Amendment conferred citizenship and all its rights and privileges to blacks. Although it was not ratified by all the states until 1868, it was an important step in protecting blacks' civil rights.

Chapter 4: The United States and the Native Americans Battle over Land Rights .

most of their land by the beginning of the twentieth century.

7. The Battle at Wounded Knee
The Battle at Wounded Knee was the last major
uprising staged by the Native Americans. Hundreds of Sioux were killed, and the battle marked
the final surrender of the Indians.

Chapter 5: The Gilded Age

1. The Industrial Revolution
In the Gilded Age, discoveries of abundant natural
resources, such as oil and iron, and technological
innovations contributed to the Industrial Revolution. America shifted from an agricultural society
to an industrial society.

2. Capitalism and Social Darwinism
Charles Darwin's theory of evolution characterized by the "survival of the fittest" was applied to
entrepreneurs and industrialists of the Gilded Age.
The strongest of society were extremely successful
and wealthy and others suffered terrible poverty.

3. The Growth of the Railroads
The expansion of transcontinental railroads benefited the economy and job market during the
Gilded Age. It not only improved transportation
for people and goods, but also freed up revenue
for investments and the market economy.

4. Immigration
The Gilded Age saw an enormous surge of immigrants from Europe and Asia. Drawn to America
by tales of wealth and opportunity, foreigners enjoyed more prosperity than at home, but also suffered from poverty and racism.

D uring the sixteenth century, events occurred in North America that would change the course of American history. In 1512, Spanish explorer Juan Ponce de León led the first European expedition to Florida. French navigator Jean Ribault established the first French colony in America at Fort Caroline in 1564. Over a decade later, in 1579, English pirate Francis Drake landed near San Francisco and claimed the country for England.

These three seemingly random events happened in different decades, occurred in various regions of America, and involved three different European nations. However, each discrete occurrence was part of a larger movement for European dominance over the New World. During the sixteenth century, Spain, France, and England vied for control of what was later to become the United States. Each nation was to leave behind a legacy that would shape the political structure, language, culture, and customs of the American people.

Examining such seemingly disparate events in tandem can help to emphasize the connections between them and generate an appreciation for the larger global forces of which they were a part. Greenhaven Press's American History by Era series provides students with a unique tool for examining American history in a way that allows them to see such connections. This series divides American history—from the time that the first people arrived in the New World from Asia to the September 11 terrorist attacks—into nine discrete periods. Each volume then presents a collection of both primary and secondary documents that describe the major events of the period in chronological order. This structure provides students with a snapshot of events occurring simultaneously in all parts of America. The reader can then gain an appreciation for the political, social, and cultural movements and trends that shaped the nation. Students reading about the adventures of individual European explorers, for instance, are invited to consider how such expeditions compared in purpose and consequence to earlier and later expeditions. Rather than simply learning that Ponce de León was the first Spaniard to try to colonize Florida, for example, students can begin to understand his expedition in a larger context. Indeed, Ponce's voyage was an extension of Spain's desire to conquer the Caribbean and Mexico, and his expedition was to inspire other Spanish explorers to head north from Hispaniola and New Spain in search of rich empires to conquer.

Another benefit of studying eras is that students can view a "snapshot" of America at any given moment of time and see the various social, cultural, and political events that occurred simultaneously. For example, during the period between 1920 and 1945, Charles Lindbergh became the first to make a solo transatlantic flight, Babe Ruth broke the record for the most home runs in one season, and the United States dropped the atomic bomb on Hiroshima. Random events occurring in post–Cold War America included the torching of the Branch Davidian compound in Waco, Texas, the emergence of the World Wide Web, and the 2000 presidential election debacle in which ballot miscounts in Florida held up election results for weeks.

Each volume in this series offers features to enhance students' understanding of the era of American history under discussion. An introductory essay provides an overview of the period, supplying essential context for the readings that follow. An annotated table of contents highlights the main point of each selection. A more in-depth introduction precedes each document, placing it in its particular historical context and offering biographical information about the author. A thorough chronology and index allow students to quickly reference specific events and dates. Finally, a bibliography opens up additional avenues of research. These features help to make the American History by Era series an extremely valuable tool for students researching the political upheavals, wars, cultural movements, scientific and technological advancements, and other events that mark the unfolding of American history.

During the Civil War era the U.S. government struggled to consolidate various states and territories, each of which had their own interests and concerns, into a single, unified nation. The North and the South were separate entities without much in common. Their differences became entrenched over the issue of slavery, and a war was fought to force the two virtually separate nations into a single nation under a single government. The Union victory ensured that the United States would continue to include its Southern portion, but since the victory was a military one, social issues such as slavery, states' rights, and westward expansion, remained. The government attempted to rectify some of these social problems during Reconstruction, but political conflicts slowed the reassimilation of Southern states into the Union and prevented unification.

After the Civil War the strength and unity of the fledgling country was tested. The government faced the daunting task of organizing a vast expanse of land into a unified nation. The fact that its citizens differed violently over how that land should be organized made the task even more difficult. The solution to the irreconcilable differences between the North and the South—the Civil War—eradicated the evil of slavery and sealed the splintered nation, but at an enormous cost. Thousands of lives were lost, and the Southern economy and landscape were devastated for generations. The Civil War era's legacy of racism and sectional controversy haunts America today.

SECTIONALISM AND POLITICAL REALIGNMENT

Two distinct Americas existed during the nineteenth century: the North and the South. New England and the mid-Atlantic states were the main centers of manufacturing, commerce, and finance, and their key products were textiles, machinery, woolen goods, clothing, leather, and lumber. The concentration of industry and factories in the North brought thousands of immigrants to its shores and greatly increased its population. The South remained primarily an agrarian society, and its population stagnated. The South produced mainly cotton but also rice, sugar, and tobacco. Unlike the North, the South had few manufacturing plants, which contributed to its defeat in the Civil War.

The economic systems of the North and the South motivated their respective positions on slavery. Cotton had been the largest and most important American export since the invention of the cotton gin in 1793. Northerners and Southerners alike depended on the valuable crop; the South produced thousands of bales of raw cotton that Northern manufacturers and shippers bought and profited from. By the 1850s, however, the Northern economy had expanded to include various industries, factories, crops, and transportation systems that relied on paid labor instead of slave labor. Northerners began to view slavery as unnecessary and inhumane, but Southerners still depended on slavery as their main source of labor. Although slaves were costly, supporting them was far more affordable to planters than paying free laborers to toil in the vast cotton fields.

While Northern industries began using paid labor, the South continued to rely on slave labor to maintain its cotton plantations.

Slavery soon became the major dissenting issue between the North and the South. The publication of Harriet Beecher Stowe's *Uncle Tom's Cabin* in 1854 fueled the growing antislavery movement in the North. The novel portrayed the brutality of slavery and how slave and free societies were fundamentally incompatible. Prior to the novel's publication, most of the antislavery groups were relatively moderate. Many suggested that slaves could be slowly assimilated into society, and that slaveholders should be compensated for the loss of their property. After the publication of Stowe's book, antislavery factions became more militant and demanded the complete abolition of slavery in the South. They also demanded that the territory acquired though the Mexican-American War, also known as the Mexican cession, be declared free areas. In response, Southerners argued that without the slave system, the South would be unable to produce the raw materials, such as cotton, that were necessary to the North's industrial economy.

Politics of the 1850s reflected much of this sectional unrest. The existing two-party political system of Whigs and Democrats was collapsing; the Whig party dissolved, and the Democratic Party splintered into Northern and Southern factions. A population boom in the North resulted in larger representation—and therefore stronger antislavery forces—in government. Southerners not only resented Northern antislavery activists, but they also thought that Northerners had an unfair majority in Congress. The conflict over slavery focused primarily on whether to admit the land acquired from Mexico in 1848 as slave or free.

SLAVERY AND WESTWARD EXPANSION

The Mexican-American War ended in 1848, and the United States won a large amount of land that would eventually become the states of California, Colorado, Nevada, Arizona, New Mexico, and Utah. Northerners wanted the new land to be admitted to the Union as free territory, and Southerners argued for popular sovereignty, which would allow the inhabitants of the territories to decide the issue of slavery. The Compromise of 1850 settled the slavery issues over the Mexican cession and temporarily resolved the dispute. Among its many provisions, the compromise allowed California to be admitted to the Union as a free state, but slavery would be legal in the other territories gained from Mexico. The compromise also granted Southern demands for protection of the interstate slave trade and a more stringent fugitive slave law.

Despite concessions to the North and the South, the North got the better end of the compromise. During the 1850s the South had an equal—if not slightly greater—voice in Congress as the North, but Southerners rightfully feared the ever-tipping political balance against slavery. California's admittance to the Union as a free state permanently swayed the senatorial balance in favor of the North. Even though slavery was legal in the other territories acquired from Mexico, Southerners knew that it was only a matter of time before the growing antislavery faction declared the area free. In addition, the new Fugitive Slave Law caused intense acrimony between the North and the South because the law required severe punishment for anyone who helped slaves escape their masters. Some Northerners were even required to assist slave catchers in hunting down fugitive slaves. Northerners resented being forced to perpetuate an institution that they were against, and Southerners protested Northern interference in the maintenance of their "property." These events deepened the chasm between the North and the South and brought the nation closer to war.

Though the Compromise of 1850 kept an uneasy peace between the North and the South, it made it difficult to resolve issues related to future territory. After the territory acquired from Mexico had been coordinated, attention turned to an expanse of unorganized territory now known as Kansas and Nebraska. Northerners wanted the area organized as free territory, and Southerners wanted slavery to be permitted. To resolve the dispute, Democratic senator Stephen A. Douglas introduced the Kansas-Nebraska Act, which decreed that the people who lived in those areas would decide the issue of slavery. Although the act intended to further westward expansion and settlement, it inflamed Northern abolitionist sentiment and exacerbated the conflict between the North and the South. Proslavery supporters celebrated the bill because it validated the constitutionality of slavery. Antislavery advocates were furious because the act repealed the Missouri Compromise, which prohibited slavery north of latitude 36°30'. They feared that the act heralded the expansion of slavery into western territories. In a direct response to the Kansas-Nebraska Act, antislavery activists formed a new political party—the Republican Party—whose primary agenda was to restrict the expansion of slavery into the territories.

THE ELECTION OF 1860 AND SECESSION

In 1858 little-known Illinois attorney Abraham Lincoln ran for the U.S. Senate against incumbent Democrat Stephen A. Douglas. Although Douglas won the election, their explosive debates made headlines, and Lincoln's perspectives on slavery gained him national attention. Lincoln was not an abolitionist—he maintained that the Constitution protected slavery in slave states—but he was opposed to the expansion of slavery and advocated free territory in the West. Lincoln claimed that the issue of slavery in the territories was crucial to the nation as a whole, and therefore could not be decided only by the inhabitants of the territories. His goal was to maintain the union of the United States, as secessionist rumblings could be heard from the South. The burgeoning Republican Party chose Lincoln as their candidate for the 1860 presidential election.

Southerners were outraged by the Republican nomination of Lincoln, whom they perceived as an ardent abolitionist. Douglas, the Democratic candidate, continued to advocate popular sovereignty in the territories, but his moderate position alienated his Southern constituency, who wanted him to take a more proslavery stance. Southern Democrats, therefore, nominated their own presidential candidate, John C. Breckinridge. Finally, the small Constitutional Union Party nominated John Bell as their candidate. Four candidates now competed for the votes of U.S. citizens.

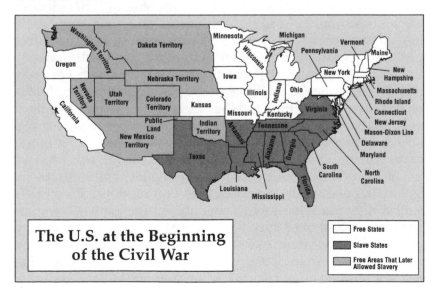

The U.S. at the Beginning of the Civil War

☐ Free States
■ Slave States
■ Free Areas That Later Allowed Slavery

Lincoln won the election by a narrow margin; he garnered only 40 percent of the popular vote, but he carried 180 electoral votes. South Carolina saw Lincoln's victory as a direct affront to the South and seceded on December 20, 1860. Several other states soon followed South Carolina's lead. The states seceded for a variety of reasons, most of which were related to slavery. They were alarmed by the shifting political balance against them, what they called the "despotic majority of numbers." They were disconcerted by the Northern Republican Party, whose growing support threatened the South's waning political power. Moreover, none of the states felt that they were doing anything wrong or immoral by leaving the Union. Most of them maintained that they were acting on the precedent of self-determination set by George Washington and the American Revolution in 1776: They were throwing off the yoke of an unreasonable ruler and forging their own destiny. Lincoln and other Northerners, however, argued that secession was a direct affront to the heroes of the American Revolution because it tore apart the very nation that Washington and others had struggled to liberate. Lincoln's goal, therefore, was to regain control of the seceded states and reunite the nation.

THE CONFEDERACY ATTACKS FORT SUMTER AND BEGINS THE CIVIL WAR

After South Carolina and the six other states seceded, the rebel South was now in possession of several federal forts. Lincoln was determined to hold onto the forts, and Southern rebels vowed to oust Union soldiers. When Confederate brigadier general Pierre G.T. Beauregard demanded that Union major Robert Anderson vacate Fort Sumter in Charleston, South Carolina, Anderson refused. On April 12, 1861, Confederate forces fired the first shot of the Civil War on Fort Sumter, and two days of shelling ensued. The fort was evacuated on April 14, and President Lincoln called for seventy-five thousand militiamen to prepare for war.

The Confederacy trounced the Union army in the first several battles of the war, including both battles of Bull Run, Fredericksburg, and Shiloh. However, the Union army grew considerably in size over the course of the war by enlisting blacks and immigrants, and it eventually outnumbered Confederate soldiers by five to two. Being primarily a war of attrition, this meant that the Union had the advantage in the war. Federals

On April 12, 1861, Confederate forces fired on Fort Sumter, signaling the beginning of the Civil War.

also bottled up the Confederate harbor, and plantation owners and farmers could not export cotton, which hurt the Confederate economy. The South lacked manufacturing plants for weapons and clothing; Rebel soldiers soon wore homespun uniforms and toted broken guns. As the war progressed, Union leadership combined with industrial and manpower advantages portended defeat for the Confederacy.

The Battle of Gettysburg in Pennsylvania brought these factors to a head. On July 1, 1863, Confederate soldiers invaded the town of Gettysburg in search of much-needed supplies and clashed with the Union army. Three days of intense fighting followed between Union general George McClellan's army and Confederate general Robert E. Lee's troops. Gettysburg was the bloodiest battle of the war; McClellan lost about twenty-three thousand men, and Lee lost about thirty-one thousand. Despite the fact that the Confederacy continued to fight for two more years, Gettysburg was a decisive victory for the North. The battle fired the morale of the Northern troops, and the loss of so many soldiers devastated the Rebel army.

The Civil War ended in April 1865 at Appomattox Court House, Virginia. General Lee had suffered a series of defeats and heavy losses. He attempted to retreat south along the line of the Appomattox River, but Union general Ulysses S. Grant

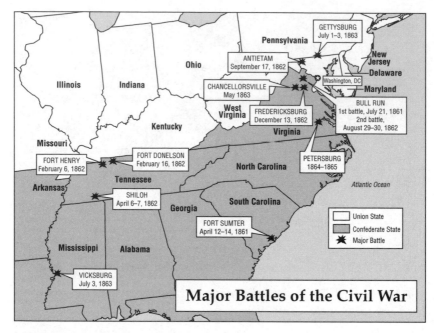

Major Battles of the Civil War

(Map labels: Illinois, Indiana, Ohio, Pennsylvania, New Jersey, Delaware, Maryland, Missouri, Kentucky, West Virginia, Virginia, North Carolina, Arkansas, Tennessee, South Carolina, Georgia, Mississippi, Alabama, Washington, DC, Atlantic Ocean)

GETTYSBURG July 1–3, 1863

ANTIETAM September 17, 1862

CHANCELLORSVILLE May 1863

BULL RUN 1st battle, July 21, 1861 2nd battle, August 29–30, 1862

FREDERICKSBURG December 13, 1862

FORT DONELSON February 16, 1862

PETERSBURG 1864–1865

FORT HENRY February 6, 1862

SHILOH April 6–7, 1862

FORT SUMTER April 12–14, 1861

VICKSBURG July 3, 1863

Union State
Confederate State
Major Battle

blocked him at every turn. Finally, Lee arrived at Appomattox Courthouse and found that the rations he had expected were not waiting for him. By this time Grant had cut off any further retreat. On April 9, 1865, General Robert E. Lee surrendered his army to General Grant and effectively ended the Civil War. The war officially ended on May 26, 1865.

Except for World War II, the Civil War was the most deadly in American history: In all, more than 1 million men were seriously injured or killed, and about 600,000 were killed in action or by disease. Every death was an American death. The white South lost almost an entire generation of young men. Total monetary costs of the war exceeded $15 billion, but other costs, such as broken families, fatherless children, destitute neighborhoods, and bitter memories, cannot be calculated. Despite these tragedies, most people would agree that the benefits of the Civil War far outweighed its negative consequences. The Union was once again physically whole, even though sectional bitterness and resentment would prohibit spiritual unity for decades.

RECONSTRUCTION AND POLITICAL DISSENSION

The ravages of war were evident in the South's landscape. Once-thriving cities such as Atlanta and Charleston had been gutted by invading armies. Social institutions were battered and dilapidated, churches were burned, schools were destroyed, and many teachers were killed in battle. Transportation avenues were devastated, and many miles of train tracks had been torn up, their rails heated and deformed. Agriculture, the mainstay of Southerners, was in shambles, as invading Union soldiers had ransacked plantations, burned cotton stores, plundered gardens, and slaughtered livestock. Seeds were scarce, and the once-flourishing cotton plantations now produced a bumper crop of weeds. Their labor source gone, formerly rich planters turned an awkward hand to plows, and magnolia-white Southern belles traded their prized pallor for the day laborer's burnished tan.

As Southerners struggled to find food and rebuild their lives, politicians in Washington, D.C., considered how to reconstruct the United States. The government was unsure of the constitutional status of the defeated states. President Lincoln and Congress debated whether the states had ever legally been out of the Union and whether to readmit them as states or as conquered provinces. Even before the war was over, the president and Congress bickered over how to treat the seceded states. Lincoln was more inclined to readmit the Confederacy as states of the Union, but radical members of Congress insisted that they were conquered territory that belonged to the federal government. In 1863 Lincoln introduced his 10-Percent Plan, which

Abraham Lincoln

promised recognition to the states that accepted his Emancipation Proclamation in which at least 10 percent of the voters would take an oath of allegiance to the Union. In 1864 radical Republicans responded to Lincoln's moderate plan with the Wade-Davis Bill. The Wade-Davis Bill required a provisional Union government in the Southern states until the end of the war and decreed that civil government would only be reestablished when 50 percent of the white male population took an oath of loyalty to the Union. It also prohibited any Southern man from voting if he had ranked a colonel or higher in the Confederate military. Lincoln pocket vetoed the bill—failed to

sign the bill within the ten days allowed by the Constitution—
and infuriated radical members of Congress.

After Lincoln's assassination in April 1865, radical Republicans realized that his successor, Andrew Johnson, would oppose them even more strongly than Lincoln had. Following Lincoln's plan, Johnson recognized the four Southern state governments that Lincoln had set up, and he began to organize provisional governments for the remaining seven states. In response, congressional radicals headed by Senator Thaddeus Stevens created the Joint Committee on Reconstruction. The committee enthusiastically endorsed the Fourteenth Amendment and demanded that no state be readmitted until it had ratified the amendment. The amendment declared that African Americans were citizens of the United States and also of the states in which they lived, and it granted them all the rights and privileges that citizenship conferred. Moreover, it provided that any state which denied blacks the vote would have its representation in Congress proportionately reduced. Although radicals hoped to guarantee a large portion of the former slave vote in their favor, many were also genuinely concerned with the welfare of the freedmen.

SOUTHERNERS AND CIVIL RIGHTS

Meanwhile, former Confederates struggled to regain local supremacy in the South. Unable to vote, white Southerners instituted new policies designed to oust the Republican government and dominate freedmen. Among these programs were the infamous Black Codes, first enacted by Mississippi in 1865. Black Codes were designed to regulate and inhibit the lives of former slaves; they controlled nearly every aspect of life and prohibited blacks from enjoying the freedom that they had just won. Mississippi's Black Code was one of the most rigid, and it demanded that freedmen work and refrain from idleness and vagrancy. It also dictated the work hours, duties, and acceptable behavior of former slaves.

Southerners also organized groups that strove to eliminate the Republican regime and maintain white superiority in the South. The most notorious of these groups was the Ku Klux Klan, first organized in Pulaski, Tennessee, in 1866. During the Reconstruction era, local government was weak or nonexistent, and there were fears of black outrages or even insurrections. In retaliation, unofficial vigilante groups sprouted in nearly every community in the South. Klansmen were widely known for their white robes, midnight rides, silent parades, and mysterious language and commands. They were extremely effective at playing upon fears and superstitions. Members of the Klan covered their horses in white robes and muffled their hooves; they dressed as dead Confederate soldiers returned from the battlefield in flowing white sheets and white masks, and they placed skulls at their saddle horns. Klansmen attacked mostly blacks, but they also targeted Republicans, scalawags (Southerners who had turned Republican), and carpetbaggers (Northerners who had come south seeking fortune after the war). Although they were often able to achieve their aims with terror alone, lynchings and whippings were common.

In an effort to protect blacks and manage chaotic Southern towns, Congress created the Freedmen's Bureau in March 1865, otherwise known as the Bureau of Refugees, Freedmen, and Abandoned Lands. The Freedmen's Bureau intended to help blacks in their transition from slavery to freedom. It provided food, shelter, clothing, medical care, and job services for former slaves and destitute Southern whites. It also built over one thousand black schools and helped found black colleges and teacher-training institutions. However, it had little success in safeguarding civil rights of freed slaves and controlling the lawlessness of many Southern communities. One year after the bureau's inception, President Johnson vetoed a bill extending its life, but in April 1866 such a bill passed over Johnson's veto. The Freedmen's Bureau was terminated in December 1868.

THE ELECTION OF 1876 AND THE END OF RECONSTRUCTION

The presidential election of 1876 was rife with fraud, but it effectively ended the Reconstruction era. The candidates, Republican Rutherford B. Hayes and Democrat Samuel Tilden, were both known as reformers: Tilden had almost single-handedly smashed the infamous Tweed Ring, a corrupt group of Democrats that had been running New York City for years. The era frowned on overt personal campaigning, as the presidencies of Andrew Johnson and Ulysses S. Grant—whose tenure as president from 1868 to 1876 consisted of administrative inaction and scandal—had drained much of the power and legitimacy from the office. Hayes, therefore, issued one printed statement that promised reform of civil service, education, money policy, and a pledge to serve only one term.

The election was extremely close. Tilden won the popular vote, but the count from four states—Oregon, Florida, South Carolina, and Louisiana—was disputed. Voter fraud was prevalent everywhere, as each party submitted their own vote tallies and claimed to have won the states' electors. Moreover, in the three Southern states, black voters had been kept from the polls with intimidation tactics. The Republican Party alleged that if the blacks had been allowed to vote, Hayes would have won those states. If Hayes could carry all four of the disputed states, he would win the election, but if Tilden secured any one of them, then the presidency was his.

Congress set up a bipartisan committee to solve the conflict. The committee decided that Rutherford B. Hayes would become the nineteenth president, but concessions were made to appease the Democratic South. The solution, known as the Compromise of 1877, pledged to withdraw all federal troops from the South, appoint a prominent Southern leader to the president's cabinet, and support funding for internal improvements in Southern states. Blacks called the compromise "the Great Betrayal" because withdrawal of federal troops guaranteed white rule of the South for generations. The Compromise of 1877 ended Reconstruction by returning local rule to Southern governments, but in doing so the Republican Party abandoned its commitment to black equality.

Many historians consider Reconstruction one of the most decisive failures in American government policy. The Union failed to close the social chasm between the North and the South, and attempts by Republicans to reestablish local governments in the South increased bitterness between the two parties. Northerners attempted to institute their ideals of national unity and human freedom in a region that still valued the principles of white superiority and states' rights. In hindsight, the radical Reconstruction policy might well have included social and economic improvement for blacks and whites in the South rather than treating Southerners as little more than conquered prisoners. As it was, Reconstruction failed to improve the status of black freedmen; they would have to wait almost one hundred years—until the civil rights era of the 1960s—to see justice and enjoy equal rights. Although the Union was restored, war-borne hatred and resentment continued to divide the nation.

The Civil War era answered the question that Abraham Lincoln put forth in his 1863 Gettysburg Address: whether a nation "conceived in liberty, and dedicated to the proposition that all men are created equal . . . can long endure." The chasm between the North and the South threatened the concepts of freedom, equality, and democracy that the founding fathers saw for the United States. The Union victory reaffirmed the political strength of the United States and ensured that the founding principles would continue, but the sentiment that had precipitated the split took decades to remedy. Throughout the Civil War era, America faced other challenges to its solidarity, such as assimilating Native Americans into white culture and an enormous wave of immigration just before the turn of the century. However, no challenge characterized the spirit of national unity as much as the Civil War and Reconstruction. Although Americans still struggle to cleanse the nation of the racism, bitterness, and sectional hatred that defined the Civil War era, they also enjoy the security of a unified nation.

Tension Mounts Between the North and South

CHAPTER 1

THE COMPROMISE OF 1850

ROBERT H. JONES

In 1850 arguments between proslavery and antislavery factions raged over whether to admit the new territory acquired from Mexico in 1848 as slave territory or free territory. Antislavery advocates maintained that the federal government should make slavery illegal in the territories. Proslavery groups argued for popular sovereignty, which would leave the slavery decision up to the voters in the territories. In an effort to quell the rising threat to the Union, Senator Henry Clay proposed a number of resolutions known as the Compromise of 1850. In the following article, Robert H. Jones contends that while the compromise made concessions to both the North and the South, it merely solved the immediate dispute without addressing the underlying conflict: Abolitionists favored a federal ban on slavery throughout the nation, while proslavery activists desired a state-by-state choice. Robert H. Jones is a distinguished scholar and Civil War historian.

C ongressmen who felt the preservation of the Union to be more important than sectional differences looked to Senator Henry Clay to work out a compromise. Along with many other politicians, Clay felt that if the difficult question of slavery could be ended in the political arena, the nation could deal with other demanding national problems in a less emotional atmosphere, and the danger to the Union and the division of political parties would come to an end for the time being. Clay hoped to bring "peace, concord, and harmony" to the Union.

Excerpted from *Disrupted Decades: The Civil War and Reconstruction Years* by Robert H. Jones (New York: Charles Scribner's Sons, 1973). Copyright © 1973 by Charles Scribner's Sons. Reprinted with permission.

CLAY'S PROPOSALS

On January 29, 1850, Clay introduced in the Senate a series of resolutions dealing with all the major questions at issue. They were:

1. Admit California as a free state.

2. Establish territorial governments in the remainder of the Mexican cession without any restrictions on slavery.

3. Establish a reasonable western boundary for Texas.

4. Assume the part of Texas' public debt contracted prior to annexation, provided Texas gives up her claim to part of New Mexico.

5. Abolish slavery in the District of Columbia only if the people of both Maryland and the District consent, and then only with compensation to slaveholders.

6. Prohibit the slave trade in the District of Columbia.

7. Enact a new and effective fugitive slave law.

8. Affirm that Congress has not the power to deal with the interstate slave trade.

Clay's resolutions touched off one of the greatest debates in American congressional history. For nearly nine months, not only in Congress, but across the nation, Americans wrestled with the effort to find a solution to the problems of the Union.

Clay, seventy-three years old, weak and in poor health, rose in the Senate to defend his resolutions on February 5, 1850. The galleries were so tightly packed that a correspondent for the New York *Tribune* could not get close enough to hear. Clay told the assemblage that his compromise measures would not involve the sacrifice of "any great principle" by either section. Yet concession, "not of principle, but of feeling" was necessary by both sides. The admission of California was standard procedure. But what of the application of the Wilmot Proviso [which excluded slavery from any territory acquired from Mexico] in the rest of the territory?

What do you want who reside in the free states? You want that there shall be no slavery introduced into the territories acquired from Mexico. Well, have you not got it in California already, if admitted as a state?

Have you not got it in New Mexico, in all human probability, also? What more do you want? You have what is worth a thousand Wilmot Provisos. You have got nature on your side.

On the subject of a new fugitive slave law Clay remarked that not only was it necessary in order to win Southern support for the compromise, but also "it is our duty to make the law more effective." Clay explained to the South the folly of secession. "War and dissolution of the Union are identical," he warned, painting a word picture of a fierce and bloody struggle of "interminable duration." He appealed to the common sense of both sides to prevent such a disaster, to quiet the clamor of the nation.

Senator John C. Calhoun continued the great oratorical contest with his speech on March 4, 1850. Very ill, unable to speak in person, Calhoun sat wrapped in flannels, his eyes half-closed while Virginia Senator James M. Mason read his speech. The "great and primary cause" of Southern discontent, Mason said, "is that the equilibrium between the two sections has been destroyed." . . . Many cords binding the states together had begun to snap. Religious ties had already broken, and he warned, "if the agitation goes on, the same force . . . will finally snap every cord," political and social as well as religious, and "nothing will be left to hold the states together except force."

LOOKING TO THE NORTH

The Union could be saved, Calhoun continued, but neither by Clay's compromise nor President Zachary Taylor's action. The North held the key. The North had to concede that the territories belonged to the South as well as the North, return the fugitive slaves, refrain from attacking slavery in the South, and consent to a constitutional amendment that would preserve equilibrium of the sections in Congress. California's admission to the Union would provide a test of Northern intentions, for if the North acted to admit California as a free state the North would be serving notice that it intended to "destroy irretrievably" the sectional balance. "If you who represent the stronger portion cannot agree to settle" the disputes between us "on the broad principle of justice and duty, say so; and let the states we both represent agree to separate and part in peace. . . ." Calhoun, who died within the month, had asked for complete capitulation by the North.

Three days later Senator Daniel Webster delivered his famous

"Seventh of March" speech, "the most important" of his life, he believed. Webster began: "I wish to speak today, not as a Massachusetts man, nor as a Northern man, but as an American. . . . I speak today for the preservation of the Union." He had no desire to disturb slavery where it exists, he said, and pledged "I will not violate the faith of the government." So far as California and New Mexico were concerned, Webster held "slavery to be excluded from those territories by a law even superior to that which admits and sanctions it" elsewhere. "I mean the law of nature." Webster admonished: "That law settled forever, with a strength beyond all terms of human enactment, that slavery cannot exist in California and New Mexico." For that reason, he would support "no Wilmot Proviso for the mere purpose of taunt or reproach. . . ."

On the burning question of fugitive slaves, knowing full well how his own section felt on the matter, Webster bravely asserted that he believed the complaints of the South had merit and that the North had failed to do its duty. Webster claimed Northern abolition societies were not "useful." For "the last twenty years [they] have produced nothing good or valuable," and have only added to division and perpetuated discord. Turning to the South, he warned as Clay had of the fallacy of peaceable secession. "Instead of speaking of the possibility or utility of secession, instead of dwelling in those caverns of darkness . . . let us come out into the light of day; let us enjoy the fresh air of liberty and union."

Northern reaction against Webster's speech was instantaneous. The Massachusetts legislature debated a resolution to instruct Webster to support the Wilmot Proviso, and though it failed to pass, social commentator Horace Mann lamented "Webster is a fallen star!" Congressman Theodore Parker, in a meeting at Boston's Faneuil Hall, said that he knew "no deed in American history done by a son of New England to which I can compare this but the act of traitor Benedict Arnold." Webster had slapped the abolitionists hard and punched them with his support of a new fugitive slave law. His career in Massachusetts seemed ended, a fact the Senator must have considered as he wrote his words. Courageously, he had been willing to trade his career and reputation for the preservation of the Union. Yet near the end of March 1850, eight hundred men of Boston sent him a testimonial for his "broad, national, and patriotic views." Webster won praise from the Washington, D.C., newspapers, and from the Charleston *Mercury.* Calhoun thought Webster showed a commendable "yielding on the part of the North."

Yet Webster changed few votes. Northern Whigs still remained faithful to Taylor; Southern Whigs divided between Clay and the Democrats; and the Democrats remained divided between Calhoun and those who followed Douglas, who supported Clay. Outside of Congress, Webster probably swung a segment of Northern opinion toward compromise.

OPPOSING ARGUMENTS

Senator William H. Seward spoke on March 11, 1850. Although a novice in Congress, he was well known as a former governor of New York and as an able lawyer. Seward echoed the antislavery views of his friend John Quincy Adams, and his fellow Whigs knew he would lash out against the compromise. They were not disappointed. Supporting the admission of California, Seward stated, "I am opposed to any such compromise, in any and all the forms in which it has been proposed." He told the South they were "entitled to no more stringent [fugitive slave] laws; and that such laws would be useless," for no government has ever succeeded in "changing the moral convictions of its subjects by force." In regard to the territories, Seward remarked that although the Constitution regulated the nation's stewardship, "there is a higher law than the Constitution." On the question of secesssion he proved more prophetic than any of the other speakers. He asked his audience whether the Union should remain as it is and slavery be gradually removed by peaceful means, or whether the Union should be dissolved and civil war follow, "bringing on violent but complete and immediate emancipation." The South balked at Seward's assumption that slavery would perish one way or another, but that was Seward's view, and in that light the sectional quarrel was useless. "You cannot roll back the tide of social progress." Seward closed with an appeal for the Union.

A friend of President Taylor and a leader of the "conscience" Whigs of the North, Seward had shocked no one by his support of Taylor's position on California nor by his defense of Northern efforts to protect fugitive slaves nor by his desire to keep slavery out of the territories. What stunned Southerners and disturbed even Taylor was Seward's reference to "a higher law." That also troubled New York political boss Thurlow Weed, an associate of Seward's. Seward had put into political terms the notion that manmade laws and God's laws must be compatible for law to be meaningful, a notion Transcendentalists like Ralph Waldo Emerson had propounded earlier.

Senator Jefferson Davis spoke on March 13, 1850. He advocated nonintervention in Southern affairs and equal rights in the territories. He agreed to an extension of the Missouri Compromise line west through the territories acquired from Mexico. By mid-March all positions had been heard. Clay, the Southern Whig, spoke for his compromise; Calhoun, the Southern Democrat, had denounced it; Webster, the Northern Whig, had supported it; Seward, another Northern Whig had opposed it; and Davis, another Southern Democrat, had opposed it. Others spoke, echoing or expanding the speeches of these men. The debate became so heated that the venerable Senator Thomas Hart Benton of Missouri physically threatened Senator Henry S. Foote of Mississippi who had taunted him as a traitor to the South. Benton chased Foote from his seat. Foote fled to the foot of the rostrum, drew a loaded revolver, and aimed at Benton. Their colleagues intervened in the nick of time.

On April 18, 1850, Clay's resolutions were referred to a fairly moderate committee chosen on sectional lines. On May 8 they reported back to the Senate a somewhat altered set of resolutions, and the debate continued for another five months. Senators Clay, Webster, Cass, Douglas, and Foote argued in favor of the committee position; Senators Seward, Chase, Benton, and Davis joined President Taylor in opposition. Ironically, the opposition included the Northern Whig and Southern Democrat extremists, while the supporters included Whig and Democrat moderates from both sections. Hanging over a successful compromise bill, should one pass, was the cloud of Taylor's possible veto.

PUBLIC SUPPORT

Outside of Congress, as the spring and summer of 1850 wore on, public sentiment appeared to favor adoption of the compromise. The nation enjoyed the rising prosperity that followed the expansion of the railroads, the influx of gold from California's mines, the increase of foreign trade, and the growth of industry. Businessmen hesitated to support any measure but compromise for fear of blocking the road to increased profits with sectional disruption. Northern merchants and manufacturers hoped to conciliate the angry South and preserve their lucrative markets, and Southern cotton producers and brokers wanted nothing to interrupt their booming foreign trade. The moderates took over the Nashville convention and recessed to watch the outcome of events in Congress.

During the summer the various impediments to compromise began to dissolve. President Taylor died July 9, of an illness that began July 4, probably acute gastroenteritis. Millard Fillmore of New York, a Whig who had supported John Quincy Adams in the House fight over the gag rule, succeeded to the presidency. Fillmore appointed Webster to the top State Department post, and Clay became a White House spokesman. The compromise now received the backing of the administration. Clay, worn out by his futile attempts to get his omnibus measure passed and by the summer's heat in Washington, left the capital early in August for a month's rest in New England by the sea. Inadvertently, by keeping the compromise measures together in one bill, the "omnibus bill," had drawn "all the malcontents" into combination against it. Clay's absence gave Illinois Senator Stephen A. Douglas the opportunity to submit the compromise as a series of individual bills, which he believed would pass singly, with different majorities on each. Where it had been impossible to obtain a single majority for the omnibus bill, it was now possible to win the vote. In order of passage, the Compromise of 1850 included these separate laws as it left the Senate:

1. Texas relinquished her claim to New Mexico's territory for $10,000,000 (the vote was 30 to 20, with the opposition including 12 Southerners and 8 Northerners, mainly extremists from both sections).

2. California was admitted as a free state (the vote was 34 to 18, with 26 of the yea votes from Northern Democrats and Whigs, and all of the negative votes from Southerners, mostly Democrats).

3. New Mexico was created as a territory without reference to the Wilmot Proviso (27 to 10, all negatives from the North).

4. A new and tougher fugitive slave law was enacted (27 to 12, 8 Northern Whigs, 3 Northern Democrats, and Free-Soiler Chase opposed; 15 Northern senators did not vote).

5. Slave trade in the District of Columbia was abol-

ished (33 to 19, 13 Southern Democrats and 6 Southern Whigs opposed).

Douglas had been correct. He had succeeded in getting the Senate to pass the measures individually, and in so doing, was able to pass the substance of Clay's compromise.

The House of Representatives made a few changes in the final compromise, but the whole secured easier approval than in the Senate. As signed by Fillmore in September, the final version looked like this:

1. New Mexico was created a territory without the Wilmot Proviso, and Texas's claim to part of New Mexico was vacated for an indemnity of $10,000,000.

2. California was admitted as a free state.

3. Utah was created a territory without the Wilmot Proviso.

4. A more stringent fugitive slave law was enacted.

5. The slave trade was abolished in the District of Columbia.

SUBSEQUENT TENSIONS

America remained on edge even after the compromise passed, for it meant nothing if the nation did not accept it. The political parties were badly scarred by the sectional issues, a bad omen indeed. The Nashville Convention [a group of Southern politicians that favored slavery] reassembled in November, denounced the Compromise of 1850, and urged that a new convention meet to discuss ways of protecting slavery or to consider secession. Alabama, Georgia, Mississippi, and South Carolina convoked special state conventions to discuss secession, and hope for the compromise looked bleak. But the Nashville Convention's recommendations were not followed; in the last analysis none of the four state conventions favored secession, although South Carolina would have moved in that direction had she had support. Sentiment throughout the South echoed the Georgia convention's resolutions: Georgia accepted the compromise as a "permanent" solution to the problem of sectionalism but warned the North that preservation of the Union depended upon how well the North observed the new fugitive slave law.

That new fugitive slave law was bitter medicine for the North. Under the new provisions, anyone accused of being a fugitive was not allowed to testify, had no right to a jury trial, and could be turned over to his master or his master's agent with only an affidavit or a sworn statement that the fugitive belonged to the master. The fugitive's fate was decided by either a federal judge or a court-appointed commissioner. The act contained *ex post facto* provisions, for it applied to any slave who had escaped at any time in the past. A commissioner earned $10 for a decision in favor of the master, $5 for one in favor of the fugitive. Federal marshals and their deputies were directed to enforce the act, and anyone convicted of aiding a fugitive faced a fine of up to $1,000 or six months in prison, plus liability in a civil suit of $1,000 damages to the slave owner. Obviously the law was aimed squarely at the abolitionists.

Fillmore might have vetoed the act had it appeared clearly unconstitutional to him, and he was not certain but that it would fail to stand up to Supreme Court scrutiny. Yet Attorney General John J. Crittenden advised Fillmore the law was constitutional, and so did Webster, whose opinion Fillmore also sought. Constitutionality aside, if Fillmore had vetoed the measure, he would probably have destroyed the compromise and reopened the entire slavery debate. He had little choice.

BLACKS REJECT THE COMPROMISE

In Boston, within days of the passage of the fugitive slave act, 40 former slaves departed for Canada. Before the law was signed, an estimated 200 blacks left Pittsburgh for north of the border, and 600 more joined them shortly. Others followed. Black churches suddenly lost their members. Other blacks remained to fight. Throughout the North, antifugitive slave law meetings were held. A particularly large one took place in New York in October, where about 1,500 black New Yorkers listened to Speaker William P. Powell; asked if they would submit peacefully, if they would kiss their chains, they shouted in reply, "No, no!" They dispatched petitions denouncing the law to the state legislature and to Congress. Black commentator Robert Purvis told a meeting of the Pennsylvania Anti-Slavery Society that if "any pale-faced spectre" entered his house to execute the fugitive slave law, "I'll seek his life, I'll shed his blood." All across the North, the reaction of the black community was similar.

Northern white reaction was divided. At Faneuil Hall in

Boston on October 14, Congressman Charles Francis Adams presided over a meeting where politicians Theodore Parker and Wendell Phillips urged the audience to action, denouncing the fugitive slave law as contrary to God's law, the Declaration of Independence, and the Constitution. In Chicago, almost half a continent away, the city council agreed and likened those who voted for the law to the "traitors Benedict Arnold and Judas Iscariot." Yet in November, Congressman Charles Sumner told another meeting at Faneuil Hall that he advised "no violence" on the question. Let the power of public opinion make the bill "a dead letter," he said. Sumner's moderation was taken a step farther by Douglas at a large meeting in Chicago, where he pushed through a resolution that all of Congress's laws ought to be obeyed.

In fact, most Northern agitations seemed to be in support of the compromise. Bostonians saluted the measure with a hundred-gun salute fired on the Commons. Called by a petition said to be signed by 10,000 people, a Union meeting in New York City enthusiastically approved the compromise, including the fugitive slave law. Other large meetings in New York, Pennsylvania, and Ohio thundered their approval as well. In January 1851, 44 congressmen from both major parties and sections signed a pledge to oppose any candidate for office who did not accept the compromise as final.

THE FUGITIVE SLAVE LAW OF 1850

STANLEY FELDSTEIN

One of the provisions of the Compromise of 1850 was the Fugitive Slave Law. According to Stanley Feldstein, the law empowered marshals to arrest suspected fugitives and return them to slavery without the benefit of a trial. It required civilians to assist marshals in the capture of alleged runaways in both slave states and free states. Feldstein contends that Southern slaveholders celebrated the law because it allowed them unrestricted power to apprehend their runaway slaves. Northern free-state citizens argued that the law enabled other states to usurp laws that protected freedom in free states. The law intensified the strained relations between the North and South and brought the Union closer to war. Feldstein is the author of *Once a Slave: The Slaves' View of Slavery* and *The Land That I Show You: Three Centuries of Jewish Life in America*.

A n analysis of [slave] narratives indicates that perhaps the single most significant issue of the mid–nineteenth century was the enactment, interpretation, enforcement, and effect of the Fugitive Slave Law of 1850. So great was their concern about this matter, and so thorough was their analysis of it, that the gamut of their emotional responses to it ranged from anger and fear to relief and gratitude.

William Green, for example, felt that although the law caused a great deal of misery, it also did a great deal of good, in that it caused many hitherto docile fugitives to seek the sanctuary of

Canada and it aroused the abolitionist sentiments of many previously apathetic free whites.

Green asserted that with the passage of this law, Negroes, both free and bond, recognized that in the land of their birth and of their fathers they could no longer find repose under the Constitution. Many realized that they must now flee from the land of republicanism to a monarchial one, in order to enjoy freedom. By this law, passed in Congress in 1850, all slaves who had escaped from bondage and had taken refuge in the free states were subject to recapture at any subsequent time. James Watkins said, "so cruel and relentless it is, that it makes punishable with fine and imprisonment any parties who may be convicted of giving even a cup of cold water to one of these sons of sorrow and wretchedness."

VIOLATING THE RIGHT TO DUE PROCESS

According to Watkins, the sixth section of the law alone, which stated, "In no trial or hearing under this act shall the testimony of such alleged fugitive be admitted in evidence," was enough to condemn the whole act, for it was a clear violation of the Fifth Amendment's due process guarantee. It was, said Watkins, also a violation of the Constitution of each free state, which guaranteed personal liberty to all, unless deprived of it by "due process of law," and maintained that the right of trial by jury shall be inviolate.

As interpreted by the courts, the bare testimony of the slaveholder was sufficient evidence of his right to the return of the fugitive, and the alleged fugitive was not permitted to procure or produce evidence to establish his freedom. Watkins reported a case in Detroit, where a Negro was brought before the court as a fugitive. Counsel for the defendant presented an affidavit of the slave which averred that he was manumitted by deed of his claimants for seven hundred dollars, which they had received, and that the deed was in the possession of the defendant's friends in Cincinnati. Based upon this affidavit, counsel moved that the case be continued until the deeds of emancipation could be procured and brought to court. The court denied the motion on the ground that a continuance was unnecessary as the deed would be inadmissible even if produced; that the court had no power to inquire into any defense the Negro might have against the claim; and that its jurisdiction was limited to a determination of whether the case presented on the part of the claimants was sufficient to entitle them to a certificate of removal for the Negro. This being the decision of the court, Watkins claimed that "no coloured man North can be safe for a single day."

According to Watkins, the worst part of the law to the non-slaveholders was that, by its seventh section, this "atrocious and abominable law made it a crime, punishable with heavy fines and imprisonment, to be either directly or indirectly a party to the escape of a slave." In addition, the slave hunters were empowered to call for the aid of free citizens in carrying out these provisions, and any one who refused was also exposed to a heavy penalty. What was most astounding to Watkins was that this law had "the patronage and support of the ministers of religions in the slaveholding states."

Ex-slave Harriet Tubman asserted that she could "trust Uncle Sam wid my people no longer," and that the law had "brought 'em all clear off to Canada." She claimed that while the free states sustained the law which hurled the fugitives back into slavery, it was impossible for the Negro to become a man.

CONTROLLING FREE STATES

Ex-slave Austin Steward felt that with the passage of this law, the free states had no right to feel that they owned no slaves or were not connected with the system. It might have been true that the law of the free states prohibited the holding of slaves, but

> is the poor, flying fugitive from the house of bondage, safe one moment within your borders? Will he be welcome to your homes, tables, your firesides? Will your clergyman bid you clothe and feed him, or give him a cup of cold water. . . . Or will your own miserable Fugitive Slave Law close the mouth of your clergy, crush down the rising benevolence of your heart; and convert you into a human blood hound, to hunt down the panting fugitive, and return him to the hell of slavery?

Steward recognized, of course, that there were some in the free states who would violate the law. A few did remain who "in defiance of iniquitous laws, throw open wide their doors to the trembling, fleeing bondman." These people, he claimed, did help the fugitive on his way to Canada, but it was done at night and quietly, making no noise, "lest an United States' marshall wrest from you the object of your Christian sympathy, and impose on you a heavy fine, for your daring to do to another as you would he should do to you."

Slave hunting in the free states was, according to ex-slave Linda Brent, "the beginning of a reign of terror to the colored population." Many families who had lived in freedom for years fled from it now. A slave discovered that his husband or wife was formerly a fugitive and had to escape to insure his own safety. Even worse, because a child followed the condition of its mother, the Negro discovered that the children of a family with even one slave parent were liable to be seized and carried into slavery. In every free state there was consternation and anguish, but, asked Miss Brent, "what cared the legislators of the 'dominant race' for the blood they were crushing out of trampled hearts?"

FUGITIVE SLAVE MISERIES

Miss Brent described some of the miseries brought on by the passage of this law. Few Negroes ventured into the streets; only when necessary did they leave their homes, and when they did, they traveled as much as possible through back streets. They considered it a disgrace for a city to call itself free, when "inhabitants, guiltless of offense, and seeking to perform their duties conscientiously, should be condemned to live in such incessant fear, and have nowhere to turn for protection!" Impromptu vigilance committees were formed. Every black person and every friend of the Negro was on constant watch, and evening newspapers were examined carefully "to see what Southerners had put up at the hotels."

Ex-slave William Parker confirmed the reports of Linda Brent, and stated that in the free cities, both whites and blacks were fully resolved to leave no means untried to thwart "the barbarous and inhuman monsters who crawled in the gloom of midnight, like the ferocious tiger, and, stealthily springing on their unsuspecting victims, seized, bound, and hurled them into the ever open jaws of slavery." Parker reported that the anti-slavery people united together, regardless of all personal considerations, to save the fugitive from capture. They thoroughly examined all matters connected with the law, and were cognizant of the plans adopted to carry it out. This was generally accomplished through correspondence with reliable persons in various sections of the slave states, and thus the vigilance com-

mittees knew the slave hunters, their agents, spies and betray-
ers. Parker asserted that the business of slave hunting was conducted by only a few men "willing to degrade themselves by
doing the dirty work of four-legged blood hounds." According
to Parker, the slave hunters consorted with constables, police
officers, aldermen, and even with mentors of the legal profes-
sions "who disgraced their respectable calling by low, con-
temptible acts, and were willing to clasp hands with the lowest
ruffian in order to pocket the reward that was the price of
blood." Every official facility was offered the slave hunter, and

> whether it was night or day, it was only necessary to
> whisper in a certain circle that a negro was to be
> caught, and horses and wagons, men and officers,
> spies and betrayers, were ready, at the shortest notice,
> armed and equipped, and eager for the chase.

The Fugitive Slave Law, asserted ex-slave Samuel R. Ward,
stripped the Negro of all manner of protection, of the writ of
habeas corpus, of trial by jury, or of any other law of civilized nations. There were no longer any legal safeguards of personal liberty, and the fugitive was thrown back upon only the natural
rights of self-defense and self-protection. The law solemnly referred to each Negro, fugitive and free, the question of whether
he would submit to being enslaved or whether he would protect himself, even if in so doing he risked his life. It gave the
fugitive the alternative of dying free or living as a slave. Thus,
Ward warned,

> Let the men who would execute this bill beware. Let
> them know that the business of catching slaves, or
> kidnapping freemen, is an open warfare upon the
> rights and liberties of the black men of the North. Let
> them know that to enlist in that warfare is present,
> certain, inevitable death and damnation. Let us teach
> them, that none should engage in this business, but
> those who are ready to be offered up on the polluted
> altar of accursed slavery . . . let all the black men of
> America say, and we shall teach Southern slavecrats,
> and Northern dough-faces, that to perpetuate the
> union, they must beware how they expose *us* to slav-
> ery, and themselves to death and destruction, present
> and future, temporal and eternal!

UNCLE TOM'S CABIN

HARRIET BEECHER STOWE

When President Abraham Lincoln met Harriet Beecher Stowe in 1863, he referred to her as "the little lady who made this big war." *Uncle Tom's Cabin* strengthened the animosity between the North and South. Northerners were shocked by Stowe's portrayal of the cruelties that slaves endured, and Southerners maintained that she exaggerated the evils of slavery and slaveholders. The following excerpt from the novel comes from a chapter entitled "A Select Incident of Lawful Trade." Haley is a slave-trader and has already bought Tom, the main character. On a boat trip down the Ohio River with Tom, Haley stops and buys other slaves at several auctions, including a young woman named Lucy and her baby. Haley's treatment of Lucy and her baby defines the indifference with which many slave-traders separated families and the agony that slaves suffered at the loss of their loved ones. Harriet Beecher Stowe (1811–1896) was the daughter and sister of two nineteenth-century American theologians.

M r. Haley pulled out of his pocket sundry newspapers, and began looking over their advertisements, with absorbed interest. He was not a remarkably fluent reader, and was in the habit of reading in a sort of recitative half-aloud, by way of calling in his ears to verify the deductions of his eyes. In this tone he slowly recited the following paragraph:

"EXECUTOR'S SALE,—NEGROES!—*Agreeably to order of court, will be sold, on Tuesday, February 20, before the Court-house door, in the town of Washington, Kentucky, the following negroes: Hagar, aged 60; John, aged 30; Ben, aged*

Excerpted from *Uncle Tom's Cabin* by Harriet Beecher Stowe (New York: Penguin, 1852).

21; Saul, aged 25; Albert, aged 14. Sold for the benefit of the creditors and heirs of the estate of Jesse Blutchford, Esq.

SAMUEL MORRIS,
THOMAS FLINT,
Executors."

"This yer I must look at," said he to Tom, for want of somebody else to talk to.

"Ye see, I'm going to get up a prime gang to take down with ye, Tom; it'll make it sociable and pleasant like,—good company will, ye know. We must drive right to Washington first and foremost, and then I'll clap you into jail, while I does the business.". . .

About eleven o'clock the next day, a mixed throng was gathered around the court-house steps,—smoking, chewing, spitting, swearing, and conversing, according to their respective tastes and turns,—waiting for the auction to commence. The men and women to be sold sat in a group apart, talking in a low tone to each other. The woman who had been advertised by the name of Hagar was a regular African in feature and figure. She might have been sixty, but was older than that by hard work and disease, was partially blind, and somewhat crippled with rheumatism. By her side stood her only remaining son, Albert, a bright-looking little fellow of fourteen years. The boy was the only survivor of a large family, who had been successively sold away from her to a southern market. The mother held on to him with both her shaking hands, and eyed with intense trepidation every one who walked up to examine him.

"Don't be feard, Aunt Hagar," said the oldest of the men, "I spoke to Mas'r Thomas 'bout it, and he thought he might manage to sell you in a lot both together."

"Dey needn't call me worn out yet," said she, lifting her shaking hands. "I can cook yet, and scrub, and scour,—I'm wuth a buying, if I do come cheap;—tell em dat ar,—you *tell* em," she added, earnestly.

Haley here forced his way into the group, walked up to the old man, pulled his mouth open and looked in, felt of his teeth, made him stand and straighten himself, bend his back, and perform various evolutions to show his muscles; and then passed on to the next, and put him through the same trial. Walking up last to the boy, he felt of his arms, straightened his hands, and looked at his fingers, and made him jump, to show his agility.

"He an't gwine to be sold widout me!" said the old woman, with passionate eagerness; "he and I goes in a lot together; I's rail strong yet, Mas'r and can do heaps o' work,—heaps on it, Mas'r."

"On plantation?" said Haley, with a contemptuous glance. "Likely story!" and, as if satisfied with his examination, he walked out and looked, and stood with his hands in his pocket, his cigar in his mouth, and his hat cocked on one side, ready for action.

"What think of 'em?" said a man who had been following Haley's examination, as if to make up his own mind from it.

"Wal," said Haley, spitting, "I shall put in, I think, for the youngerly ones and the boy."

"They want to sell the boy and the old woman together," said the man.

"'Find it a tight pull;—why, she's an old rack o' bones,—not worth her salt."

"You wouldn't then?" said the man.

"Anybody 'd be a fool 't would. She's half blind, crooked with rheumatis, and foolish to boot."

"Some buys up these yer old critturs, and ses there's a sight more wear in 'em than a body 'd think," said the man, reflectively.

"No go, 't all," said Haley; "wouldn't take her for a present,—fact,—I've *seen*, now."

"Wal, 't is kinder pity, now, not to buy her with her son,—her heart seems so sot on him,—s'pose they fling her in cheap."

"Them that's got money to spend that ar way, it's all well enough. I shall bid off on that ar boy for a plantation-hand;—wouldn't be bothered with her, no way,—not if they'd give her to me," said Haley.

"She'll take on desp't," said the man.

"Nat'lly, she will," said the trader, coolly.

The conversation was here interrupted by a busy hum in the audience; and the auctioneer, a short, bustling, important fellow, elbowed his way into the crowd. The old woman drew in her breath, and caught instinctively at her son.

"Keep close to yer mammy, Albert,—close,—dey'll put us up togedder," she said.

"O, mammy, I'm feard they won't," said the boy.

"Dey must, child; I can't live, no ways, if they don't" said the old creature, vehemently.

The stentorian tones of the auctioneer, calling out to clear the way, now announced that the sale was about to commence. A place was cleared, and the bidding began. The different men on the list were soon knocked off at prices which showed a pretty brisk demand in the market; two of them fell to Haley.

"Come, now, young un," said the auctioneer, giving the boy a touch with his hammer, "be up and show your springs, now."

"Put us two up togedder, togedder,—do please, Mas'r," said the old woman, holding fast to her boy.

"Be off," said the man, gruffly, pushing her hands away; "you come last. Now, darkey, spring;" and, with the word, he pushed the boy toward the block, while a deep, heavy groan rose behind him. The boy paused, and looked back; but there was no time to stay, and, dashing the tears from his large, bright eyes, he was up in a moment.

His fine figure, alert limbs, and bright face, raised an instant competition, and half a dozen bids simultaneously met the ear of the auctioneer. Anxious, half-frightened, he looked from side to side, as he heard the clatter of contending bids,—now here, now there,—till the hammer fell. Haley had got him. He was pushed from the block toward his new master, but stopped one moment, and looked back, when his poor old mother, trembling in every limb, held out her shaking hands toward him.

"Buy me too, Mas'r, for de dear Lord's sake!—buy me,—I shall die if you don't!"

"You'll die if I do, that's the kink of it," said Haley,—"no!" And he turned on his heel.

The bidding for the poor old creature was summary. The man who had addressed Haley, and who seemed not destitute of compassion, bought her for a trifle, and the spectators began to disperse.

The poor victims of the sale, who had been brought up in one place together for years, gathered round the despairing old mother, whose agony was pitiful to see.

"Couldn't dey leave me one? Mas'r allers said I should have one,—he did," she repeated over and over, in heart-broken tones.

"Trust in the Lord, Aunt Hagar," said the oldest of the men, sorrowfully.

"What good will it do?" said she, sobbing passionately.

"Mother, mother,—don't! don't!" said the boy. "They say you's got a good master."

"I don't care,—I don't care. O, Albert! oh, my boy! you's my last baby. Lord, how ken I?"

"Come, take her off, can't some of ye?" said Haley, dryly; "don't do no good for her to go on that ar way."

The old men of the company, partly by persuasion and partly by force, loosed the poor creature's last despairing hold, and, as they led her off to her new master's wagon, strove to comfort her.

"Now!" said Haley, pushing his three purchases together, and producing a bundle of handcuffs, which he proceeded to put on their wrists; and fastening each handcuff to a long chain, he drove them before him to the jail.

Harriet Beecher Stowe

A few days saw Haley, with his possessions, safely deposited on one of the Ohio boats. It was the commencement of his gang, to be augmented, as the boat moved on, by various other merchandise of the same kind, which he, or his agent, had stored for him in various points along shore.

The La Belle Rivière, as brave and beautiful a boat as ever walked the waters of her namesake river, was floating gayly down the stream, under a brilliant sky, the stripes and stars of free America waving and fluttering over head; the guards crowded with well-dressed ladies and gentlemen walking and enjoying the delightful day. All was full of life, buoyant and rejoicing;—all but Haley's gang, who were stored, with other freight, on the lower deck, and who, somehow, did not seem to appreciate their various privileges, as they sat in a knot, talking to each other in low tones.

"Boys," said Haley, coming up, briskly, "I hope you keep up good heart, and are cheerful. Now, no sulks, ye see; keep stiff upper lip, boys; do well by me, and I'll do well by you."

The boys addressed responded the invariable "Yes, Mas'r," for ages the watchword of poor Africa; but it's to be owned they did not look particularly cheerful; they had their various little prejudices in favor of wives, mothers, sisters, and children, seen for the last time,—and though "they that wasted them required of them mirth," it was not instantly forthcoming.

"I've got a wife," spoke out the article enumerated as "John, aged thirty," and he laid his chained hand on Tom's knee,— "and she don't know a word about this, poor girl!"

"Where does she live?" said Tom.

"In a tavern a piece down here," said John; "I wish, now, I *could* see her once more in this world," he added.

Poor John! It *was* rather natural; and the tears that fell, as he spoke, came as naturally as if he had been a white man. Tom drew a long breath from a sore heart, and tried, in his poor way, to comfort him.

And over head, in the cabin, sat fathers and mothers, husbands and wives; and merry, dancing children moved round among them, like so many little butterflies, and everything was going on quite easy and comfortable.

"O, mamma," said a boy, who had just come up from below, "there's a negro trader on board, and he's brought four or five slaves down there."

"Poor creatures!" said the mother, in a tone between grief and indignation.

"What's that?" said another lady.

"Some poor slaves below," said the mother.

"And they've got chains on," said the boy.

"What a shame to our country that such sights are to be seen!" said another lady.

"O, there's a great deal to be said on both sides of the subject," said a genteel woman, who sat at her state-room door sewing, while her little girl and boy were playing round her. "I've been south, and I must say I think the negroes are better off than they would be to be free."

"In some respects, some of them are well off, I grant," said the lady to whose remark she had answered. "The most dreadful part of slavery, to my-mind, is its outrages on the feelings and affections,—the separating of families, for example."

"That *is* a bad thing, certainly," said the other lady, holding up a baby's dress she had just completed, and looking intently on its trimmings; "but then, I fancy, it don't occur often."

"O, it does," said the first lady, eagerly; "I've lived many years in Kentucky and Virginia both, and I've seen enough to make any one's heart sick. Suppose, ma'am, your two children, there, should be taken from you, and sold?"

"We can't reason from our feelings to those of this class of persons," said the other lady, sorting out some worsteds on her lap.

"Indeed, ma'am, you can know nothing of them, if you say so," answered the first lady, warmly. "I was born and brought up among them. I know they *do* feel, just as keenly,—even more so, perhaps,—as we do."

The lady said "Indeed!" yawned, and looked out the cabin window, and finally repeated, for a finale, the remark with which she had begun,—"After all, I think they are better off than they would be to be free.". . .

Tom, whose fetters did not prevent his taking a moderate circuit, had drawn near the side of the boat, and stood listlessly gazing over the railing. After a time, he saw the trader returning, with an alert step, in company with a colored woman, bearing in her arms a young child. She was dressed quite respectably, and a colored man followed her, bringing along a small trunk. The woman came cheerfully onward, talking, as she came, with the man who bore her trunk, and so passed up the plank into the boat. The bell rung, the steamer whizzed, the engine groaned and coughed, and away swept the boat down the river.

The woman walked forward among the boxes and bales of the lower deck, and, sitting down, busied herself with chirruping to her baby. . . .

The woman looked calm, as the boat went on; and a beautiful soft summer breeze passed like a compassionate spirit over her head,—the gentle breeze, that never inquires whether the brow is dusky or fair that it fans. And she saw sunshine sparkling on the water, in golden ripples, and heard gay voices, full of ease and pleasure, talking around her everywhere; but her heart lay as if a great stone had fallen on it. Her baby raised himself up against her, and stroked her cheeks with his little hands; and, springing up and down, crowing and chatting, seemed determined to arouse her. She strained him suddenly and tightly in her arms, and slowly one tear after another fell on his wondering, unconscious face; and gradually she seemed, and little by little, to grow calmer, and busied herself with tending and nursing him.

The child, a boy of ten months, was uncommonly large and strong of his age, and very vigorous in his limbs. Never, for a moment, still, he kept his mother constantly busy in holding him, and guarding his springing activity.

"That's a fine chap!" said a man, suddenly stopping opposite to him, with his hands in his pockets. "How old is he?"

"Ten months and a half," said the mother.

The man whistled to the boy, and offered him part of a stick of candy, which he eagerly grabbed at, and very soon had it in a baby's general depository, to wit, his mouth.

"Rum fellow!" said the man "Knows what's what!" and he whistled, and walked on. When he had got to the other side of the boat, he came across Haley, who was smoking on top of a pile of boxes.

The stranger produced a match, and lighted a cigar, saying, as he did so,

"Decentish kind o' wench you've got round there, stranger."

"Why, I reckon she *is* tol'able fair," said Haley, blowing the smoke out of his mouth.

"Taking her down south?" said the man.

Haley nodded, and smoked on.

"Plantation hand?" said the man.

"Wal," said Haley, "I'm fillin' out an order for a plantation, and I think I shall put her in. They told me she was a good cook; and they can use her for that, or set her at the cotton-picking. She's got the right fingers for that; I looked at 'em. Sell well, either way;" and Haley resumed his cigar.

"They won't want the young 'un on the plantation," said the man.

"I shall sell him, first chance I find," said Haley, lighting another cigar.

"S'pose you'd be selling him tol'able cheap," said the stranger, mounting the pile of boxes, and sitting down comfortably.

"Don't know 'bout that," said Haley; "he's a pretty smart young 'un,—straight, fat, strong; flesh as hard as a brick!"

"Very true, but then there's the bother and expense of raisin'."

"Nonsense!" said Haley; "they is raised as easy as any kind of critter there is going; they an't a bit more trouble than pups. This yer chap will be running all around, in a month."

"I've got a good place for raisin', and I thought of takin' in a little more stock," said the man. "One cook lost a young 'un last week,—got drownded in a washtub, while she was a hangin' out the clothes,—and I reckon it would be well enough to set her to raisin' this yer."...

"I'll give thirty for him," said the stranger, "but not a cent more."

"Now, I'll tell ye what I will do," said Haley, spitting again, with renewed decision. "I'll split the difference, and say forty-five; and that's the most I will do."

"Well, agreed!" said the man, after an interval.

"Done!" said Haley. "Where do you land?"

"At Louisville," said the man.

"Louisville," said Haley. "Very fair, we get there about dusk. Chap will be asleep,—all fair,—get him off quietly, and no screaming,—happens beautiful,—I like to do everything quietly,—I hates all kind of agitation and fluster." And so, after a transfer of certain bills had passed from the man's pocket-book to the trader's, he resumed his cigar.

It was a bright, tranquil evening when the boat stopped at the wharf at Louisville. The woman had been sitting with her baby in her arms, now wrapped in a heavy sleep. When she heard the name of the place called out, she hastily laid the child down in a little cradle formed by the hollow among the boxes, first carefully spreading under it her cloak; and then she sprung to the side of the boat, in hopes that, among the various hotel-waiters who thronged the wharf, she might see her husband. In this hope, she pressed forward to the front rails, and, stretching far over them, strained her eyes intently on the moving heads on the shore, and the crowd pressed in between her and the child.

"Now's your time," said Haley, taking the sleeping child up, and handing him to the stranger. "Don't wake him up, and set him to crying, now; it would make a devil of a fuss with the gal." The man took the bundle carefully, and was soon lost in the crowd that went up the wharf.

When the boat, creaking, and groaning, and puffing, had loosed from the wharf, and was beginning slowly to strain herself along, the woman returned to her old seat. The trader was sitting there,—the child was gone!

"Why, why,—where?" she began, in bewildered surprise.

"Lucy," said the trader, "your child's gone; you may as well know it first as last. You see, I know'd you couldn't take him down south; and I got a chance to sell him to a first-rate family, that'll raise him better than you can."

The trader had arrived at that stage of Christian and political perfection which has been recommended by some preachers and politicians of the north, lately, in which he had completely overcome every humane weakness and prejudice. His heart was exactly where yours, sir, and mine could be brought, with proper effort and cultivation. The wild look of anguish and utter despair that the woman cast on him might have disturbed one less practised; but he was used to it. He had seen that same look hundreds of times. You can get used to such things, too, my friend; and it is the great object of recent efforts to make our whole northern community used to them, for the glory of the Union. So the trader only regarded the mortal anguish which he saw working in those dark features, those clenched hands, and suffocating breathings, as necessary incidents of the trade, and merely calculated whether she was going to scream, and get up a commotion on the boat; for, like other supporters of our peculiar institution, he decidedly disliked agitation.

But the woman did not scream. The shot had passed too straight and direct through the heart, for cry or tear.

Dizzily she sat down. Her slack hands fell lifeless by her side. Her eyes looked straight forward, but she saw nothing. All the noise and hum of the boat, the groaning of the machinery, mingled dreamily to her bewildered ear; and the poor, dumb-stricken heart had neither cry nor tear to show for its utter misery. She was quite calm.

The trader, who, considering his advantages, was almost as humane as some of our politicians, seemed to feel called on to administer such consolation as the case admitted of.

"I know this yer comes kinder hard, at first, Lucy," said he; "but such a smart, sensible gal as you are, won't give way to it. You see it's *necessary,* and can't be helped!"

"O! don't, Mas'r, don't!" said the woman, with a voice like one that is smothering.

"You're a smart wench, Lucy," he persisted; "I mean to do well by ye, and get ye a nice place down river; and you'll soon get another husband,—such a likely gal as you—"

"O! Mas'r, if you *only* won't talk to me now," said the woman, in a voice of such quick and living anguish that the trader felt that there was something at present in the case beyond his style of operation. He got up, and the woman turned away, and buried her head in her cloak. . . .

Tom drew near, and tried to say something; but she only groaned. Honestly, and with tears running down his own cheeks, he spoke of a heart of love in the skies, of a pitying Jesus, and an eternal home; but the ear was deaf with anguish, and the palsied heart could not feel.

PROSLAVERY SENTIMENT

WILLIAM SUMNER JENKINS

The existence of slavery in the United States contradicts the principles that the country was founded upon: freedom and democracy. To avoid what modern society might label blatant hypocrisy, slaveholders needed to justify their theft of another person's right to life and liberty. Proslavery defenses ranged from Christian arguments that quoted the Bible to theories that blacks were inherently suited for physical labor. In the following article, William Sumner Jenkins describes a social theory argument in favor of slavery that allocated manual labor and drudgery to the African American slave class and left the white race free for cultural and philosophical pursuits. He maintains that Southern society considered this division of labor appropriate to each race's inherent qualities. At the heart of this and other proslavery arguments is a belief in the inferiority of the black race without regard to individual intelligence or ability. At the time his book was published, William Sumner Jenkins was an assistant professor of political science at the University of North Carolina.

T he slaveholder believed that he lived in a perfectly ordered society, where each class filled a natural position for the advancement of civilization. Governor George McDuffie gave expression to the theory when he said: "In the very nature of things there must be classes of persons to discharge all the different offices of society. Some of those offices are regarded as degrading, though they must and will be per-

Excerpted from *Pro-Slavery Thought in the Old South* by William Sumner Jenkins (Chapel Hill: University of North Carolina Press, 1935). Copyright © 1935 by the University of North Carolina Press. Reprinted with permission.

formed." Southerners contended that they had made a contri-
bution to the science of society in that they had perfected a division of labor between classes naturally constituted for their
particular functions. As John C. Calhoun so vividly pictured it,
the unequal races occupied "the front and rear ranks in the
march of progress."

The menial and laborious tasks, which were always distasteful to man, had to be performed by some class. Here was the office of the slave class. Beverley Tucker, of Virginia, thought that
"it is here on this point, of the necessity of forcing those to labor
who are unable to live honestly without labor, that we base the
defense of our system." Likewise, Governor James Henry Hammond expressed the view that "this idea that slavery is so necessary to the performance of the drudgery so essential to the
subsistence of man, and the advance of civilization, is undoubtedly the ground on which the reason of the institution
rests." From this idea, he developed his famous mud-sill theory
of the structural basis of all society:

> In all social systems there must be a class to do the
> menial duties, to perform the drudgery of life. That is,
> a class requiring but a low order of intellect and but
> little skill. Its requisites are vigor, docility, fidelity.
> Such a class you must have or you would not have
> that other class which leads progress, civilization, and
> refinement. It constitutes the very mud-sill of society
> and of political government; and you might as well
> attempt to build a house in the air, as to build either
> the one or the other, except on this mud-sill. Fortu-
> nately for the South, she found a race adapted to that
> purpose to her hand. . . . We use them for our purpose
> and call them slaves. . . .

Since slave labor filled the low and degrading stations, doing
all the tasks of mere brute strength, the freeman did the services
that required trust, confidence, and skill. These gave him a
sense of respectability, made him more honorable, chivalrous
and self-governed, and fitted him to be the director. Slave society was often pictured as a great organism where the mind of
the master directed the physical faculties of the slave. Moreover,
the system made possible a large leisure class which devoted its
attention to the cultural and political spheres of life. The Southerner was proud of naming the great political leaders produced

under slavery and of boasting of the culture attained on the Southern plantation.

CLASS DIVISIONS AMONG WHITES

It is erroneous, of course, to think of the whites as a single class in society. They were sub-divided among themselves into a number of classes. But the argument of the slaveholder was that domestic slavery caused an identity of interests among all the whites to the extent that they approached singleness of class. Color really became the badge of distinction and all classes of whites were interested in maintaining that distinction. Color, so noticeable to the eye, inspired the most humble white man to a sense of his comparative dignity and importance. As one writer remarked, "however poor, or ignorant, or miserable he may be, he has yet the consoling consciousness that there is a still lower condition to which he can never be reduced." But beyond the color line which was the basis of class unity, in slave society the interests of the different orders were the most identical, their habits the most uniform, and their pursuits the most permanent. And this resulted from two principal reasons—the upper order were all owners of slaves and cultivators of the soil. Whatever of diversity was maintained in their occupations, the largest interest of all was in their slaves. This reasoning led Judge Abel P. Upshur to declare: "We have among us, but one great class, and all who belong to it have a necessary sympathy with one another; we have but one great interest, and all who possess it are equally ready to maintain and protect it."

The charge was often made that this caste system of Southern society was aristocratic in its nature, and, consequently, denied the genius of free institutions. The slaveholder admitted that it was indeed aristocratic. For example, Governor Hammond remarked that "slavery does indeed create an aristocracy—an aristocracy of talents, of virtue, of generosity and courage. . . . It is a government of the best, combining all the advantages and possessing but few of the disadvantages of the aristocracy of the old world." Instead of fostering "the pride, the exclusiveness, the selfishness, the thirst for sway, the contempt for the right of others" which characterized European nobility, it provided "their education, their polish, their munificence, their high honor, their undaunted spirit." In fact, every freeman in slave society was an aristocrat. In the same strain of thought Chancellor Robert G. Harper explained that "ours is indeed an aristocracy, founded on the distinction of races, and conformable, as we believe, to the order of nature." To him it had the advantage "that the privileged class is larger in proportion to the whole society." He thought that the advantage of rank was conferred on a larger number than the world had known in any other society. . . .

Holding to the aristocratic nature of society was far from admitting the second contention—that slavery destroyed free institutions. The slaveholder argued that free institutions had their only natural basis in slave society. It was because of the aristocracy in the first place that there was "less of any other invidiously aristocratic distinction, and that every freeman may claim to be the peer of any other freeman," according to Chancellor Harper. Here arose one of the most important elements in the slavery defense, the reconciliation of slavery with the principles of republican liberty. In order to do so, the opinion of Edmund Burke was cited as authority. The influence of Burke upon Southern minds was probably as great as that of either Thomas Carlyle or Aristotle. He was considered "the most profound of political philosophers." More quotations probably can be found from his speech on conciliation with America than from any single work of any other writer. At the time of the Revolution he had declared: "These people of the Southern (American) colonies are much more strongly, and with a higher and more stubborn spirit, attached to liberty than those of the northward.". . ."It is because freedom is to them not only an enjoyment, but a kind of rank and privilege."

Again, they often pointed to the fact that it was in the ancient republics of Greece and Rome, where slavery flourished, that the spirit of freedom was born. This fact led Senator Robert L. Toombs to remark that "public liberty and domestic slavery were cradled together." Another line of argument pointed to the fact that the old whig principle of liberty, which restricted the powers of government to the limits of the Constitution, had always maintained its stronghold in the slaveholding States of the South. They had ever been the chief barrier to centralization which they viewed as the greatest destroyer of local freedom.

SOUTHERN SOCIAL ORGANIZATION

Beverley Tucker thought that the influence of slavery as a preservative of the spirit of freedom grew out of the peculiar organization of Southern society. He held that there was an element in every community that must be restricted by coercion to its proper place, the performance of labor; but, "if there is strength enough in the frame of government to make this coercion effectual, that strength may be dangerous to the freedom of all." In the slave régimes of the past it was necessary for the government to possess too much power in order to maintain them. However, where society was so organized, as in the South, "that the element in question can be restrained and directed by other energies than those of government, we escape the difficulty." Tucker was continually emphasizing the fact that the peculiar organization of slave society narrowed the scope of powers that it was necessary to vest in government. . . .

Returning to the question of republican liberty, it was contended that its true basis, actual equality, was attained only in slave society. Professor Thomas R. Dew declared that in the South had been accomplished equality among the whites "as nearly as can be expected or desired in the world." Their very sympathy, which arose from their identity of interests was favorable to equality. Judge Upshur explained the effect of slavery as an equalizer of wealth. He recognized that no government could preserve an equality of wealth, even for a day. But he thought that domestic slavery "approaches that result much more nearly than any other civil institution, and it prevents, in a very great degree, if not entirely, that gross inequality among the different *classes* of society, from which alone liberty has anything to fear." In free society there was no such influence and there, the Southerner pointed out, the basis of class was wealth. The only force acting to maintain the equality in the Northern States was the westward movement of the population, which acted as a safety valve to those who were falling behind in the race of life.

PROTECTING PROPERTY

But there was another reason why this aristocracy of race and color really maintained the true republican principles. This was because it offered the only sure protection of property. The poorest man in slave society felt an interest in the laws which protected the rights of property, "for, though he has none as yet, he has the purpose and the hope to be rich before he dies, and to leave property to his children." Consequently, Tucker thought that suffrage might be given to all the whites in slave society, because the temptation of the lower class to abuse power was diminished. Where all have property, the right of property is held sacred by all; and there will be no misgovernment, for what is best for one is best for all. There could be no ground for jealousy between rich and poor. In other words, the argument of the Southerner was that all classes felt a security of rights in slave society, and therefore were in the true sense of the word freemen. There was no oppressive force of government, for this constitution of society made the tasks of government easy, since there were no classes to be reconciled. The result was domestic peace, order, and security. In the last analysis, slavery was the ideal force and security for perfect social control.

On the other hand, the slaveholder thought that if the man who had no property be allowed to vote, there could be no security to the rights of people who owned property. Property would be voted robbery. This was the cause for the weakness of universal suffrage in free society, where the large propertyless class was enfranchised. There, in place of a force acting to identify the classes, wealth was rapidly distributing men into classes of diverse interests. The progress of society would increase these diversities until the classes would begin to war upon each other. The powerful class would always sacrifice the interests of the weaker. Hence, the power of government must be increased to maintain social order and to secure the rights of individuals. But in order to do so the power of government must necessarily become burdensome upon some element.

Going a step further, the slaveholder doubted if the government based upon equal political rights in every member of the community, from the highest to the lowest, could maintain itself when society had reached the stage where wealth was centered in the hands of the few and the great number were reduced to poverty. To such a condition all free society was rapidly progressing. The agrarian spirit was already apparent in the Northern States, and here again, it was shown, only the influence of the westward movement held it in check. The final result, however, could not long be delayed and free society in the North must find some other solution for the class conflict that was imminent.

The result of the reasoning led the slaveholder to picture slavery as the strongest conservative force in society and a bulwark against agrarianism. As Judge Upshur expressed it: "There is then in this institution something which courts and solicits good order; there is a principle in it which avoids confusion and repels faction; its necessary tendency is to distract the purposes and to bind the arm of the agrarian and the leveler." This resulted from the facts that "equal in our rank, the spirit of levelling sees nothing to envy; equal in our fortune, the spirit of agrarianism sees nothing to attack." Truly the agrarian spirit was divided against itself in slave society and there were no revolutionary movements to overthrow the harmony of social order or the security of vested rights. Hence, Governor McDuffie declared that slavery was the "cornerstone of our republican edifice," and with the same confidence the Southern leaders declared that the last stronghold of republicanism would be in the slaveholding States. Consequently, South Carolina, when she came to secede from the Union, declared "we are vindicating the great cause of free government, more important, perhaps, to the world, than the existence of all the United States."

THE KANSAS-NEBRASKA ACT OF 1854

J.G. RANDALL AND DAVID DONALD

J.G. Randall and David Donald explain how the Kansas-Nebraska Act of 1854 fueled sectional unrest and civil war. The act repealed a provision of the Compromise of 1850 that barred slavery from the territory and left the decision of slavery up to the voters of the states, coining the term "popular sovereignty." Northerners were so incensed at the repeal of the Missouri Compromise that many united to form the Republican Party to fight the expansion of slavery into the territories. J.G. Randall was a history professor at the University of Illinois, and David Donald was a Harry C. Black professor of American history at the Johns Hopkins University.

For the settlement of [the slavery issue within] the territories question three solutions were prominently urged. First, there was the Wilmot proviso, associated with the Free-Soilers and the Republican party: the doctrine that slavery in all national territory ought to be definitely prohibited by Congress. Second, at the other extreme there was the doctrine of the Southern Democracy that it was the duty of the Federal government to extend positive protection to slavery in the territories—i.e. not merely to permit it, but to maintain and protect it. This solution was soon to be powerfully supported by both the President and the Supreme Court of the United States.

Excerpted from *The Civil War and Reconstruction* by J.G. Randall and David Donald (Lexington, MA: D.C. Heath and Company, 1969). Copyright © 1969 by Raytheon Education Company. Reprinted with permission.

Third, there was the "popular sovereignty" program associated with the policy of Senator Stephen A. Douglas and the anti-James Buchanan Democrats. Briefly, its purport was that slavery should be neither positively established nor arbitrarily prohibited in any territory by national action, but that the issue should be settled on the broad American principle of local self-determination by leaving the people of each territory free to deal with the matter as the majority by conventional political processes should decide.

THE RISE OF STEPHEN A. DOUGLAS

It is to the last-mentioned program that attention must now turn. In the slavery legislation of 1850 the principle of popular sovereignty had been applied to the Mexican acquisition; and now under President Franklin Pierce a more famous instance of its application was to be seen in Douglas's Kansas-Nebraska bill of 1854. So truculent was the controversy waged concerning this piece of legislation that it is hard to penetrate the mists of vituperation and to isolate the causes and essential elements of the situation. A reappraisal of the much maligned Douglas will be of assistance in understanding the problem. Few men have presented so notable an example of rapid rise to political leadership. Born in Vermont, he struggled for some years as a lawyer in Illinois, became active in promoting the Democratic organization of his state, and served in the legislature simultaneously with Lincoln. For two years he was a member of the supreme court of Illinois; and the title "Judge Douglas" lasted through life. After serving briefly but brilliantly in the House of Representatives, he held the office of senator from Illinois during the critical years from 1847 to 1861, by which time he was the foremost Democrat of the North. His forthrightness, vigor, and aggressiveness, his force as a debater and talent as political strategist, had made a deep impression; and the breadth of his national vision had given him a peculiar distinction in an age when the sectionalism of many of the nation's leaders was all too evident.

Western problems and territorial issues had been a specialty of Douglas, who had since 1847 been chairman of the committee on territories of the United States Senate after having held a similar chairmanship in the House. Questions of territorial organization, involving far-reaching phases of the westward movement, necessarily awaited his action in the formulation and recommendation of policies. It has already been noted that his part in the Compromise of 1850 was as vital as that of Henry Clay himself; in 1854 no man was more thoroughly conversant than he with the whole background of territorial politics. By this time the territorial organization of the vast "Platte country" was overdue.

ORGANIZING THE PLATTE

Speaking for his committee, Douglas reported a bill for the territorial organization of the Platte country on January 4, 1854. Most of its provisions were conventional, but those concerning slavery attracted attention. Douglas declared that his bill was in tune with "certain great principles," which had already been enacted into law in 1850. "Your committee," he said, "deem it fortunate . . . that the controversy then resulted in the adoption of the compromise measures, which the two great political parties . . . have affirmed . . . and proclaimed . . . as a final settlement of the controversy and an end of the agitation." Briefly, these principles, as he stated them, were that the people, through their representatives in the legislature, should decide as to slavery in the territories with the right of appeal on matters of constitutionality to the Supreme Court of the United States.

Historians have long argued over Douglas's motives in introducing this measure, which seemed indirectly to repeal the Missouri Compromise of 1850 ban on slavery in the Nebraska region and thus reopened the sectional conflict. Some critics have maintained that Douglas had a material interest in the promotion of slavery, since his first wife had inherited a plantation with 150 slaves. More frequently it has been argued that Douglas was angling for the Democratic presidential nomination in 1856 and hoped to win Southern support. Refuting these charges, friendly historians have suggested instead that Douglas wished to assist Senator David R. Atchison in his campaign for re-election in Missouri, that he desired to promote the building of a transcontinental railroad with eastern termini at Chicago and St. Louis, or that he hoped to give the floundering Democratic party a fresh issue upon which it could appeal to the voters. Recently the argument has been settled by the discovery of a contemporary letter in which Douglas himself explained his motives. His purpose in introducing the Kansas-Nebraska bill, Douglas declared, was to remove the "barbarian wall" of Indian tribes checking further settlement in the central plains and "to authorize and encourage a continuous line of settlements to the Pacific Ocean." His central idea of continental expansion included railroad development. As he explained:

> How are we to develope [sic], cherish and protect our immense interests and possessions in the Pacific, with a vast wilderness fifteen hundred miles in breadth, filled with hostile savages, and cutting off direct communication. The Indian barrier must be removed. The tide of emigration and civilization must be permitted to roll onward until it rushes through the passes of the mountains, and spreads over the plains, and mingles with the waters of the Pacific. Continuous lines of settlements with civil, political and religious institutions all under the protection of law, are imperiously demanded by the highest national considerations. These are essential, but they are not sufficient. . . . We must therefore have Rail Roads and Telegraphs from the Atlantic to the Pacific, through our own territory. Not one line only, but many lines, for the valley of the Mississippi will require as many Rail Roads to the Pacific as to the Atlantic, and will not venture to limit the number.

Intent upon opening the West to further development, Douglas wished to ignore or by-pass the slavery question. Knowing that he had no chance whatever of getting a territorial bill adopted without Southern votes, he presented a deliberately ambiguous measure, which did not explicitly exclude slavery from the area, but which almost certainly would have left the Missouri Compromise prohibition in effect during the territorial stage of its development. Personally hostile to slavery, Douglas did not think the South's peculiar institution could ever extend into the great plains; consequently he believed that his token concession to the South in no sense endangered liberty. "It is to be hoped," he argued, "that the necessity and importance of the measure are manifest to the whole country, and that so far as the slavery question is concerned, all will be willing to sanction and affirm the principles established by the Compromise measures of 1850."

But once the measure was presented to the Senate, it became the object of intense political pressure. Excited Free Soilers attempted to add amendments reaffirming the Missouri Compromise ban on slavery. Angered by these maneuvers, Southerners informed Douglas that slavery must be permitted in the Nebraska country during the territorial phase of its organization. Reluctantly yielding to this latter pressure, Douglas on January 10 brought forward an additional section of his bill, which, he asserted, had previously been omitted through "clerical error"; it provided "that all questions pertaining to slavery in the Territories, and in the new States to be formed therefrom, are to be left to the people residing therein, through their appropriate representatives." Though this provision plainly implied the repeal of the Missouri Compromise, proslavery leaders were still not satisfied, and Douglas was obliged to add a further amendment declaring the Missouri Compromise "inoperative and void." At the same time his bill was modified in another important fashion by dividing the area under consideration into the two separate territories of Kansas and Nebraska. Thus the final version of the Kansas-Nebraska bill was not Douglas's alone; it was, as Roy F. Nichols has said, "the work of many hands and the fruit of much strategic planning." Assisted by relentless pressure from the Pierce administration, the bill, after months of riotous debate, was passed; the fateful measure became law on May 30, 1854.

THE DOGS OF WAR

It was at once apparent that this legislation had let loose the dogs of war. While Southerners at first showed either indifference or resentment toward the act as one that offered them insufficient protection, they soon came enthusiastically to endorse it as "a measure . . . just in regards to the rights of the South, and . . . reasonable in its operation and effect" [as stated by Nichols]. In the North Douglas's bill furiously aroused antislavery sentiment, and free-soil men in both parties took steps to have the action of Congress repudiated. Salmon P. Chase of Ohio, a puritan in politics who had labored in the Liberty party of 1840 and with the Free-Soilers of '48, now headed a movement to capture the Democratic party for the cause of antislavery. In his "Appeal to the Independent Democrats" he denounced Douglas's action as a violation of a solemn pledge, predicted its dire effect upon immigration to the West, warned the country that freedom and union were in peril, and besought all Christians to rise in protest against this "enormous crime." The vocabulary of abuse was exhausted in the attacks upon Douglas: "never before has a public man been so hunted and hounded." As he himself declared, he could have traveled from Boston to Chicago by the light of his burning effigies. Even in his home state he was vigorously condemned. Both in Chicago and in downstate Illinois he encountered abuse and insult when he tried to defend his course, but he managed to strike home with his argument that it was the extremists on both sides, not himself, who were responsible for the storm of sectionalism.

In keeping with the prevailing tendency toward political realignment, and as a direct result of the Kansas-Nebraska act, a new political party now came into being. Wilmot-proviso sentiment caused various diverse elements here and there to fuse into organizations, which sometimes bore the awkward designation of "anti-Nebraska" parties, but which soon came to be known as the "Republican" party. There has been some dispute as to the exact time and place where the party was "born." Coalition movements of a similar sort were afoot in many parts of the country at about the same time, and such a dispute is of little importance. The name "Republican" was adopted at a mass meeting on July 6, 1854, at Jackson, Michigan; prior to this, however, while the repeal of the Missouri compromise was pending in Congress, a similar mass meeting at Ripon, Wisconsin, had resolved that in the event of such repeal old party organizations would be discarded and a new party would be built "on the sole issue of the non-extension of slavery." Elsewhere in the country local conventions followed suit; and by late summer of 1854 the new party movement was well under way. Made up of old-line Whigs, many of whom, such as Edward Bates of Missouri and Orville Browning of Illinois, preserved the Southern conservative tradition, together with radical antislavery men such as Charles Sumner and G.W. Julian, Knownothings, and free-soil Democrats such as Lyman Trumbull and Chase, the new party combined many diverse ingredients; the force that cemented them (at the outset) was common opposition to the further extension of slavery in the territories.

The outcome of Douglas's policy had been the opposite of his intentions. So far from allaying sectional conflict and uniting his party, he had reopened the strife, which he himself had designated the "fearful struggle of 1850"; he had split the historic Democratic party; he had supplied the occasion for the entrance of a wholly sectional party onto the scene; and he had driven many Northern Democrats into the ranks of this sectional group.

THE *DRED SCOTT* CASE

DON E. FEHRENBACHER

Dred Scott was a slave who accompanied his master on journeys to free territories over a period of several years. Upon the death of his master, Dred Scott petitioned for his freedom on the grounds that he had lived in free territory for a significant length of time. After a series of appeals, the case landed in the Supreme Court in 1857 where the court denied Scott his petition for freedom. Chief Justice Roger B. Taney, who wrote the opinion, concluded that although blacks could become citizens of states, they could not become citizens of the nation, because they were not considered citizens when the Constitution was drafted. Southerners rejoiced in the decision's affirmation of slavery, while Northerners considered it a distortion of history and law. According to Don E. Fehrenbacher, the case widened the rift between the proslavery and antislavery factions and brought the nation closer to civil war. Don E. Fehrenbacher was a noted Civil War scholar and won the 1979 Pulitzer Prize for his book *The Dred Scott Case: Its Significance in American Law and Politics*.

O n Friday morning, March 6, 1857—a crisp, clear day for residents of Washington, D.C.—public attention centered on a dusky, ground-level courtroom deep within the Capitol. The Senate chamber directly above was quiet; Congress had adjourned on March 3. The inauguration ceremonies of March 4 were over, and James Buchanan had begun settling into his role as the fifteenth President. Now it was the judiciary's turn to be heard, as though the three branches of government were passing in review before the American people. Ordinarily, the Supreme Court carried on its business before a small audience and with only perfunctory notice from the press, but today the journalists were out in force and the courtroom was packed with spectators. A murmur of expectancy ran through the crowd and greeted the nine black-robed jurists as they filed into view at eleven o'clock, led by the aged Chief Justice. Acrimonious debate in the recent Congress had once again failed to settle the paramount constitutional and political issue of the decade. The Court, however, was ready to terminate the long struggle over slavery in the territories and, incidentally, decide the fate of a man named Dred Scott.

Neither of the two litigants was present in the courtroom. Scott remained at home in St. Louis, still a hired-out slave eleven years after he had taken the first legal step in his long battle for freedom. As for his alleged owner, John F.A. Sanford languished in an insane asylum and within two months would be dead. But then, both men had been dwarfed by the implications of their case and were now mere pawns in a much larger contest.

Roger B. Taney, who in eleven days would be eighty years old, began reading from a manuscript held in tremulous hands. For more than two hours the audience strained to hear his steadily weakening voice as he delivered the opinion of the Court in *Dred Scott v. Sandford.** Other opinions followed from some of the concurring justices and from the two dissenters. When they were finished at the end of the next day, only one thing was absolutely clear. Nine distinguished white men, by a vote of 7 to 2, had decided in the court of last resort that an insignificant, elderly black man and his family were still slaves and not free citizens, as they claimed.

SUBSEQUENT CONTROVERSY

What else had been decided was fiercely debated then and ever afterward. Critics argued that on some points Taney did not speak for a majority of the justices. Yet none of his eight colleagues directly challenged Taney's explicit assertion that his was the official opinion of the Court, and in popular usage on all sides the "Dred Scott decision" came to mean the opinion read by the Chief Justice. Critics also insisted that Taney's most

---

*The defendant's name, John F.A. Sanford, was misspelled in the official Supreme Court report.

important pronouncement was extrajudicial, but only the Court itself, in later decisions, could legally settle such a question by accepting or rejecting the pronouncement as established precedent. Rightly or not, permanently or not, the Supreme Court had written two new and provocative rules into the fundamental law of the nation: first, that no Negro could be a United States citizen or even a state citizen "within the meaning of the Constitution"; and second, that Congress had no power to exclude slavery from the federal territories, and that accordingly the Missouri Compromise of 1820, together with all other legislation embodying such exclusion, was unconstitutional.

Public reaction was prompt and often intense, as countless lawyers, politicians, editors, and preachers reached for their pens or cleared their throats for oratory. The outpouring of comment gathered into three major streams of opinion. Most conspicuous by far was the roar of anger and defiance from antislavery voices throughout the North, well illustrated in the notorious remark of the New York *Tribune* conceding the decision "just so much moral weight as . . . the judgment of a majority of those congregated in any Washington bar-room." From southerners, in contrast, came expressions of satisfaction and renewed sectional confidence at this overdue vindication of their constitutional rights. Meanwhile, northern Democrats and certain other conservatives were confining themselves, for the most part, to exclamations of relief at the settlement of a dangerous issue and pious lectures on the duty of every citizen to accept the wise judgment of the Court.

In the years immediately following, the response to the decision proved to be much more important than its direct legal effect. As law, the decision legitimized and encouraged an expansion of slavery that never took place; it denied freedom to a slave who was then quickly manumitted. But as a public event, the decision aggravated an already bitter sectional conflict and to some degree determined the shape of the final crisis.

FANNING THE FLAMES OF WAR

There is irony here, of course, if one views the Court's action as an effort at judicial statesmanship, intended to bring peace but instead pushing the nation closer to civil war. In this light, the Court majority appears incredibly unrealistic—indeed, so foolish as to pour oil rather than water on a fire. Yet Taney's opinion, carefully read, proves to be a work of unmitigated partisanship, polemical in spirit though judicial in its language, and more like an ultimatum than a formula for sectional accommodation. Peace on Taney's terms resembled the peace implicit in a demand for unconditional surrender. As one scholar has written, "The Dred Scott decision was nothing less than a summons to the Republicans to disband."

Thus perceived, the decision falls logically into place as one unusually bold venture in a desperate struggle for power, rather than being an evenhanded effort to resolve that struggle. And under close study it proves to be no less meaningful as a historical consequence than as a historical cause.

There are sharply defined historical events through which, like the neck of an hourglass, great causal forces appear to flow, emerging converted into significant consequences. Strictly speaking, this is illusion, and the translation is essentially a verbal one; for "cause" and "consequence" are subjective categories that serve to simplify and make intelligible the highly complex relationships among objective historical phenomena. Yet all explanation, being in some degree selective and synthetic, is to some degree a distortion of reality. The hourglass construct at least incorporates the flow of time and is chronologically sound. Like biography, moreover, the history of a single event provides a firm and convenient vantage point from which to observe the sweep of historical forces. The principal fallacy to be avoided is a tendency to view one's subject as the matrix of forces when it is usually instead a mere channel of their passage.

DECLARING A LAW UNCONSTITUTIONAL

The Dred Scott decision, for example, was the Supreme Court's first invalidation of a major federal law. It is therefore a landmark in the history of judicial review. But the power to declare an act of Congress unconstitutional had frequently been asserted or implied in earlier decisions, and the existence of such power was widely assumed by the American people. That the power would have been exercised eventually, if not in 1857, seems about as certain as that someone else would have discovered America if Columbus had failed to do so. Thus the Dred Scott decision should probably be regarded as a prominent point of reference, but not as a major turning point, in the development of judicial review. And yet, since it was in 1857 that the Supreme Court first took this important step, it was in 1857 that Americans for the first time had to consider the operational scope and meaning of judicial review in national politics. What was the effect of such a decision beyond the specific judgment rendered? To what extent, for instance, would it inhibit the subsequent deliberations of Congress, and what recourse was left for the bitter critics of the decision? The heated argument of these constitutional questions had unmistakable political consequences.

The answer of Republicans like Abraham Lincoln was that a decision so defective in its logic, so contrary to precedent, and so repugnant to a large part of the population did not immediately become binding on the other branches of the government or upon the American people as settled law of the land. Republicans, for their part, would not defy the decision but instead work to have it reversed. This reversal obviously could be accomplished only by changing the personnel of the Supreme Court, which in turn depended upon control of the presidency. Thus the South's judicial victory was to be challenged at the polls, and southerners had another strong reason to fear a Republican in the White House. That is one plainly observable link between the Dred Scott decision and the secession crisis of 1860–61.

There were other links, of course, such as the divisive influence of the decision within the Democratic party and its reinforcement of northern fear of an "aggressive slave power." No doubt the Dred Scott decision is of historical significance primarily because of its place in the configuration of forces and events that produced the Civil War. But the decision also has revelatory value in the study of other forces at work and other historical problems. For instance, unlike Taney's pronouncements on slavery, which defended a minority section with partisan fervor, the racial theory underlying his opinion was majoritarian. For proof of the Negro's degraded status, he relied heavily upon examples taken from the free states. Without the northern record of increasing discrimination he would have found it much more difficult to exclude Negroes from citizenship. Thus, although the principal conclusions of Taney's opinion were soon wiped away by the Civil War and subsequent constitutional amendments, the spirit of the opinion survived for a century in the racial sequel to emancipation.

COURTS AS VEHICLES FOR SOCIAL CHANGE

Furthermore, although the Dred Scott decision was essentially a vain effort to turn back the clock of civilization and permanently legitimate a "relic of barbarism," in at least one respect it had a distinctly modern ring. American courts in the late twentieth century are no longer mere constitutional censors of public policies fashioned by other hands. They have also become initiators of social change. Government by judiciary is now, in a sense, democracy's non-democratic alternative to representative government when the latter bogs down in failure or inaction. The Dred Scott decision nevertheless remains the most striking instance of the Supreme Court's attempting to play the role of *deus ex machina* in a setting of national crisis. The decision, in fact, provided an early indication of the vast judicial power that could be generated if political issues were converted by definition into constitutional questions.

Much of the American past clung to the Dred Scott case, and some of the American future was embodied in it. But this had not always been true. For most of its eleven-year history, Scott's legal struggle for freedom aroused scarcely any public interest as it proceeded by an anomalous route from a Missouri trial court to the Supreme Court of the United States. In the beginning, it posed a fairly simple legal problem for which precedent seemed to provide a ready-made solution. At each stage of litigation, however, new and bigger issues were injected into the case. Thus it grew steadily more complex and in the end became critically important to the entire nation.

The confusion still surrounding the case reflects the confusion with which it was handled by the Court, and both are attributable in part to its legal complexity but in larger measure to the enormous range of its scrutiny and implication. In his opinion, Taney issued pronouncements on the relationship between the Constitution and the Articles of Confederation, on the limits of congressional power, on the geographic extent of the Bill of Rights, on constitutional authority for territorial expansion, on the rights of private property, on comity between states, and on the nature of the Federal Union. He defined the power of naturalization, the legal status of Indian tribes, and the criteria for citizenship, state and federal. He introduced a new meaning of "due process" into federal law and virtually rewrote the privileges-and-immunities clause of the Constitution. These, moreover, were merely connotative aspects of the opinion.

The three *principal* subjects with which Taney dealt at length were: (1) the Negro race generally and free Negroes in particular; (2) the institution of slavery; and (3) the territorial system.

Of these, the first is not mentioned at all in the Constitution; the second is referred to in three separate passages, but never by name; and the third is treated in one brief and ambiguous clause. The textual basis for constitutional interpretation was therefore meager. In each instance, moreover, there was a peculiar hybridism that fostered confusion. The so-called free Negro, though not a slave, was excluded from many of the privileges and opportunities associated with American freedom. Slaves were in some respects persons and in other respects property. And territories were likewise something betwixt and between, being neither colonies nor self-governing states but rather a distinctive American combination of the two.

FREEDOM OF INTERPRETATION

Altogether, the Dred Scott case was legally complex and invited a judicial investigation of remarkable scope into matters of perplexing ambiguity for which the constitutional guidelines were often vague and discrepant. The Court, as a consequence, had much freedom of choice and found it easy to treat broad political and historical questions as though they were legal issues susceptible of judicial settlement. Indeed, citation of legal rules and precedents was only a secondary bulwark of Taney's opinion; which depended primarily upon the interpretation of American history that he proposed to write into constitutional law.

Such an event cannot be examined in any narrow context without the risk of considerable misunderstanding. For it is integrally part of a complex pattern of thoughts and actions extending far backward and well forward in time from the year 1857. Studied in breadth and depth, the Dred Scott decision becomes a point of illumination, casting light upon more than a century of American history.

The Civil War

CHAPTER 2

FORT SUMTER

JAMES FORD RHODES

The first shot of the Civil War was fired at Fort Sumter, South Carolina, on April 12, 1861. Confederate general Pierre Beauregard had demanded the evacuation of the fort on April 10, but Union major Robert Anderson had refused to carry out the order. Beauregard responded with an onslaught of cannons and bullets that Union soldiers were not able to defeat, and Anderson surrendered the fort on April 13. Although no one was killed, the bombardment of Fort Sumter was the opening engagement of the Civil War. In the following article, James Ford Rhodes describes the attack on Fort Sumter and the events that led up to it. James Ford Rhodes is a renowned historian and the author of *History of the United States from the Compromise of 1850*.

D uring the progress of the secession, the forts, arsenals, custom-houses and other property of the Federal government within the limits of the cotton States were taken possession of by these States and, in due time, all this property was turned over to the Southern Confederacy, so that on March 4, 1861, all that President Abraham Lincoln controlled was four military posts, of which Fort Sumter, commanding Charleston, was much the most important. Since the very beginning of the secession movement, the eyes of the North had been upon South Carolina. For many years she had been restive under the bonds of the Union; her chief city, Charleston, had witnessed the disruption of the Democratic national convention, and the consequent split in the party which made certain the Republican success of 1860, that in turn had led to the secession of the State and the formation of the Southern Confederacy. Fort Sumter had fixed the attention of the Northern mind

Excerpted from *History of the Civil War* by James Ford Rhodes (New York: Frederick Ungar, 1961). Copyright © 1961 by Frederick Ungar Publishing Company, Inc. Reprinted with permission.

by an occurrence in December, 1860. Major Robert Anderson with a small garrison of United States troops had occupied Fort Moultrie; but, convinced that he could not defend that fort against any attack from Charleston, he had, secretly on the night after Christmas, withdrawn his force to Fort Sumter, a much stronger post. Next morning, when the movement was discovered, Charleston fumed with rage whilst the North, on hearing the news, was jubilant and made a hero of Anderson. Lincoln recognized the importance of holding Fort Sumter but he also purposed to use all means short of the compromise of his deepest convictions to retain the border slave States and North Carolina, Tennessee and Arkansas in the Union. The action of these three turned upon Virginia, whose convention was in session, ready to take any action which the posture of affairs seemed to demand. The fundamental difficulty now asserted itself. To hold Fort Sumter was to Lincoln a bounden duty but to the Virginians it savored of coercion; and coercion in this case meant forcing a State which had seceded, back into the Union. If an attempt was made to coerce a State, Virginia would join the Southern Confederacy. The Confederate States now regarded the old Union as a foreign power whose possession of a fort within their limits, flying the American flag, was a daily insult. They attempted to secure Sumter by an indirect negotiation with the Washington government and were encouraged by the assurances of William Seward, Lincoln's Secretary of State and most trusted counsellor. Had the President known of Seward's intimation, which was almost a promise, that Sumter would be evacuated, he would have been greatly perturbed and would have called a halt in the negotiations to the end that the Southern commissioners be undeceived. On April 1, 1861, he was further troubled by a paper, "Some Thoughts for the President's Consideration," which Seward had privately submitted to him as an outline of the fit policy to be pursued. This was briefly: the evacuation of Fort Sumter; the reënforcement of the other posts in the South; a demand at once for explanations from Spain and France and, if they were not satisfactory, a call of a special session of Congress to declare war against those two nations; also explanations to be sought from Great Britain and Russia. With that same rash disregard of his chief and blind reliance on his own notions of statecraft which he had shown in his negotiations with Justice John Campbell, the intermediary between himself and the Southern commissioners, who had been sent to

Washington by Jefferson Davis, he gave the President a strong hint that the execution of this policy should be devolved upon some member of the Cabinet and that member, himself. The proposed foreign policy was reckless and wholly unwarranted. Our relations with these four powers were entirely peaceful; to use Seward's own words less than three months before, "there is not a nation on earth that is not an interested, admiring friend." Seward had got it into his head that, if our nation should provoke a foreign war, the cotton States would unite in amity with the North and like brothers fight the common foe under the old flag. Lincoln of course saw that the foreign policy proposed was wild and foolish but ignored it in his considerate reply to "Some Thoughts for the President's Consideration"; he kept the existence of the paper rigidly a secret; he did not demand the Secretary's resignation; he had for him no word of sarcasm or reproach.

OFFICE SEEKERS

The President submitted to another drain on his time and strength in the persistent scramble for office. "The grounds, halls, stairways, closets of the White House," wrote Seward, are filled with office seekers; and Lincoln said, "I seem like one sitting in a palace assigning apartments to importunate applicants, while the structure is on fire and likely soon to perish in ashes." When he ought to have been able to concentrate his mind on the proper attitude to the seceding States, he was hampered by the ceaseless demands for a lucrative recognition from his supporters and by the irrational proposals of the chief of his Cabinet.

The great problem now was Sumter. What should be done about it? On the day after his inauguration, the President was informed that Major Anderson believed a reënforcement of 20,000 men necessary for the defence of the post; after being transported to the neighborhood by sea, they must fight their way through to the fort. For the South Carolinians had been steadily at work on the islands in Charleston harbor erecting batteries and strengthening the forts which bore on Sumter. Moreover, Anderson's provisions would not last beyond the middle of April. General Winfield Scott, the head of the army, advised the evacuation of Sumter, a logical step in the course of action toward the South, which he and other men of influence had advocated and which he expressed in the pertinent words, "Wayward sisters depart in peace." At the Cabinet meeting of

March 15, 1861, the President asked his advisers, If it be possible to provision Fort Sumter, is it wise to attempt it? Four agreed with Seward, saying, No; only two gave an affirmative answer. Lincoln undoubtedly had moments of thinking that the Fort must be evacuated. With his eye upon Virginia, whose convention he hoped might adjourn without action, he may have promised one of her representatives that he would withdraw Anderson, provided the Virginia convention, always a menace of secession while it continued to sit, would adjourn *sine die*. The evidence is too conflicting to justify a positive assertion; but if such a proposal were made, it was never transmitted to and acted upon by the convention.

In the final decision, the sentiment of the North had to be taken into account. To abandon Sumter would seem to indicate that a peaceful separation would follow; that the principle of the sovereignty of the States and secession had triumphed. Finally, with increasing support in his Cabinet, Lincoln came to a wise decision. Reënforcement from a military point of view was impracticable; to reach the fort the North might have to fire the first shot. But, as a political measure, he decided to "send bread to Anderson," so that Sumter would not have to be evacuated from lack of food. In accordance with his previous promise, he sent word to the Governor of South Carolina of his intention. General Pierre Beauregard, commander of the Confederate troops at Charleston, who in company with the Governor heard the formal notification, telegraphed it to the Confederate Secretary of War at Montgomery, receiving two days later [April 10, 1861] the order to demand the evacuation of Fort Sumter and, if this was refused, to proceed to reduce it.

The demand was made; and when Anderson had written his refusal to comply with it he observed to the Confederate aides, the bearers of Beauregard's note, "If you do not batter the fort to pieces about us we shall be starved out in a few days." Beauregard, acting with caution, transmitted this remark to Montgomery where equal caution not to precipitate hostilities was shown in the reply: "Do not desire needlessly to bombard Fort Sumter. If Major Anderson will state the time at which . . . he will evacuate Sumter . . . you are authorized thus to avoid the effusion of blood." Evacuation was redemanded by Beauregard's aides at three quarters of an hour after midnight of April 11. This was again refused, but Anderson wrote, "I will . . . evacuate Fort Sumter by noon on the 15th instant . . . should I not re-

ceive prior to that time controlling instructions from my government or additional supplies." The aides considered these
terms "manifestly futile" and, acting in accordance with the letter of their instructions, they gave the order to Fort Johnson to
open fire; the first shell was fired at half past four on the morning of April 12. This shot, the signal for the bombardment to begin, caused a profound thrill throughout the United States and
in point of fact it inaugurated four years of civil war.

The bombardment was unnecessary. Sumter might have been
had without it. Beauregard was needlessly alarmed over the relief expedition that was bringing bread to Anderson. He feared
a descent upon the South Carolina coast by "the United States
fleet then lying at the entrance of the harbor" for the supposed
purpose of reënforcing Fort Sumter. One of his aides reported
that "four large steamers are plainly in view standing off the
bar." The people in Charleston thought that there were six men-
of-war in the offing. In connection with the general alarm on
shore, it is interesting to note the actual mishaps of the relief expedition. This was intended to consist of four war-ships, three
steam-tugs and the merchant steamer *Baltic*. The *Baltic*, with
G.V. Fox, who had command of the expedition, on board, arrived off Charleston one hour and a half before the bombardment began, but found there only one warship. Another arrived
at seven in the morning; but without the *Powhatan*, the most important of the war-ships and the one carrying the equipment
necessary for the undertaking, nothing could be accomplished,
and no attempt was made to provision the fort. Administrative
inefficiency, Seward's meddlesomeness and a heavy storm at
sea conjoined to cause the failure of the expedition. Fox and his
companions watched the bombardment, chafing at their powerlessness to render their brothers-in-arms any assistance.

BOMBARDMENT OF FORT SUMTER

Before leaving Sumter, Beauregard's aides notified Anderson in
writing that in an hour their batteries would open on the fort.
Anderson and his officers went through the casemates where
the men were sleeping, waked them, told them of the impending attack and of his decision not to return the fire until after
daylight. The first shell was from Fort Johnson; at half past four,
it "rose high in air and curving in its course burst almost directly over the fort." The next shot came from Cummings Point,
fired, it is said, by a venerable secessionist from Virginia who

had long awaited the glory of this day. The official account does not confirm the popular impression, but the Lieutenant-Colonel in command wrote that his men were "greatly incited" by the "enthusiasm and example" of this old Virginian who was at one of the Cummings Point batteries "during the greater part of the bombardment." After Cummings Point all the batteries opened in quick succession; Sumter was "surrounded by a circle of fire." Meanwhile the men in the fort, alive to the novelty of the scene, watched the shot and shell directed at them, until, realizing the danger of exposure, they retired to the bomb-proofs to await the usual roll-call and order for breakfast. Having no more bread, they ate pork and damaged rice. At seven o'clock, Anderson gave the order and Sumter discharged its first gun at Cummings Point, following up this shot with a vigorous fire. An hour and a half later Sumter opened upon Moultrie and from that time "a steady and continuous fire" between the two "was kept up throughout the day." For the people of Charleston who gathered on the housetops and thronged to the wharves and to their favorite promenade, the Battery, this artillery duel was a mighty spectacle. They had lost all love for the Union; they hated the American flag . . . and, though apprehensive of danger to their husbands, sons and brothers, they rejoiced that the time was drawing near when the enemy should no longer hold a fort commanding their harbor and city.

In the early afternoon the fire of Sumter slackened; cartridges were lacking, "although the six needles in the fort were kept steadily employed" until all "the extra clothing of the companies, all coarse paper and extra hospital sheets" had been used. After dark Sumter stopped firing; the Confederate batteries continued to throw shells, though at longer intervals. As, during the dark and stormy night, "it was almost confidently expected that the United States fleet would attempt to land troops upon the islands or to throw men into Fort Sumter by means of boats," there was ceaseless vigilance on Morris and Sullivan's islands. Early on Saturday morning [April 13, 1861] the bombardment was renewed. The men in the fort ate the last of the damaged rice with pork, but they sprang briskly to their work. "Fort Sumter opened early and spitefully and paid especial attention to Fort Moultrie," wrote Moultrie's commander. Soon hot shot from Moultrie and other batteries set the officers' quarters on fire. The powder magazine was in danger. Anderson ordered fifty barrels removed and distributed around in the casemates, the magazine doors to be closed and packed with earth. As in the meantime the wooden barracks had taken fire, endangering the powder in the casemates, he commanded that all but five barrels should be thrown into the sea. At one o'clock the flag-staff was struck and fell; and the fallen flag, though soon hoisted again, together with the smoke and the flames gave the Confederates reason to believe that Anderson was in distress. An aide under a white flag was despatched to him from Cummings Point; three more from the city by Beauregard. Negotiations followed resulting in honorable terms. "I marched out of the fort Sunday afternoon the 14th instant," reported Anderson, "with colors flying and drums beating, bringing away company and private property, and saluting my flag with fifty guns."

No Lives Lost

In this momentous battle, no man on either side was killed. As compared with the military writing of two years later, the crudity of the contemporary correspondence and reports is grimly significant. They told of the work of boys learning the rudiments of war—boys who would soon be seasoned veterans wise in the methods of destruction. A strenuous schooling this; and the beginning of it was the artillery duel in Charleston harbor.

Beauregard's aides assumed too great a responsibility in giving the order to fire the first shot; they should have referred Anderson's reply to their chief. There can be no doubt that the Confederate States would have obtained peacefully on Monday what they got by force on Sunday. If Beauregard had had Anderson's last response, he would unquestionably have waited to ask Montgomery for further instructions. The presence of the United States fleet was of course disquieting; yet the danger from this source, even as exaggerated in Beauregard's mind, could be averted quite as well by acting on the defensive, as by the bombardment of Fort Sumter. But South Carolina was hot for possession of the fort and the aides who gave the order that precipitated hostilities were swayed by the passion of the moment.

In April, 1861, war was undoubtedly inevitable. The House divided against itself could not stand. The irrepressible conflict had come to a head; words were a salve no longer. Under the circumstances it was fortunate for Lincoln that the South became the aggressor. Confederate President Jefferson Davis's elaborate apology and the writing inspired by it could never answer the questions put by Northern to Southern soldiers, when they met under a flag of truce or in the banter between Confederates and Federals when opportunities offered, "Who began the war? Who struck the first blow? Who battered the walls of Fort Sumter?"

GENERAL ROBERT E. LEE

JEFFERSON DAVIS

Confederate general Robert Edward Lee (1807–1870) was one of the most celebrated military leaders in the Civil War. His dignified presence and courteous behavior, even in defeat, helped secure his status as an American hero. Although he was ambivalent about states' rights and slavery, he resigned from the federal army when his home state of Virginia seceded in 1861. In 1862 he became the head of the Confederate Army of Northern Virginia, and proved his military genius with victories in the battles of Second Bull Run, Fredericksburg, and Chancellorsville, among others. Confederate president Jefferson Davis describes Lee's personal and military virtues in an article he wrote long after the Civil War for a publication titled the *North American Review*.

R obert Edward Lee, gentleman, scholar, gallant soldier, great general, and true Christian, was born in Westmoreland county, Va., on January 19, 1807. He was the youngest son of General Henry Lee, who was familiarly known as "Light Horse Harry" in the traditions of the war of the Revolution, and who possessed the marked confidence and personal regard of General George Washington.

R.E. Lee entered the United States Military Academy in the summer of 1825, after which my acquaintance with him commenced. He was, as I remember him, larger and looked more mature than the average "plebe." His soldierly bearing and excellent conduct caused him in due succession to rise through

Excerpted from "Jefferson Davis on Robert E. Lee," by Jefferson Davis, *North American Review*, n.d.

the several grades and to be the adjutant of the corps of cadets when he graduated. It is stated that he had not then a "demerit" mark standing against him, which is quite creditable if all "reports" against him had been canceled because they were not for wanton or intentional delinquency. Though numerically rated second in his class his proficiency was such that he was assigned to the engineer corps, which for many years he adorned both as a military and civil engineer. . . .

A SYMPATHETIC TEACHER

In 1852 Colonel Lee was made superintendent of the United States Military Academy—a position for which he seemed to be peculiarly fitted as well by his attainments as by his fondness for young people, his fine personal appearance, and impressive manners. When a year or two thereafter I visited the academy, and was surprised to see so many gray hairs on his head, he confessed that the cadets did exceedingly worry him, and then it was perceptible that his sympathy with young people was rather an impediment than a qualification for the superintendency.

In 1855 four new regiments were added to the army—two of cavalry and two of infantry. Captain Lee, of the engineers, brevet-colonel of the army, was offered the position of lieutenant-colonel of the Second regiment of cavalry, which he accepted. He was a bold, graceful horseman, and the son of Light-Horse Harry now seemed to be in his proper element; but the chief of engineers endeavored to persuade him that it was a descent to go from the engineer corps into the cavalry. Soon after the regiment was organized and assigned to duty in Texas, the colonel, Albert Sidney Johnston, was selected to command an expedition to Utah, and the command of the regiment and the protection of the frontier of Texas against Indian marauders devolved upon Colonel Lee. There, as in every position he had occupied, diligence, sound judgment, and soldierly endowment made his service successful. In 1859, being on leave of absence in Virginia, he was made available for the suppression of the John Brown [slave] raid. As soon as relieved from that special assignment he returned to his command in Texas, and on April 25, 1861, resigned from the United States army.

THE TEST OF ALLEGIANCE

Then was his devotion to principle subjected to a crucial test, the severity of which can only be fully realized by a "West-

Pointer" whose life has been spent in the army. That it was to
sever the friendships of youth, to break up the habits of inter-
course, of manners, and of thought, others may comprehend
and estimate; but the sentiment most profound in the heart of
the war-worn cadet, and which made the change [from the
Union to the Confederacy] most painful to Lee, he has partially
expressed in the letters he wrote at the time to his beloved sister and to his venerated friend and commander, General Winfield Scott.

Partizan malignants have not failed to misrepresent the conduct of Lee, even to the extent of charging him with treason and
desertion; and unable to appreciate his sacrifice to the allegiance
due to Virginia, they have blindly ascribed his action to selfish
ambition. It has been erroneously asserted that he was educated
at the expense of the General Government, and an attempt has
been made then to deduce a special obligation to adhere to it. . . .

No proposition could be more absurd than that he was
prompted by selfish ambition to join the Confederacy. With a
small part of his knowledge of the relative amount of material
of war possessed by the North and South, any one must have
seen that the chances of war were against us; but if thrice-armed
Justice should enable the South to maintain her independence,
as our fathers had done, notwithstanding the unequal contest,
what selfish advantage could it bring Lee? If, as some among us
yet expected, many hoped, and all wished, there should be a
peaceful separation, he would have left behind him all he had
gained by long and brilliant service, and could not leave in our
small army greater rank than was proffered to him in the larger
one he had left. If active hostilities were prosecuted, his large
property would be so exposed as to incur serious injury, if not
destruction. His mother, Virginia, had revoked the grants she
had voluntarily made to the Federal Government, and asserted
the State sovereignty and independence she had won from the
mother-country by the war of the Revolution; and thus, it was
regarded, the allegiance of her sons became wholly her own.
Above the voice of his friends at Washington, advising and en-
treating him to stay with them, rose the cry of Virginia calling
her sons to defend her against threatened invasion. Lee heeded
this cry only—alone he rode forth . . . his guiding star being
duty, and offered his sword to Virginia. His offer was accepted,
and he was appointed to the chief command of the forces of the
State. Though his reception was most flattering, and the confi-

dence manifested in him unlimited, his conduct was conspicuous for the modesty and moderation which had always been characteristic of him.

THE STATE OF THE CONFEDERACY

The South had been involved in war without having made due preparations for it. She was without a navy, without even a merchant marine commensurate with her wants during peace; without arsenals, armories, foundries, manufactories, or stores on hand to supply those wants. Lee exerted himself to the utmost to raise and organize troops in Virginia, and when the State joined the Confederacy he was invited to come to [the Confederate capital] Montgomery, Alabama, and explain the condition of his command; but his engagements were so pressing that he sent his second officer, General J.E. Johnston, to furnish the desired information.

When the capital of the Confederacy was removed from Montgomery to Richmond, Virginia, Lee, under the orders of the President Jefferson Davis, was charged with the general direction of army affairs. In this position the same pleasant relations which had always existed between them continued, and Lee's indefatigable attention to the details of the various commands was of much benefit to the public service. In the meantime disasters, confusion, and disagreement among the commands in western Virginia made it necessary to send there an officer of higher rank than any then on duty in that section. The service was disagreeable, toilsome, and in no wise promising to give distinction to a commander. Passing by all reference to others, suffice it to say that at last Lee was asked to go, and, not counting the cost, he unhesitatingly prepared to start. By concentrating the troops, and by a judicious selection of the position he compelled the enemy finally to retreat.

A COMPASSIONATE COMMANDER

There is an incident in this campaign which has never been reported, save as it was orally given to me by General Lee, with a request that I should take no official notice of it. A strong division of the enemy was reported to be encamped in a valley, which one of the colonels said he had found by reconnaissance could readily be approached on one side, and he proposed with his regiment to surprise and attack. General Lee accepted his proposition, but told him that he himself would, in the mean-

time, with several regiments, ascend the mountain that over-
looked the valley on the other side, and at dawn of day, on a
morning fixed, the Colonel was to make his assault. His firing
was to be the signal for a joint attack from three directions. During the night Lee made a toilsome ascent of the mountain and
was in position at the time agreed upon. The valley was covered
by a dense fog. Not hearing the signal, he went by a winding
path down the side of the mountain and saw the enemy prepar-

*Robert E. Lee's military intelligence, integrity, and concern for his
men earned him the respect of his superiors and his soldiers.*

ing breakfast and otherwise so engaged as to indicate that they were entirely ignorant of any danger. Lee returned to his own command, told them what he had seen, and though the expected signal had not been given by which the attacking regiment and another detachment were to engage in the assault, he proposed that the regiments then with him should surprise the camp, which he believed, under the circumstances, might successfully be done. The colonels went to consult their men, and returned to inform that they were so cold, wet, and hungry, as to be unfit for the enterprise. The fog was then lifting, and it was necessary to attack immediately or to withdraw before being discovered by the much larger force in the valley. Lee therefore withdrew his small command and safely conducted them to his encampment.

The colonel who was to give the signal for the joint attack, mis-apprehending the purpose, reported that when he arrived upon the ground he found the encampment protected by a heavy abattis, which prevented him from making a sudden charge, as he had expected, not understanding that if he had fired his guns at any distance he would have secured the joint attack of the other detachments, and probably brought about an entire victory. Lee generously forebore to exonerate himself when the newspapers in Richmond criticised him severely, one denying him any other consideration except that which he enjoyed as "the President's pet."

It was an embarrassment to the Executive to be deprived of the advice of General Lee, but it was deemed necessary again to detach him to look after affairs on the coast of Carolina and Georgia, and so violent had been the unmerited attacks upon him by the Richmond press that it was thought proper to give him a letter to the Governor of South Carolina, stating what manner of man had been sent to him. There his skill as an engineer was manifested in the defenses he constructed and devised. On his return to Richmond he resumed his functions of general supervisor of military affairs. . . .

LEE'S STRATEGY

There was never a greater mistake than that which was attributed to General Lee what General Charles Lee, in his reply to General Washington, called the "rascally virtue." I have had occasion to remonstrate with General Lee for exposing himself, as I thought, unnecessarily in reconnaissance, but he justified himself by saying he "could not understand things so well unless he saw them." In the excitement of battle his natural combativeness would sometimes overcome his habitual self-control; thus it twice occurred in the campaign against Grant that the men seized his bridle to restrain him from his purpose to lead them in a charge.

He was always careful not to wound the sensibilities of any one, and sometimes with an exterior jest or compliment, would give what, if properly appreciated, was instruction for the better performance of some duty: for example, if he thought a general officer was not visiting his command as early and as often as was desirable, he might admire his horse and suggest that the animal would be improved by more exercise.

He was not of the grave, formal nature that he seemed to some who only knew him when sad realities cast dark shadows upon him; but even then the humor natural to him would occasionally break out. For instance, General Lee called at my office for a ride to the defense of Richmond, then under construction. He was mounted on a stallion which some kind friend had recently sent him. As I mounted my horse, his was restive and kicked at mine. We rode on quietly together, though Lee was watchful to keep his horse in order. Passing by an encampment, we saw near a tent two stallions tied at a safe distance from one another. "There," said he, "is a man worse off than I am." When asked to explain, he said: "Don't you see, he has two stallions? I have but one."

His habits had always been rigidly temperate, and his fare in camp was of the simplest. I remember on one battle-field riding past where he and his staff were taking their luncheon. He invited me to share it, and when I dismounted for the purpose, it proved to have consisted only of bacon and cornbread. The bacon had all been eaten, and there were only some crusts of cornbread left, which, however, having been saturated with the bacon gravy, were in those hard times altogether acceptable, as General Lee was assured, in order to silence his regrets. . . .

AFTER THE WAR

After the close of the war, while I was in prison and Lee was on parole, we were both indicted on a charge of treason; but, in hot haste to get in their work, the indictment was drawn with the fatal omission of an overt act. General Grant interposed in the case of General Lee, on the ground that he had taken his parole and that he was, therefore, not subject to arrest. Another grand

jury was summoned and a bill was presented against me alone
and amended by inserting specifications of overt acts. General
Lee was summoned as a witness before that grand jury, the object being to prove by him that I was responsible for certain
things done by him during the war. I was in Richmond, having
been released by virtue of the writ of habeas corpus. General
Lee met me very soon after having given his testimony before
the grand jury, and told me that to the inquiry whether he had
not, in the specified cases, acted under my orders, he said that
he had always consulted me when he had the opportunity, both
on the field and elsewhere; that after discussion, if not before,
we had always agreed, and therefore he had done with my consent and approval only what he might have done if he had not
consulted me, and that he accepted the full responsibility for his
acts. He said he had endeavored to present the matter as distinctly as he could, and looked up to see what effect he was producing upon the grand jury. Immediately before him sat a big
black negro, whose head had fallen back on the rail of the bench
he sat on; his mouth was wide open, and he was fast asleep.
General Lee pleasantly added that, if he had had any vanity as
an orator, it would have received a rude check.

The evident purpose was to offer to Lee a chance to escape
by transferring to me the responsibility for overt acts. Not only
to repel the suggestion, but unequivocally to avow his individual responsibility, with all that, under existing circumstances,
was implied in this, was the highest reach of moral courage and
gentlemanly pride. Those circumstances were exceptionally per-
ilous to him. He had been indicted for treason; the United States
President had vindictively threatened to make treason odious;
the dregs of society had been thrown to the surface; judicial
seats were held by political adventurers; the United States judge
of the Virginia district had answered to a committee of Congress
that he could pack a jury so as to convict Davis or Lee—and it
was under such surroundings that he met the grand jury and
testified as stated above. Arbitrary power might pervert justice
and trample on right, but could not turn the knightly Lee from
the path of honor and truth.

Descended from a long line of illustrious warriors and states-
men, Robert Edward Lee added new glory to the name he bore,
and, whether measured by a martial or an intellectual standard,
will compare favorably with those whose reputation it devolved upon him to sustain and emulate.

THE BATTLE OF BULL RUN

R. ERNEST DUPUY AND TREVOR N. DUPUY

The First Battle of Bull Run (Manassas), on July 21, 1861, marked the first serious battle of the Civil War. The Union and Confederate armies approached the battlefield with patriotic fervor and enthusiasm, but very few of the soldiers had any military training. The battle from both sides was poorly organized, and the battlefield was characterized by confusion and chaos. Many soldiers were accidentally killed by their comrades in the melee. Although most consider it a Confederate victory, the fight proved that neither the Yankees nor the Rebels were prepared for war. In the following article, R. Ernest Dupuy and Trevor N. Dupuy describe the landmark battle that fired the enthusiasm of the Southerners and pricked the confidence of the Unionists. R. Ernest Dupuy was the author of several military books, including *Where They Have Trod* and *Civilian Defense of the U.S.* His son, coauthor Trevor N. Dupuy, was the author of *Brave Men and Great Captains* and *First Book of Civil War Land Battles*.

I t was sunny and hot, that Sunday morning of July 21, 1861, and fashionable Washington, it seemed, had gone picnicking across to Virginia heedless of the church bells. Fine ladies in barouches, their parasols mushrooming above them; smart gentlemen tooling gigs or astride horses, packed the dusty Warrenton Turnpike. They were bound for Centreville to see Union General Irvin McDowell trounce his West Point classmate General Pierre Beauregard, commanding the Confederates at Manassas. Hampers and saddlebags were packed with goodies—

Excerpted from *The Compact History of the Civil War* by R. Ernest Dupuy and Trevor N. Dupuy (New York: Hawthorn, 1960). Copyright © 1960 by Hawthorn Books, Inc. Reprinted with permission.

solid and liquid—and everyone was in holiday spirit, despite the heat and the dust and the delays incident to threading their way through a straggling column of men in blue uniform, bound in the opposite direction. These were militiamen hurrying homeward, their three-months' service completed, oblivious of the rumble of cannonading behind them. The merrymakers' only worry, on the other hand, was that they might miss something of the splendid opportunity to see a real battle. As it turned out, their curiosity was more than satisfied. It was also the last picnic that Washingtonians would indulge in for a long time.

THE CALL TO ARMS

Three months of patriotic fervor had come to its frothing climax. Since President Lincoln issued his first call for militia the response of the Northern states had been overwhelming. Uniformed hordes in variegated costumes poured into Washington, bedded down in public buildings, huddled in tented camps, roistered in the streets. Two things they all had in common: determination to crush rebellion; and, with the exception of a few regiments, an almost complete ignorance of soldiering. There had been some difficulty in getting there; the 6th Massachusetts—first to answer the call—had had to fight its way through a secessionist mob in Baltimore, at a cost of four men killed and thirty-one wounded. New York's "silk stocking" 7th Regiment, next to arrive, had been detoured around Baltimore, taking steamboats at Perryville for Annapolis.

The match was soon applied to this collective powder-keg. The Northern public and press, enraged by the fall of Fort Sumter, and united for victory, clamored for an immediate advance. Here were the men; there, at Manassas, was the enemy. What were we waiting for?

Further Union irritation was caused by a clash on June 10, at Big Bethel Church near Yorktown. The Southerners were commanded by General John B. Magruder, holding the Peninsula against the threat of Butler's Union forces assembled at Fortress Monroe. Butler had attempted a surprise move toward Yorktown, but the green Federal troops collided with one another and the clumsy assault was handily thrown back by a small number of Confederate troops. The Southerners, equally green, were led by Colonel D.H. Hill, West Pointer and ex-Regular.

Physically nothing more than a skirmish—the Federals lost

seventy-six men and the Confederates eleven—psychologically this clash brought exultation to Southern adherents, the *Richmond Dispatch* hailing it as one of the most extraordinary victories in the annals of war. To the North, Big Bethel was just another infuriation. The pressure on the administration became overwhelming.

PRESSURE TO ATTACK

McDowell had been wrestling with the Augean task of trying to create soldiers overnight. Under the pressure for action, he reluctantly brought out a plan. He would move on the Manassas Confederate concentration, turn its position by a wide flanking envelopment, and eject his enemy "by threatening or seizing his communications." Approved June 24, 1861, the plan was ordered into execution July 8. Vital to success would be the Federal government's ability to keep Confederate concentrations in the lower Shenandoah Valley from reinforcing Beauregard at Manassas. General Winfield Scott sent urgent orders to General Robert Patterson to keep General Joseph Johnston pinned down near Winchester.

Not until July 16 was McDowell able to begin his move, for not until that very day had he been able to organize his so-called army into brigades or divisions. The long, ungainly column marched bravely out from Alexandria, banners streaming, to inchworm through Fairfax Courthouse and on to Centreville. In all that mass of 38,000 men there were not 2,000 professionals.

It took the Union army the better part of two days to concentrate about Centreville, and McDowell wasted two more days in determining how best to tackle his enemy. The Confederates, he knew, lay behind the steep tree-lined banks of Bull Run, which meandered generally southeast across the Warrenton Pike about four miles west of Centreville. Their line apparently ran seven miles, from the Stone Bridge carrying the Pike, down to the Orange and Alexandria Railroad trestle across Bull Run at Union Mills.

MCDOWELL'S STRATEGY

On the eighteenth, a Federal reconnaissance, moving in force against the approximate center of the Confederate position, directly south of Centreville, met with bloody repulse in front of Mitchell's and Blackburn's Fords. To turn the Confederate right presented difficulties; neither the terrain nor the water courses favored such approach. But McDowell's engineers, reconnoitering to the northwest, found favorable ground. Believing he had more men than Beauregard, McDowell decided he would turn the Southern left flank. Starting in the morning hours of darkness on July 21, two divisions—McDowell would lead them in person—were to make a twelve-mile circuitous march west from Centreville, cross Bull Run at Sudley Springs ford well beyond Beauregard's left—then strike due south down the Manassas-Sudley road. Another division would drive directly west along the Turnpike and across the Stone Bridge. A detached brigade would make a feint against the fords directly south of Centreville where the Union fingers had been burned on the eighteenth. Back at Centreville another division would lie in reserve. The remaining Union division was scattered along the line of communications all the way back to Washington; it would take no part in the battle. The total combat force available for battle was 32,000 men.

The plan was ambitious, with success dependent upon the coordination of the movements of three widely separated forces. Given competent commanders, an efficient staff and highly-trained troops, it might well have worked. But it was far beyond the capability of a poorly-trained, just-organized team, running out on the field for its first tussle. What McDowell didn't know, when he issued his order on the evening of July 20, was that his offensive plans were known to the enemy high command even before he left Washington; that Beauregard had expected to be attacked on the seventeenth; and that Johnston, deftly screening his move from doddering Patterson's Winchester front, had left the Shenandoah Valley for Manassas. Actually Johnston and the bulk of his troops, moving by rail—the first time the railroad played a strategic role in war—had joined Beauregard. Johnston's last element, Edmund Kirby Smith's brigade, would be rattling down the Manassas Gap Railroad from Strasburg next morning. In addition, Holmes' brigade from Aquia Creek had also arrived.

Two strikes, then, had been called on McDowell before he came up to the plate. Confederate intelligence had diagnosed the Union intentions and strength. The railroad had furnished the Confederacy the strategic mobility with which to concentrate on interior lines. As a result, McDowell's available 32,000 strength would be pitted in an offensive against 35,000 men who lay in a defensive position on very favorable terrain. Beauregard's elements covered all the Bun Run crossings. The bulk of his strength, including Johnston's newly arrived troops, lay opposite Centreville for a very good reason. Beauregard intended to take the offensive himself, driving between Centreville and Fairfax Courthouse and cutting McDowell's exposed communications. Johnston, who was senior to Beauregard, assumed command on arrival, but approved Beauregard's dispositions for the battle and, for all practical purposes, left the immediate, tactical control to him.

YANKEE MISHAPS

On the Union side, things went wrong from the first, that Sunday morning. The feint against the fords never materialized. The main effort, 12,000 strong, was delayed in getting away. It didn't reach the Sudley Spring ford until after nine o'clock. The secondary attack, against Beauregard's extreme left at the Stone Bridge, was pushed so half-heartedly that the local Confederate commander, wily Brigadier General Nathan G. ("Shanks") Evans suspected that it was not the main attack. A courier from a Confederate picket at Sudley Springs brought word of Federal troops moving south on the Manassas-Sudley road, and this was confirmed by flag signals. So Evans shifted the major part of his command—a little more than one regiment—to the left rear onto high ground not far north of the turnpike, just in time to meet the main Union advance.

Evans' action changed the entire complexion of the battle. His small force, far out on the Confederate left, was at once involved in hot engagement as McDowell attacked and the Federal artillery came into action. Beauregard, who early that morning had become convinced that the Union commander was committing himself to an attack along the Warrenton Pike in the Stone Bridge area, had begun, with Johnston's approval, to shift his reserves—Johnston's troops from Winchester—to back up that sector. At the same time, also with Johnston's approval, he ordered his own attack. His right center would cross Bull Run on its front and hit the Federal left and rear at Centreville.

REBEL MISHAPS

But it was now the Confederates' turn to stumble. The attack order, because of faulty staff work, never reached the brigade commander who was to lead it. Since he didn't move, neither did the others. By 10:30 A.M., when Beauregard discovered that his plan had miscarried, the sound of battle on his left indicated a serious engagement, although the point of impact and the Union objective were still both nebulous.

Johnston and Beauregard, galloping to the sound of the guns, found that Evans, together with two reinforcing brigades, was being driven back eastward upon the Henry House Hill—a flattish ridge pointing into the southeastern angle between the Turnpike and the Manassas-Sudley road. In overwhelming force, the Federal attack was overlapping the Confederate left on this new battlefront, while Brigadier General William T. Sherman's Union brigade, fording Bull Run west of the Stone Bridge, was threatening its right. The sole remaining Confederate local reserve was Brigadier General Thomas J. Jackson's Virginia brigade, just arrived on the Henry House Hill.

Johnston, putting Beauregard in charge of the combat area, established his command post further behind the line and busied himself with withdrawing the remaining Southern forces originally lining Bull Run and disposing them to meet the new situation.

Meanwhile, Jackson, picking his terrain carefully, formed his brigade on the northeastern side of the Henry House Hill, to cover the disorganized retreat of the Southern troops recoiling from McDowell's assault. The immovable Virginians checked the Union advance and the retreating troops reformed behind them. "There stands Jackson like a stone wall!" cried Confederate General Barnard E. Bee as he rallied the fugitives.

STRENGTH IN NUMBERS

But McDowell still had twice the strength of the Confederates at Henry House Hill, and his men had plenty of fight left in them. He pressed on.

The Federals gained the northwestern edge of the ridge, their lines lapping around the Henry House Hill. Two Union artillery batteries came slashing into action in close support of the infantry, but they dropped trails within musket-shot of woods on their right, from which Confederate sharpshooters began picking off horses and cannoneers. A squadron of Southern cavalry—J.E.B. Stuart's—scattered the Union infantry near the guns and overran the batteries. Immediately, additional Union infantry moved in to regain them.

Three times the silent guns were taken and retaken as the

fighting surged back and forth. Then McDowell's rear guard brigade, his last reserve south of the stream, arrived on the field, extending the Union line to the right. Victory, it seemed, was almost in the Federal general's hands; Beauregard's left was again outflanked.

But up from the railroad at Manassas Junction came Kirby Smith's brigade, just in from Winchester. Johnston threw it against the Federal right. Hot on its heels, ordered from its position at the lower fords on the original Confederate right, came Early's brigade. McDowell's offensive collapsed; the Northern soldiers who had now been marching and fighting for twelve hours could do no more against these fresh troops. The blue lines melted, soldiers simply leaving their ranks and starting back the way they had come, heedless of their officers. By 4:30 P.M., not a Union soldier remained on the battlefield, except for the dead and the wounded.

UNION RETREAT

Protected by the Regulars—William H. Sikes' infantry battalion and J.M. Palmer's cavalry—who never broke formation, the Federal horde went trudging back to the turnpike west of Bull Run. Most of the Confederates on the field were themselves too tired and too disorganized to make any great effort. Stuart's cavalry made a few passes but the dogged Regulars easily beat them off. Federal losses were 481 killed, 1,011 wounded and 1,216 missing (many of these prisoners). The Confederates lost 387 men killed, 1,582 wounded and 13 missing.

For a while the steady tide of Federal defeat flowed eastward, with the Washington picnickers and their transport scattered amidst the men, guns and wagons crowding the road. Then across the field from the lower fords of Bull Run came R.C.W. Radford's squadron of Confederate cavalry, with a four-gun battery, to make a tentative jab at the pike. The fugitives hurried their pace. Two miles east of the Stone Bridge, a lucky Southern shell smashed a wagon and momentarily blocked passage. That did it. Panic flared and the entire mob stampeded. Except for the little clump of Regulars, protecting the rear, McDowell's army evaporated in the dusk.

The Union's bright bubble of enthusiasm had been pricked. The last of the tattered refugees were still crossing the Long Bridge into Washington next morning. It took another twenty-four hours to pick up the wounded from the battlefield. In the

Southern Confederacy hopes soared high. Its combat superiority had been proven on a stricken field, for all the world to see. Virginia in particular was justly proud of herself; Virginia troops had made up a good twenty-five per cent of the victorious army.

While Confederate pickets roamed the Potomac heights within sight of a dazed capital, President Abraham Lincoln now began wrestling with the problem to plague him for three more years to come: he had to find a general. Out of the ruck and frustration [the] meteoric personality [of Ulysses S. Grant] was to soar into view.

THE BATTLE AT ANTIETAM CREEK

EYEWITNESS

The Battle of Antietam on September 17, 1862, was the single bloodiest day of war in American history. Union and Confederate casualties totaled more than twenty-three thousand, and only the fatigue of the soldiers ended the battle. Although technically the battle ended in a draw, it was a strategic victory for the North, because Confederate general Robert E. Lee retreated across the Potomac the next night. The following article excerpts two Union soldiers' firsthand accounts of the battle and their reactions to the carnage.

G eneral Robert E. Lee's first invasion of the North was a huge gamble that held the potential of very great rewards. Lee's campaign could win Maryland for the Confederacy, earn diplomatic recognition from Britain and France, and perhaps even force the Union to sue for peace. It would also take his troops out of war-ravaged Virginia during harvest time, and enable his troops to live off the enemy's country for a while. Following his victory at the Second Battle of Bull Run Lee led his ragtag army northward across the Potomac River and into Union territory.

The ensuing battle on September 17, 1862, produced the bloodiest day in American combat history with over 23,000 casualties on both sides. More than twice as many Americans were killed or mortally wounded in combat at Antietam that day as in the War of 1812, the Mexican War, and the Spanish-American War combined.

The two armies met in the Maryland farm fields bordering the trickling Antietam Creek near the town of Sharpsburg. The Union named the conflict the Battle of Antietam in honor of the creek while the South called it the Battle of Sharpsburg in honor of the town. From dawn till dark on the 17th the two armies threw frontal attacks at each other, littering the fields with their dead and wounded. "The whole landscape for an instant turned red," one northern soldier later wrote. Another veteran recalled, "[The cornfield] was so full of bodies that a man could have walked through it without stepping on the ground." No clear victor emerged and the fighting stopped out of shear exhaustion. Lee withdrew during the night of September 18, and re-crossed the Potomac. Tactically, the battle ended in a draw. Strategically, it was a victory for the Union.

Baptism of Fire at Bloody Lane

Some of the day's most brutal combat occurred during the late morning along a sunken road held by the Confederates. For two and one half hours Union troops threw themselves at the entrenched Confederates finally dislodging them. The murderous fire from both sides left the battlefield strewn with corpses giving the road the name "Bloody Lane." Lt. Frederick Hitchcock was a member of the 132d Pennsylvania Volunteers and experienced his first combat that day.

"We . . . moved, as I thought, rather leisurely for upwards of two miles, crossing Antietam Creek, which our men waded nearly waist deep, emerging, of course, soaked through, our first experience of this kind. It was a hot morning and, therefore, the only ill effect of this wading was the discomfort to the men of marching with soaked feet. It was now quite evident that a great battle was in progress. A deafening pandemonium of cannonading, with shrieking and bursting shells, filled the air beyond us, towards which we were marching. An occasional shell whizzed by or over, reminding us that we were rapidly approaching the 'debatable ground.'

"Soon we began to hear a most ominous sound which we had never before heard, except in the far distance at South Mountain, namely, the rattle of musketry. It had none of the deafening bluster of the cannonading so terrifying to new troops, but to those who had once experienced its effects, it was infinitely more to be dreaded. These volleys of musketry we were approaching sounded in the distance like the rapid pouring of shot upon a tinpan, or the tearing of heavy canvas, with slight pauses interspersed with single shots, or desultory shooting."

"All this presaged fearful work in store for us, with what results to each personally in the future, measured probably by moments, would reveal. How does one feel under such conditions? To tell the truth, I realized the situation most keenly and felt very uncomfortable. Lest there might be some undue manifestation of this feeling on my conduct, I said to myself, this is the duty I undertook to perform for my country, and now I'll do it, and leave the results with God. My greater fear was not that I might be killed, but that I might be grievously wounded and left a victim suffering on the field. The nervous strain was plainly visible upon all of us. All moved doggedly forward in obedience to orders, in absolute silence so far as talking was concerned. The compressed lip and set teeth showed that nerve and resolution had been summoned to the discharge of duty. A few temporarily fell out, unable to endure the nervous strain."

WITH BURNSIDE AT ANTIETAM CREEK

On the night of September 16, the 9th New York Volunteers took up their position opposite a stone bridge crossing Antietam Creek and awaited orders. As dawn broke, the soldiers could hear the sounds of battle on their right and left but no orders were given to advance. By afternoon, as the fighting ebbed and flowed on other parts of the battlefield, General Ambrose Burnside gave the order for his troops to attack the Confederates positioned across the Antietam Creek. David Thompson, a member of the 9th N.Y. volunteers describes his experience:

"So the morning wore away and the fighting on the right ceased entirely. That was fresh anxiety—the scales were turning perhaps, but which way? About noon the battle began afresh. This must have been Franklin's men of the Sixth Corps, for the firing was nearer, and they came up behind the center. Suddenly a stir beginning far upon the right, and running like a wave along the line, brought the regiment to its feet. A silence fell on every one at once, for each felt that the momentous 'now' had come. Just as we started I saw, with a little shock, a line-officer take out his watch to note the hour, as though the affair beyond the creek were a business appointment which he was going to keep."

"When we reached the brow of the hill the fringe of trees along the creek screened the fighting entire, and we were deployed as skirmishers under their cover. We sat there two hours. All that time the rest of corps had been moving over the stone bridge and going into position on the other side of the creek. Then we were ordered over a ford which had been found below the bridge, where the water was waist deep. One man was shot in mid-stream.

"At the foot of the slope on the opposite side the line was formed and we moved up through the thin woods. Reaching the level we lay down behind a battery which seemed to have been disabled. There, if anywhere, I should have remembered that I was soaking wet from my waist down. So great was the excitement, however, that I have never been able to recall it. Here some of the men, going to the rear for water, discovered in the ashes of some hay-ricks which had been fired by our shells the charred remains of several Confederates. After long waiting it became noised along the line that we were to take a battery that was at work several yards ahead on the top of a hill. This narrowed the field and brought us to consider the work before us more attentively.

"Right across our front, two hundred feet or so away, ran a country road bordered on each side by a snake fence. Beyond this road stretched a plowed field several hundred feet in length, sloping up to the battery which was hidden in a corn field. A stone fence, breast-high, inclosed the field on the left,

The Battle of Antietam was the single bloodiest day of war in American history, with casualties totaling more than twenty-three thousand.

and behind it lay a regiment of Confederates, who would be directly on our flank if we should attempt the slope. The prospect was far from encouraging, but the order came to get ready for the attempt.

RUSHING THE ENEMY

"Our knapsacks were left on the ground behind us. At the word a rush was made for the fences. The line was so disordered by the time the second fence was passed that we hurried forward to a shallow undulation a few feet ahead, and lay down among the furrows to re-form, doing so by crawling up into line. A hundred feet or so ahead was a similar undulation to which we ran for a second shelter. The battery, which at first had not seemed to notice us, now, apprised of its danger, opened fire upon us. We were getting ready now for the charge proper, but were still lying on our faces. Lieutenant-Colonel John W. Kimball was ramping up and down the line. The discreet regiment behind the fence was silent. Now and then a bullet from them cut the air over our head, but generally they were reserving their fire for that better show which they knew they would get in a few minutes. The battery, however, whose shots at first went over our heads, had depressed its guns so as to shave the surface of the ground. Its fire was beginning to tell.

"I remember looking behind and seeing an officer riding diagonally across the field—a most inviting target—instinctively bending his head down over his horse's neck, as though he were riding through driving rain. While my eye was on him I saw, between me and him a rolled overcoat with its traps on bound into the air and fall among the furrows. One of the enemy's grape-shot had plowed a groove in the skull of a young fellow and had cut his overcoat from his shoulders. He never stirred from his position, but lay there face downward, a dreadful spectacle. A moment after, I heard a man cursing a comrade for lying on him heavily. He was cursing a dying man.

"As the range grew better, the firing became more rapid, the situation desperate and exasperating to the last degree. Human nature was on the race, and there burst forth from it the most vehement, terrible swearing I have ever heard. Certainly the joy of conflict was not ours that day. The suspense was only for a moment, however, for the order to charge came just after. Whether the regiment was thrown into disorder or not, I never knew. I only remember that as we rose, and started all the fire that had been held back so long was loosed. In a second the air was full of the hiss of bullets and the hurtle of grape-shot. The mental strain was so great that I saw at the moment the singular effect mentioned, I think, in the life of Goethe on a similar occasion—the whole landscape for an instant turned slight red.

"I see again, as I saw it then in a flash, a man just in front of me drop his musket and throw up his hands, stung into vigorous swearing by a bullet behind the ear. Many men fell going up the hill, but it seemed to be all over in a moment, and I found myself passing a hollow where a dozen wounded men lay—among them our sergeant-major who was calling me to come down. He had caught sight of the blanket rolled across my back, and called me to unroll it and help to carry from the field one of our wounded lieutenants."

THE BATTLE OF GETTYSBURG

FRANK ARETAS HASKELL

The Battle of Gettysburg, fought during the first few days of July 1863, was a significant turning point in the Civil War. Unionists and Confederates believed that Southern victory at Gettysburg would probably end the war in favor of the Confederacy. During the bloodiest battle ever to take place in the United States, more than 28,000 Confederates were killed compared with 23,000 Union soldiers. Rebel general Robert E. Lee lost nearly one-third of his army, and the remaining soldiers were forced out of the North. For the rest of the war, the Yankees fought with renewed confidence and vigor that resulted in their ultimate victory in 1865. Frank Aretas Haskell, a staff officer for Union general John Gibbon, describes the violent Battle of Gettysburg in a letter he wrote to his brother in 1863.

The great battle of Gettysburg is now an event of the past. The composition and strength of the armies, their leaders, the strategy, the tactics, the result, of that field are today by the side of those of Waterloo—matters of history. A few days ago these things were otherwise. This great event did not so "cast its shadow before," as to moderate the hot sunshine that streamed upon our preceding march, or to relieve our minds of all apprehension of the result of the second great Rebel invasion of the soil North of the Potomac. . . .

Without a topographical map, some description of the ground and location is necessary to a clear understanding of the battle. . . . The line of battle as it was established, on the evening

Excerpted from *Excerpt of the Battle of Gettysburg* by Frank Aretas Haskell (Frank Aretas Haskell, 1863).

of the first, and morning of the second of July was in the form of the letter "U," the troops facing outwards. And the "Cemetery," which is at the point of the sharpest curvature of the line, being due South of the town of Gettysburg. "Round Top," the extreme left of the line, is a small, woody, rocky elevation, a very little West of South of the town, and nearly two miles from it. . . .

So, before a great battle, was ranged the [Union] Army of the Potomac. The day wore on, the weather still sultry, and the sky overcast, with a mizzling effort at rain. When the audience has all assembled, time seems long until the curtain rises; so today. "Will there be a battle to-day?" "Shall we attack the Rebel?" "Will he attack us?" These and similar questions, later in the morning, were thought or asked a million times.

Meanwhile, on our part, all was put in the last state of readiness for battle. Surgeons were busy riding about selecting eligible places for Hospitals, and hunting streams, and springs, and wells. Ambulances, and ambulance men, were brought up near the lines, and stretchers gotten ready for use. Who of us could tell but that he would be the first to need them? . . .

Skillful generalship and good fighting are the jewels of war. These concurring are difficult to overcome; and these, not numbers, must determine this battle. . . .

THE FIGHTING BEGINS

The Third Corps now became the absorbing object of interest of all eyes. The Second Corps took arms, and the 1st Division of this Corps was ordered to be in readiness to support the Third Corps, should circumstances render support necessary. As the Third Corps was the extreme left of our line, as it advanced, if the enemy was assembling to the West of Round Top with a view to turn our left, as we had heard, there would be nothing between the left flank of the Corps and the enemy, and the enemy would be square upon its flank by the time it had attained the road. So when this advance line came near the Emmetsburg road, and we saw the squadrons of cavalry mentioned, come dashing back from their position as flankers, and the smoke of some guns, and we heard the reports away to General Daniel Sickles' left, anxiety became an element in our interest in these movements.

The enemy opened slowly at first, and from long range; but he was square upon Sickles' left flank. General John Caldwell was ordered at once to put his Division—the 1st of the Second

Corps, as mentioned—in motion, and to take post in the woods at the left slope of Round Top, in such a manner as to resist the enemy should he attempt to come around Sickles' left and gain his rear. . . . So the plot thickened. As the enemy opened upon Sickles with his batteries, some five or six in all, I suppose, firing slowly, Sickles with as many replied, and with much more spirit. The artillery fire became quite animated, soon; but the enemy was forced to withdraw his guns farther and farther away, and ours advanced upon him. It was not long before the cannonade ceased altogether, the enemy having retired out of range, and Sickles, having temporarily halted his command, pending this, moved forward again to the position he desired, or nearly that. It was now about five o'clock, and we shall soon see what Sickles gained by his move. First we hear more artillery firing upon Sickles' left—the enemy seems to be opening again, and as we watch the Rebel batteries seem to be advancing there. The cannonade is soon opened again, and with great spirit upon both sides. The enemy's batteries press those of Sickles, and pound the shot upon them, and this time they in turn begin to retire to position nearer the infantry.

The enemy seems to be fearfully in earnest this time. And what is more ominous than the thunder or the shot of his advancing guns, this time, in the intervals between his batteries, far to Sickles' left, appear the long lines and the columns of the Rebel infantry, now unmistakably moving out to the attack. The position of the Third Corps becomes at once one of great peril, and it is probable that its commander by this time began to realize his true situation. All was astir now on our crest. Generals and their Staffs were galloping hither and thither—the men were all in their places, and you might have heard the rattle of ten thousand ramrods as they drove home and "thugged" upon the little globes and cones of lead. As the enemy was advancing upon Sickles' flank, he commenced a change, or at least a partial one, of front, by swinging back his left and throwing forward his right, in order that his lines might be parallel to those of his adversary, his batteries meantime doing what they could to check the enemy's advance; but this movement was not completely executed before new Rebel batteries opened upon Sickles' right flank—his former front—and in the same quarter appeared the Rebel infantry also.

Now came the dreadful battle picture, of which we for a time could be but spectators. Upon the front and right flank of Sickles came sweeping the infantry of Lieutenant General James Longstreet and Lieutenant General A.P. Hill. Hitherto there had been skirmishing and artillery practice—now the battle began; for amid the heavier smoke and larger tongues of flame of the batteries, now began to appear the countless flashes, and the long fiery sheets of the muskets, and the rattle of the volleys, mingled with the thunder of the guns. We see the long gray lines come sweeping down upon Sickles' front, and mix with the battle smoke; now the same colors emerge from the bushes and orchards upon his right, and envelope his flank in the confusion of the conflict. . . .

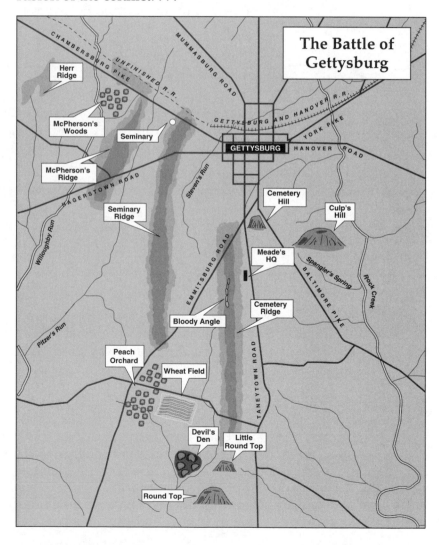

SMOKE AND FIRE

The fire all along our crest is terrific, and it is a wonder how anything human could have stood before it, and yet the madness of the enemy drove them on, clear up to the muzzle of the guns, clear up to the lines of our infantry—but the lines stood right in their places. Gen. Winfield Scott Hancock and his Aides rode up to General John Gibbon's Division, under the smoke. Gen. Gibbon, with myself, was near, and there was a flag dimly visible, coming towards us from the direction of the enemy. "Here, what are these men falling back for?" said Hancock. The flag was no more than fifty yards away, but it was the head of a Rebel column, which at once opened fire with a volley. Lieut. Miller, Gen. Hancock's Aide, fell, twice struck, but the General was unharmed. . . . Such fighting as this cannot last long. It is now near sundown, and the battle has gone on wonderfully long already. But if you will stop to notice it, a change has occurred. The Rebel cry has ceased, and the men of the Union begin to shout there, under the smoke, and their lines to advance. See, the Rebels are breaking! They are in confusion in all our front! The wave has rolled upon the rock, and the rock has smashed it. Let us shout, too! . . .

Not less, I estimate, than twenty thousand men were killed or wounded in this fight. Our own losses must have been nearly half this number,—about four thousand in the Third Corps, fully two thousand in the Second, and I think two thousand in the Fifth, and I think the losses of the First, Twelfth, and a little more than a brigade of the Sixth—all of that Corps which was actually engaged—would reach nearly two thousand more. Of course it will never be possible to know the numbers upon either side who fell in this particular part of the general battle, but from the position of the enemy and his numbers, and the appearance of the field, his loss must have been as heavy, or as I think much heavier than our own, and my estimates are probably short of the actual loss.

AN EERIE STILLNESS

The fight done, the sudden revulsions of sense and feeling follow, which more or less characterize all similar occasions. How strange the stillness seems! The whole air roared with the conflict but a moment since—now all is silent; not a gunshot sound is heard, and the silence comes distinctly, almost painfully to the senses. And the sun purples the clouds in the West, and the sultry evening steals on as if there had been no battle, and the furious shout and the cannon's roar had never shaken the earth. And how look these fields? We may see them before dark—the ripening grain, the luxuriant corn, the orchards, the grassy meadows, and in their midst the rural cottage of brick or wood. They were beautiful this morning. They are desolate now—trampled by the countless feet of the combatants, plowed and scored by the shot and shell, the orchards splintered, the fences prostrate, the harvest trodden in the mud. And more dreadful than the sight of all this, thickly strewn over all their length and breadth, are the habiliments of the soldiers, the knapsacks cast aside in the stress of the fight, or after the fatal lead had struck; haversacks, yawning with the rations the owner will never call for; canteens of cedar of the Rebel men of Jackson, and of cloth-covered tin of the men of the Union; blankets and trousers, and coats, and caps, and some are blue and some are gray; muskets and ramrods, and bayonets, and swords, and scabbards and belts, some bent and cut by the shot or shell; broken wheels, exploded caissons, and limber-boxes, and dismantled guns, and all these are sprinkled with blood; horses, some dead, a mangled heap of carnage, some alive, with a leg shot clear off, or other frightful wounds, appealing to you with almost more than brute gaze as you pass; and last, but not least numerous, many thousands of men—and there was no rebellion here now—the men of South Carolina were quiet by the side of those of Massachusetts, some composed, with upturned faces, sleeping the last sleep, some mutilated and frightful, some wretched, fallen, bathed in blood, survivors still and unwilling witnesses of the rage of Gettysburg.

Our loss was light, almost nothing in this fight—the next morning the enemy's dead were thick all along this part of the line. Near eleven o'clock the enemy, wearied with his disastrous work, desisted, and thereafter until morning, not a shot was heard in all the armies. . . .

I am weary and sleepy, almost to such an extent as not to be able to sit on my horse. And my horse can hardly move—the spur will not start him—what can be the reason? I know that he has been touched by two or three bullets to-day, but not to wound or lame him to speak of. Then, in riding by a horse that is hitched, in the dark, I got kicked; had I not a very thick boot, the blow would have been likely to have broken my ankle—it did break my temper as it was—and, as if it would cure matters, I foolishly spurred my horse again. No use, he would but walk. I dismounted; I could not lead him along at all, so out of temper I rode at the slowest possible walk to the Headquarters, which I reached at last. Generals Hancock and Gibbon were asleep in the ambulance. With a light I found what was the matter with "Billy." A bullet had entered his chest just in front of my left leg, as I was mounted, and the blood was running down all his side and leg, and the air from his lungs came out of the bullet-hole. I begged his pardon mentally for my cruelty in spurring him, and should have done so in words if he could have understood me. Kind treatment as is due to the wounded he could understand and he had it. Poor Billy! He and I were first under fire together, and I rode him at the second Bull Run and the first and second Fredericksburg, and at Antietam after brave "Joe" was killed; but I shall never mount him again— Billy's battles are over. . . .

At four o'clock on the morning of the Third, I was awakened by Gen. Gibbon's pulling me by the foot and saying: "Come, don't you hear that?" I sprang up to my feet. . . .

The house which was General George Meade's headquarters was shot through several times, and a great many horses of officers and orderlies were lying dead around it. Riderless horses, galloping madly through the fields, were brought up, or down rather, by these invisible horse-tamers, and they would not run any more. Mules with ammunition, pigs wallowing about, cows in the pastures, whatever was animate or inanimate, in all this broad range, were no exception to their blind havoc. The percussion shells would strike, and thunder, and scatter the earth and their whistling fragments; the Whitworth bolts would pound and ricochet, and bowl far away sputtering, with the sound of a mass of hot iron plunged in water; and the great solid shot would smite the unresisting ground with a sounding "thud," as the strong boxer crashes his iron fist into the jaws of his unguarded adversary. Such were some of the sights and sounds of this great iron battle of missiles. Our artillerymen upon the crest budged not an inch, nor intermitted, but, though caisson and limber were smashed, and the guns dismantled, and men and horses killed, there amidst smoke and sweat, they gave back, without grudge, or loss of time in the sending, in kind whatever the enemy sent, globe, and cone, and bolt, hollow or solid, an iron greeting to the rebellion, the compliments of the wrathful Republic. An hour has droned its flight since first the war began. There is no sign of weariness or abatement on either side. So long it seemed, that the din and crashing around began to appear the normal condition of nature there, and fighting man's element. The General proposed to go among the men and over to the front of the batteries, so at about two o'clock he and I started. We went along the lines of the infantry as they lay there flat upon the earth, a little to the front of the batteries. They were suffering little, and were quiet and cool. How glad we were that the enemy were no better gunners, and that they cut the shell fuses too long. To the question asked the men, "What do you think of this?" the replies would be, "O, this is bully," "We are getting to like it," "O, we don't mind this." And so they lay under the heaviest cannonade that ever shook the continent, and among them a thousand times more jokes than heads were cracked. . . .

THE LAST SKIRMISH OF GETTYSBURG

There was a pause between acts, with the curtain down, soon to rise upon the final act, and catastrophe of Gettysburg. We have passed by the left of the Second Division, coming from the First; when we crossed the crest the enemy was not in sight, and all was still—we walked slowly along in the rear of the troops, by the ridge cut off now from a view of the enemy in his position, and were returning to the spot where we had left our horses. General Gibbon had just said that he inclined to the belief that the enemy was falling back, and that the cannonade was only one of his noisy modes of covering the movement. I said that I thought that fifteen minutes would show that, by all his bowling, the Rebel did not mean retreat. We were near our horses when we noticed Brigadier General Henry Hunt, Chief of Artillery of the Army, near Woodruff's Battery, swiftly moving about on horseback, and apparently in a rapid manner giving some orders about the guns. Thought we, what could this mean? In a moment afterwards we met Captain Wessels and the orderlies who had our horses; they were on foot leading the horses. Captain Wessels was pale, and he said, excited: "General, they say the enemy's infantry is advancing." We sprang into our saddles, a score of bounds brought us upon the all-seeing crest. . . .

Our skirmishers open a spattering fire along the front, and, fighting, retire upon the main line—the first drops, the heralds of the storm, sounding on our windows. Then the thunders of our guns, first Arnold's, then Cushing's and Woodruff's and the rest, shake and reverberate again through the air, and their sounding shells smite the enemy. The General said I had better go and tell General Meade of this advance. To gallop to General Meade's headquarters, to learn there that he had changed them to another part of the field, to dispatch to him by the Signal Corps in General Gibbon's name the message, "The enemy is advancing his infantry in force upon my front," and to be again upon the crest, were but the work of a minute. All our available guns are now active, and from the fire of shells, as the range grows shorter and shorter, they change to shrapnel, and from shrapnel to canister; but in spite of shells, and shrapnel and canister, without wavering or halt, the hardy lines of the enemy continue to move on. . . .

The color sergeant . . . , grasping the stump of the severed lance in both his hands, waved the flag above his head and rushed towards the wall. "Will you see your color storm the wall alone?" One man only starts to follow. Almost half way to the wall, down go color bearer and color to the ground—the gallant sergeant is dead. The line springs—the crest of the solid ground with a great roar, heaves forward its maddened load, men, arms, smoke, fire, a fighting mass. It rolls to the wall— flash meets flash, the wall is crossed—a moment ensues of thrusts, yells, blows, shots, and undistinguishable conflict, followed by a shout universal that makes the welkin ring again, and the last and bloodiest fight of the great battle of Gettysburg is ended and won.

Many things cannot be described by pen or pencil—such a fight is one. Some hints and incidents may be given, but a description or picture never. From what is told the imagination may for itself construct the scene; otherwise he who never saw can have no adequate idea of what such a battle is. . . .

Already, as I rode down from the heights, nature's mysterious loom was at work, joining and weaving on her ceaseless web the shells had broken there. Another spring shall green these trampled slopes, and flowers, planted by unseen hands, shall bloom upon these graves; another autumn and the yellow harvest shall ripen there—all not in less, but in higher perfection for this poured out blood. In another decade of years, in another century, or age, we hope that the Union, by the same means, may repose in a securer peace and bloom in a higher civilization. Then what matters it if lame Tradition glean on this field and hand down her garbled sheaf—if deft story with furtive fingers plait her ballad wreaths, deeds of her heroes here? or if stately history fill as she list her arbitrary tablet, the sounding record of this fight? Tradition, story, history—all will not efface the true, grand epic of Gettysburg.

THE PATH TO EMANCIPATION

HARRY HANSEN

Congress took the first step toward abolition in 1862 when it declared the District of Columbia and all federal territories free. In 1863, President Abraham Lincoln announced his Emancipation Proclamation, which freed slaves that were held in the Confederate states. The proclamation precluded any legal action against those states, because they were governed by the Confederacy, but it was a symbolic step toward complete emancipation. The Thirteenth Amendment, ratified on December 6, 1865, not only freed all existing slaves, but also ensured that no human would serve in slavery again in the United States. In the following article, Harry Hansen relates the events that led to emancipation and the terms of the Thirteenth Amendment. Harry Hansen is the author of several books on American history, including *The Civil War* and *Midwest Portraits: A Book of Memories and Friendships.*

If the government of the United States was opposed to slavery, why didn't it free the slaves? This question was asked with increasing irritation by citizens in the North, whether they were abolitionists, radicals, or voters who endorsed the platform of the Republican Party. President Abraham Lincoln delayed action during the first half of 1862 for several reasons. One was political: he did not want to confiscate the property of slaveholders in the border states, for Washington still feared this might swing those states into the Confederate column. He had an informal and unreported conference with members of Congress from the border states on the subject of compensating owners, possibly by a bond issue. But no practical method emerged.

THE CONFISCATION ACT

As Union reverses multiplied, anxiety increased in Congress and the conviction grew that freeing of the slaves would be strategically valuable to the North. Congress in July 1862 passed the Confiscation Act, and barely avoided a veto from the President. The act made death the penalty for treason, but gave the courts power to commute the sentence to a fine and imprisonment; it directed the President to cause the seizure of all estates, property, and possessions of military and civil officers of the Confederacy or of any of its states, and, after a sixty-day notice, to confiscate the property of all engaged "in armed rebellion" or abetting it. It freed the slaves of those convicted, as well as the slaves of "rebel owners" who took refuge within the lines of the army, and denied protection of the Fugitive Slave Law to any owners of slaves except those who were loyal to the Union. It forbade military and naval officers to surrender fugitives to claimants and authorized colonization and the use of Negroes as soldiers. It gave power to grant amnesty to rebels and to make exceptions to a general pardon.

Senator Charles Sumner of Massachusetts called it "a practical act of emancipation." Five days after Congress adjourned President Lincoln called his cabinet and read a draft of his act of emancipation. The cabinet was not wholly in favor of issuing it while the Union army was losing battles. The subject weighed heavily on Lincoln's mind all during that summer. In speaking on September 13 to a group of clergymen who had come to urge freeing the slaves, he pointed to the difficulties of enforcing such an act, when he could not even enforce the Constitution in the seceded states. He referred to the Confiscation Act, which offered protection to slaves, saying "I cannot learn that that law has caused a single slave to come over to us."

But a few days later the whole atmosphere changed. The Federal army stopped General Robert E. Lee at Antietam, and an opportunity to announce emancipation of a kind came to Lincoln. He served notice on September 22, 1862, that he meant to issue on January 1, 1863, a proclamation that all persons held as slaves in any state or part of a state at that time "in rebellion against the United States," would be forever free, and that he would recommend that owners who had remained loyal to the United States should be compensated for any losses, including loss of slaves.

CREATING SLAVERY LEGISLATION

When Congress convened on December 1, 1862, President Lincoln had reached the conclusion that the time had come to formulate legislation on slavery. He already had announced on September 22 that he meant to make emancipation effective, for specific categories and places, on the first day of the next year, and he now took the opportunity presented by his annual message to spell out a proposal for action by Congress. Thus the message of December 1, 1862, famous for its invocation of "the last best hope of earth," devotes much of its space to outlining a way of freeing the slave and letting him enter into the duties of a free citizen in a democracy.

The President said that the treaty with Great Britain for the suppression of the slave trade had been put into operation with prospect of complete success. He reported that "free Americans of African descent" had asked to be included in plans for colonizing Negroes abroad, but that several Spanish-American republics had protested against receiving such emigrants "in all the rights as freemen." Only Liberia and Haiti had offered them citizenship, but the emigrants were reluctant to go there. He then took up the subject of "compensated emancipation" mentioned in his proclamation of September 22, 1862.

President Lincoln proposed that Congress draft amendments to the Constitution, to be submitted to the states for ratification, to this effect: (1) Any state that abolished slavery before January 1, 1900, to be compensated by U.S. bonds delivered at the completion of abolition, and to forfeit these bonds if it reintroduced slavery at a later date; (2) slaves freed by the war to be forever free, but owners to be compensated at the same rate as the states if proved not to have been disloyal; (3) Congress to provide with money or otherwise for colonizing abroad free colored persons with their own consent.

The President admitted that emancipation would be unsatisfactory to advocates of perpetual slavery, but he thought the length of time for abolition, thirty-seven years, should mitigate their dissatisfaction. Liberation of slaves was, "in a certain sense," destruction of property; the people of the South, he felt, were not responsible for the original introduction of this property, while the North by using cotton and sugar shared the profits of dealing in them. While the sum required would be large, he thought it smaller than the cost of continued warfare; the ample room for expansion of population and development of natural advantages would make the postponed cost less burdensome than the immediate outlay. The President said he strongly favored colonization, but not for the reason some critics gave, that free Negroes would displace white labor and white laborers. He estimated there would be one colored person to seven whites, if evenly distributed, and he did not believe "that the freed people will swarm forth and cover the whole land." He closed this message with a famous peroration, frequently quoted, but rarely in context with the rest of his annual message. It is as follows:

> Fellow citizens, *we* can not escape history. We, of this Congress and this Administration, will be remembered in spite of ourselves. No personal significance, or insignificance, can spare one or another of us. The fiery trial through which we pass, will light us down, in honor or dishonor, to the latest generation. We *say* we are for the Union. The world will not forget that we say this. We know how to save the Union. The world knows we do know how to save it. We—even *we here*—hold the power and bear the responsibility. In *giving* freedom to the *slave*, we assure freedom to the free—honorable alike in what we give and in what we preserve. We shall nobly save, or meanly lose, the last best hope of earth. Other means may succeed; this could not fail. The way is plain, peaceful, generous, just—a way which, if followed, the world will forever applaud, and God must forever bless.

HUNTER'S PREMATURE ORDER

Like Major General John C. Frémont before him, Major General David Hunter undertook to free the slaves in his military department without notice to the Executive. On May 9, 1862, he issued an order from Hilton Head, South Carolina, headquarters of the Department of the South, announcing that since Georgia, Florida, and South Carolina, three states in his department, had taken up arms against the United States, it had become necessary to place them under martial law. "Slavery and martial law in a free country are altogether incompatible. The persons in these states heretofore held as slaves, are therefore declared forever free."

President Lincoln declared the order void and unauthorized; such a decision was a prerogative of the President and could not be left to commanders in the field. He pointed to the joint resolution of Congress, adopted on his recommendation, which said the United States should cooperate with any state that adopted a gradual abolishment of slavery and should compensate for public and private inconveniences. He appealed to the states to make this possible.

The government, in recommending that military and naval commanders employ Negroes, demanded reasonable wages for them and records showing whence they had come, as a basis for possible compensation.

The military enrollment of Negroes in 1862 gave the North the use of 130,000 soldiers, seamen, and laborers, according to President Lincoln. The Confederate government announced that neither Negro soldiers nor their white officers would be granted immunities recognized under the laws of war. President Lincoln replied at once with a general order, dated April 24, 1863, advising the Army that if an enemy did enslave or sell any captured soldier such action would call for retaliation by death. On July 30 he issued a specific order that "for every soldier of the United States killed in violation of the laws of war, a Rebel soldier shall be executed; and for every one enslaved by the enemy or sold into slavery, a Rebel soldier shall be placed at hard labor on the public works, and continued at such hard labor until the other shall be released and receive the treatment due to a prisoner of war."

PAYMENTS TO SLAVE OWNERS

Slave owners were actually paid for their slaves by Congress. That they were compensated for the loss of their slaves in the District of Columbia has been generally obscured by the greater emphasis given to national emancipation. In December, 1861, Senator Henry Wilson of Massachusetts introduced a bill providing for emancipation of slaves in the District of Columbia and for the payment of compensation to loyal slave owners, the exact amount to be determined by a board of commissioners out of $1,000,000 appropriated for that purpose. The bill passed the Senate but was fought hard in the House. It was opposed by Senator John J. Crittenden of Kentucky and by Representative Clement Vallandigham of Ohio. It was passed by a vote of 92 to 38 and received President Lincoln's signature on April 16, 1862. Payment was made to owners by the United States Treasury of sums not exceeding $300, and the total was slightly under the amount appropriated by Congress.

Negroes Become Contraband

As soon as Virginia ratified its ordinance of secession slaves began to appear at military depots of the United States to ask protection. One of the places easy of access was Fortress Monroe, where General Benjamin F. Butler was in command. On May 24, 1861, a Virginia owner demanded of Butler that he hand over three Negroes who had sought refuge at Fortress Monroe. Butler refused on the ground that the Negroes were "contraband of war," since they had worked on construction of a battery directed against the Union and were owned by the citizen of a state that had declared itself out of the United States.

This was the first time the term "contraband" was applied to refugee slaves, and it became so general that slaves who left their masters and came north were referred to as contraband. Butler notified the War Department that he intended to feed all refugees and employ the able-bodied, keeping an account of the cost. His action was approved by Secretary of War Cameron.

When Butler reported on July 30, 1861, that he now had 900 Negroes to provide for, Secretary Cameron replied: "It is the desire of the President that all existing rights in all the states be fully respected and maintained; in cases of fugitives from the loyal slave states, the enforcement of the Fugitive Slave law by the ordinary forms of judicial proceedings must be respected by the military authorities; in the disloyal states the Confiscation Act of Congress must be your guide.". . .

The Emancipation Proclamation

On January 1, 1863, President Lincoln issued the Emancipation Proclamation, as he had promised one hundred days before.

This is generally considered the act that finally freed the slaves in the United States. It did not do so; that was done by the Thirteenth Amendment to the Constitution. The Emancipation Proclamation is "a fit and necessary war measure for suppressing rebellion" and applies only to the seceded states that are not under the control of the United States armies. It makes specific exception of areas so controlled, and makes no mention of the Border States, where citizens loyal to the United States still held slaves.

The Emancipation Proclamation proclaims free all persons held as slaves in the seceded states of the Confederacy, excepting certain parishes in Louisiana and the city of New Orleans, West Virginia, and specified counties of Virginia. It asks the people who are declared free to abstain from violence except in self-defense and to work faithfully for reasonable wages, and declares that they will be accepted in the armed service of the United States. The President characterized the act as "sincerely believed to be an act of justice, warranted by the Constitution upon military necessity."

Major General Carl Schurz, who marched through the South with Sherman, wrote in his *Reminiscences:*

> One of the most remarkable features of the history of those times is the fact that most of the slaves stayed on the plantations or farms and did the accustomed work with quiet and, in the case of house servants, not seldom even with affectionate fidelity, while in their hearts they yearned for freedom and prayed for its speedy coming. Only as our armies penetrated the South, and especially when Negroes were enlisted as soldiers, did they leave their former masters in large numbers, and even then there was scarcely any instance of violent revenge on their part for any wrong or cruelty any of them may have suffered in slavery.

THE THIRTEENTH AMENDMENT

The Thirteenth Amendment to the Constitution of the United States was first proposed as a resolution in Congress and passed by the Senate, April 8, 1864, by a vote of 38 to 6. It failed to receive a two-thirds vote in the House and was called up for reconsideration there on January 6, 1865. It was passed January 31, 1865, by a vote of 119 to 56. Every Republican member of the House voted for it; ten Democrats supported it and eight were absent. Delegates from the seven territories, who did not have the right to vote, were given leave to have their approval entered in the minutes.

The adoption of the amendment created great enthusiasm in the halls of Congress and was announced to Washington by a salute from cannon outside the Capitol. It had been ratified by thirty-three of the thirty-six states of the Union when the Secretary of State proclaimed it in effect, December 18, 1865. It reads:

> Neither slavery nor involuntary servitude, except as a punishment for crime whereof the party shall have been duly convicted, shall exist within the United States, or any place subject to their jurisdiction.
>
> Congress shall have power, by appropriate legislation, to enforce the provisions of this article.

The second clause removes from the states the power to legislate on slavery. Numerous states had previously abolished slavery within their borders.

STATE ACTION AGAINST SLAVERY

Maryland voters adopted a new state constitution on October 12, 1864, which provided for immediate and unconditional emancipation. On the evening of October 19 a group of loyal Maryland men living in the District of Columbia serenaded the President. He congratulated them on the results of the vote and referred to reports that if defeated in the forthcoming election he would attempt to "ruin the government." He assured them that he was struggling to maintain the government, not to overthrow it, and to prevent others from overthrowing it; if not elected he would do his utmost "that whoever is to take the helm for the next voyage shall start with the best possible chance to save the ship."

The strongly pro-Union areas of western Virginia were powerful enough to detach themselves from the secessionist state government. A conference of leaders met in Wheeling June 11–25, 1862, organized a state government, and elected Francis H. Pierpont provisional governor. Thus West Virginia applied for statehood and on December 10, 1862, Congress passed a bill admitting it to the Union as the thirty-fifth state, which President Lincoln signed into law on December 31, 1862. The President said the action was expedient because it made slave soil free and extended the national authority; if it could be called secession [from the state of Virginia], it was secession in favor of the Constitution.

SURRENDER AT APPOMATTOX

ROBERT LECKIE

On April 9, 1865, Confederate general Robert E. Lee surrendered to Union general Ulysses S. Grant at Appomattox Courthouse in Virginia. Although the war continued until May 26, 1865, Lee's surrender represented the defeat of the entire Confederacy. Tired and hungry, Rebel soldiers had been without decent food, clothing, and supplies for months, and desertions ran high. The following article describes the battle at Appomattox and Lee's final surrender. Robert Leckie is the author of several books on American military history, including *The Wars of America: Updated and Revised, 1609–1980* and *With Fire and Sword*.

onfederate President Jefferson Davis was not the man to
listen to his own death rattle. Unbending die-hard or
eleventh-hour savior, he would not in either case be conscious of impending defeat. As the year 1864 came to a close the Confederacy had shrunk to the Carolinas and Virginia; General John Hood's army was a wreck, General William T. Sherman was poised to march north to join General Ulysses S. Grant's swelling Army of the Potomac, and General Philip Sheridan was ready to ride down to Petersburg with all his immense and veteran horsemen. Surely the South, for all its splendid fighting spirit, should fight no longer. Its economy was crippled, and its government so powerless to wage war that even the gentle General Robert E. Lee raged against congressmen who "do not seem to be able to do anything except to eat peanuts and chew tobacco, while my army is starving." Lee's army was also cold

Excerpted from *None Died in Vain* by Robert Leckie (New York: HarperCollins, 1990). Copyright © 1990 by Robert Leckie. Reprinted by permission of the publisher.

and poorly clothed, and its ranks were dwindling. Desertions were now at their height, because when Sherman menaced a hearth in Georgia or the Carolinas he twisted a heart at Petersburg. Moreover, as Grant inexorably extended his lines to his left, the outnumbered Lee had to move right to contain him, and this thinned his lines. Yet Jefferson Davis had no thought of capitulation.

SOLDIER-TO-SOLDIER COMBAT

The Confederate president, a son of the eighteenth century, if not an earlier age, still saw the war as a contest between armies, soldier to soldier, not as a conflict between nations in which capacity to fight is paramount, or a war between democracies in which the will to fight is major. Attrition and blockade had scuttled the Confederate capacity, while hunger, defeat and calculated frightfulness had worn down the will. Southern morale had also been weakened by disputes over Davis's frequent suspensions of the writ of habeas corpus, and many a brave Confederate left the trenches and headed home after being informed that the Confederate commissary was stripping his farm of food and animals. Under these conditions a peace movement was begun under the leadership of Davis's archfoe and obstructionist, Vice President Alexander Stephens. Davis agreed to ask for a peace conference, but actually only in the hope of provoking a harsh statement of Union war aims that would stiffen the Southern spine.

On February 3, 1865, Stephens and two others met President Abraham Lincoln and Secretary of State William Seward on the *River Queen* in Hampton Roads. Stephens proposed that the two camps make peace to join in evicting the French from Mexico in defense of the Monroe Doctrine. Lincoln replied that he could not enter negotiations unless the Confederacy agreed to return to the Union and abolish slavery. Such proposals, of course, could not even be considered by the Confederates—and the war went on.

It continued with General Joseph Johnston recalled to block Sherman's northward march through the Carolinas, and with Robert E. Lee at last the Confederate commander in chief. Popular resentment against Davis's conduct of the war had led to creation of this position, but the gesture came as the hands of the clock neared midnight. Lee knew that the Confederacy was teetering on the edge of disaster. Desertions had so drained his armies that the Confederacy passed a law conscripting slaves. With splendid irony the South offered blacks the equal opportunity of fighting shoulder to shoulder with whites to preserve their own enslavement.

NO SURRENDER

Nevertheless, Jefferson Davis was determined to go down to utter defeat rather than accept any terms that did not recognize Southern independence, and because it was not Lee's habit to challenge the president on matters of policy, Lee also decided to fight on. Ever the gambler, he resolved on a last, desperate chance: a breakout from Petersburg followed by a lightning march south to join Johnston and overwhelm Sherman, after which both armies would return north to defeat Grant. General John Gordon, the hero of Spotsylvania, was ordered to lead the assault on Union-held Fort Stedman directly east of Petersburg. An hour before daylight on March 25, 1865, the Rebels attacked.

They went in with a silent rush, surprising and seizing Fort Stedman and sending a spearhead ahead to pierce the Federal secondary line. If they could widen their breakthrough and hold it, Lee's army could pour through the breach and get clean away to North Carolina. But the Federals rallied. Forts to either side of Stedman refused to fall, a counter-attack was launched on Stedman, and Union artillery shattered the Rebel front. By midmorning Lee's last sally had been broken and hurled back with losses of 5,000 men. Now it was the turn of U.S. Grant.

Before Gordon's attack Grant had seen that he must crush Lee's right flank, seizing the roads and railways by which the Confederates might escape south. Heavy rains had delayed putting his plan into operation, but after Philip Sheridan arrived at Petersburg with all his cavalry Grant began to move swiftly.

On March 29, 1865, a full corps began striking Lee's right, while Sheridan led a corps of cavalry and one of infantry in a wide sweep toward Five Forks still farther to the Rebel right. If he could get in behind Lee, he would cut off the Confederate escape and practically guarantee Lee's defeat. Lee reacted swiftly, sending General George Pickett to oppose him. On March 31 the Confederates halted Sheridan's forces short of Five Forks at a place called Dinwiddie Court House. But the little Union general was not defeated. He had wisely retired to await reinforcements, and Grant sent him Brigadier General Gouverneur K. Warren's corps.

Next day Sheridan chafed at Warren's delay. Sheridan smelled victory; he could win the war that day, and he cried aloud: "This battle must be fought and won before the sun goes down!" In simple terms, Sheridan wanted to crush and scatter Pickett's force and seize the Southside Railway to his rear. Unknown to Sheridan, Pickett was not with his troops but was enjoying himself at a shad bake while his men were fighting and dying, a dereliction of duty so infuriating to Lee that he relieved him of his command. If Sheridan could capture the railroad this day it would be all over with Lee and probably for the Confederacy.

SHERIDAN'S BATTLE RAGE

At last Warren's veterans began moving into line. Sheridan was everywhere among them. When one of his skirmish lines was staggered and seemed ready to fall back, he galloped toward his faltering soldiers, shouting, "Come on—go at 'em—move on with a clean jump or you'll not catch one of them!" A soldier beside him was hit in the throat. "I'm killed!" he cried, blood spurting thickly from his jugular vein. "You're not hurt a bit!" Sheridan roared. "Pick up your gun, man, and move right on!" Obediently, the soldier trotted forward—and fell dead. Now the battle line was formed, and Sheridan shouted: "Where's my battle flag?" It was brought forward, and the general raised his little swallow-tailed red-and-white banner high over his head and rode black Rienzi up and down the line.

A bullet pierced the flag, and the sergeant who had brought it fell. Sheridan rode forward, spurring his horse toward the Rebel earthworks. After him came the yelling Federal infantry. Sheridan put Rienzi over the works in a splendid leap, and his infantry swarmed in after him. Now a perfect rage of battle had come over Sheridan, in the midst of which he relieved the unfortunate Warren of his command. It was brutal, it was probably not just, but Sheridan realized with Grant that the end of the war was within the Union grasp, and a general should be ready to press forward as obediently as the private whose lifeblood poured from his throat.

"What I want is that Southern Railway," Sheridan roared repeatedly. "I want you men to understand we have a record to make before the sun goes down that will make Hell tremble!"

Capture of the vital railway that day was not to be. Yet Pickett's force had been completely shattered and Five Forks fell to Sheridan. A jubilant Grant cabled the information to Lincoln, who relayed the information to the press. For the next few days an eager North read with drawn breath of the progress of that single win-the-war battle that had eluded the nation for four years.

Next day, April 2, Grant attacked all along the line. Row upon row of Federal gun batteries began baying in a voice of rolling thunder, hurling a dreadful weight of death and destruction upon the Rebel positions. Then came silence. Thousands upon thousands of Federal soldiers moved forward. Slowly, with a gathering rush, they struck the Confederate lines, and in the weakened center they tore them apart. One by one clusters of Rebel muskets winked out in that predawn darkness, and black gaps opened in the Southern line. Into the open spaces rushed the Federals, widening them, and a quarter hour after Major General Horatio G. Wright's corps attacked in the center a decisive breakthrough was achieved.

To the rear A.P. Hill heard of the penetration while discussing the battle with Lee. He rode forward, to receive a bullet in the heart and strip from Lee yet another of his great lieutenants. Tears in his eyes, Lee called upon James Longstreet. But Old Pete and his valiant men could not stem the rising Federal tide.

As the Sunday of April 2, 1865, grew lighter, Lee prepared to abandon Petersburg. He still hoped to join Johnston. It was a forlorn hope, and Lee doubtless knew it, yet his sense of duty kept him loyal to President Davis's designs. As 30,000 red-eyed and starving survivors of the Army of Northern Virginia began streaming west, Lee dictated the long-dreaded telegraph to the War Department.

LEE'S MESSAGE OF DOOM

Meticulously dressed in gray, cold as a marble statue, Jefferson Davis sat in the family pew at St. Paul's Episcopal Church. Surrounded mostly by women, many dressed in black, Davis heard the preacher say: "The Lord is in His holy temple; let all the earth keep silence before Him." Into that churchly silence there crept the tinkle of spurs. An officer holding his saber came striding down the aisle. He handed Davis a paper. The president unfolded it and read: "I advise that all preparation be made for leaving Richmond tonight. I will advise you later, according to circumstances."

With tight-lipped calm, Davis pocketed Lee's message of doom and walked majestically from the church. Going to the

War Department, he telegraphed Lee that to move the Confederate government that night would "involve the loss of many valuables." Lee received the protest in the field, and angrily tore it to bits with the remark: "I am sure I gave him sufficient notice." Regaining his composure, he notified Davis that it was "absolutely necessary" to move that night.

Richmond learned swiftly that the government was fleeing. Throughout that Passion Sunday civilians fought government clerks for possession of carts and wagons, carriages and gigs, while crowded streets echoed to rolling wheels or the rumbling of departing trains. The Confederate treasury—less than a half-million dollars in bullion—was placed in charge of a battalion of naval cadets. Civilians able to flee joined the government exodus. Those who could not locked their doors and closed their shutters and sat down in despair to await the Yankee invasion. Night fell and the city began to tremble to the detonation of bridges and arsenals.

Soon the city was afire. So was neighboring Manchester. They blazed like beacons in the dark while the James River lay glittering between them. Inevitably, those people of Richmond whom inflation and food shortages had transformed into wild, half-starved creatures turned to looting. Commissary depots were full of supplies never delivered to Lee's hungry army, and now that they were left unguarded they were broken into and plundered. Barrels of whiskey were also found, and soon there were drunks capering in the reflected flames of burning cotton or tobacco warehouses. Then the mob began breaking into shops and storehouses, sotted women fought each other for ostrich plumes, drunken men shot each other over boots and sashes. So the flames and the frenzy spread, and soon the only safe place in Richmond was in the green hills of Capitol Square. Here women in shawls clasped frightened children to their bosoms, and here, while the night winds whipped the fires, as tall flames roared and drunken revelers shrieked, like a shower of sparks from a falling building, the capital of the Confederacy collapsed.

The Plundered Capital

Next morning, April 3, troops from the Army of the James under Major General Godfrey Weitzel entered the ruined capital. A small guidon was raised over the State House, erstwhile capitol of the Confederacy, by Major Atherton H. Stevens, Jr., of Massachusetts. Among the weeping citizens who watched, peering through their shutter chinks, was Mrs. Mary Fontaine, who wrote: "I saw them unfurl a tiny flag, and I sank on my knees, and the bitter, bitter tears came in a torrent." At eight fifteen in the City Hall General Weitzel accepted surrender of the city. "Then the Cavalry thundered at a furious gallop . . . Then the infantry came playing 'The Girl I Left Behind Me', that dear old air that we heard our brave men so often play; then the negro troops playing 'Dixie'." Now the streets were swarming with people, many of them jubilant blacks, the men hugging each other, the women kissing. Throughout the early morning the looting continued, and the flames flickered on, until the Federal troops took charge so that the thieves were either arrested or frightened off and the fires subdued. By midafternoon Richmond was quiet again, no longer the Confederate capital but a Federal city forevermore. Eventually, President Lincoln who had been to Petersburg would arrive in Richmond, and to General Weitzel's question about how to treat the conquered people in his charge, the Rail-Splitter gave his famous reply, "If I were in your place, I'd let 'em up easy—let 'em up easy."

There was little of such sentiment in the Federal capital, however, when the telegrapher at Fort Monroe dit-dotted out the historic message: "We took Richmond at 8:15 this morning." Never before or since has the white city on the Potomac rocked and reverberated to such scenes of jubilation. Church bells pealed, fire engines clattered and clanged, railroad locomotives and riverboats screamed and whistled, while batteries of artillery thundered in a seemingly endless 800-gun salute: 300 for Petersburg, 500 for Richmond—with 100 more from the navy's massive Dahlgrens. Children dismissed from school added to the general gaiety, joined by government clerks given the day off. Everywhere were the newspaper "extras" with exultant bold, black banner headlines, an explosion of printer's ink led by the Star's firecracker string: GLORY!!! HAIL COLUMBIA!!! HALLELUJAH!!! RICHMOND OURS!!! People who did not know each other embraced and kissed, friends-turned-enemies buried the hatchet, while casual acquaintances swore eternal fidelity as all of them marched through the streets arm-in-arm singing. And of course there was much of that artificial exaltation found in bottles with every bar jam-packed and the patrons vying with one another to buy a round of drinks. One newsman declared: "A more liquorish crowd was never seen in Washington." Nor was a more vindictive one. When Edwin Stanton asked a crowd what should be done with Richmond, there came the universal vengeful cry: "BURN IT! BURN IT! LET HER BURN!"....

LEE'S LAST STAND

Robert E. Lee had a head start of one day in his race against the tenacious Grant. With this advantage, Lee believed he could get his army to Danville, the pleasant little city on the Dan River to which Jefferson Davis had already moved the government. Here he could be joined by Johnston.

On April 3, 1865, it did not seem to Lee that Grant was pursuing too rapidly. That night his ragged veterans staggered into Amelia Court House, twenty-one miles west of Petersburg. There, to his dismay, Lee found not a single ration to feed 30,000 agonizingly hungry men. He had no recourse but to halt next day while forage wagons searched the countryside for food. In the meantime, the day's head start was lost. Federal cavalry were everywhere. Close behind them hurried three eager corps of Union infantry, marching a few miles south of Lee on a straighter, parallel route. That night of April 4 some of Sheridan's riders menaced Amelia.

On the morning of April 5 the forage wagons came in, and Lee saw with concealed despair that they were nearly empty. His men must march now on their nerves alone, their hearts nourished by Lee's spirit but their bellies empty and growling with hunger. Another delay ensued: Richard Ewell and Richard Anderson were slow in closing up. Finally, the army moved south from Amelia Court House—and found Federal infantry and cavalry barring the way.

There was nothing left to do but to shift west toward Farmville, where there was hope of receiving rations from Lynchburg. This meant a night march that killed a good part of Lee's army. It was a slow stumble over crowded roads made by men with leaden limbs, men who moved like sleepwalkers. Many fell out never to return. Many were captured by Federal cavalry, which never left off nipping at Lee's heels. Grant was clinging to Lee's army, and he would not let go.

Still, Lee pressed on. On April 6 the Federals caught up at a place called Sailor's Creek. Here they overwhelmed General John Gordon, who was covering the Confederate trains, capturing the greater part of Lee's wagons, and here, as Lee watched in agony, they broke Ewell's and Anderson's corps. Sitting on Traveller and holding a red battle flag, Lee saw the wreck of shattered regiments come backwashing toward him, and he cried aloud: "My God, has the Army been dissolved?" That day Lee lost between 7,000 and 8,000 men. That night Lee's army was down to 15,000 muskets and sabers to oppose 80,000 Federal infantry and cavalry. On April 7, however, his pale and pinched veterans struggled into Farmville, where they received their first rations since the retreat began. From Farmville, Lee continued his withdrawal. He got safely across the Appomattox River and burned the bridges behind him. Some of them were saved by the Federals, however, and once more Union cavalry began to bite on Lee's rear. That night Lee received Grant's invitation to surrender. He handed it to Longstreet, who replied: "Not yet."

There was still hope. If Lee could get to a place called Appomattox Station, he could feed his men from four trains of food from Lynchburg, and then swing south to safety at Danville.

On April 8 Lee was forced to fight another rear-guard action to save his remaining wagons. As he did, Sheridan's cavalry and infantry under E.O.C. Ord swept past his southern flank and drove into Appomattox Station. They captured Lee's ration trains and put themselves across his line of march. That night Lee's army reached Appomattox Court House. Below them, across their path, lay Sheridan's force. If it was only cavalry, it might be brushed aside and the army yet saved. But if infantry were there in force, the Army of Northern Virginia would be doomed.

LEE'S SURRENDER

April 9, 1865, was a Palm Sunday. Very early that morning Robert Edward Lee put on a new gray uniform, a sash of deep red silk, the jeweled sword given him by ladies in England, beautiful red-stitched spurred boots and long gray gauntlets. An officer expressed surprise, and Lee said: "I have probably to be General Grant's prisoner and thought I must make my best appearance."

To the east, riding anxiously toward Appomattox over sloppy roads came a slender brown-bearded man wearing a mud-spattered private's blouse. His face was strained, for he had a bad headache and had been up all night bathing his feet in hot water and applying mustard plasters to his neck and wrists. Still, Ulysses S. Grant was hopeful that today would see an end to four years of blood and agony.

Yet Palm Sunday was beginning with the roar of guns. Down from Appomattox Court House charged the Rebels under General Gordon. They brushed aside the Federal outriders, and saw a solid blue phalanx of glittering bayonets to the rear. The Army of Northern Virginia had come to the end of the road. Back to Lee went Gordon's message that he could do nothing without reinforcements. "Then," said Robert E. Lee calmly, "there is nothing left for me to do but to go and see General Grant, and I would rather die a thousand deaths!"

It was the end. With cries of anguish, protesting men and officers clustered around Lee. One general proposed that the army disperse and turn to guerrilla warfare. Lee replied that to do so would make mere marauders of his soldiers and inflict anarchy upon the South. He was prepared to sacrifice his own invincible pride for the safety of his country, and as the messages went out to Grant, Phil Sheridan opposite Lee grew impatient. He had massed both his men and horse with the passionate cry: "Now smash 'em, I tell you, smash 'em!" Now his bugles blew and his blue lines leaned forward, and out from those pitiful gray ranks huddled beneath a host of battle flags a lone rider galloped. He carried a flag of truce and he told Sheridan that Lee was waiting to see Grant in the McLean House.

Skeptical at first, Sheridan finally ordered a cease-fire. Dazed,

On April 9, 1865, Confederate general Robert E. Lee surrendered to Union general Ulysses S. Grant at this home in Appomattox Courthouse, Virginia.

the two armies sat down and contemplated each other. In the spring stillness they suddenly heard bird song rather than bullets. Then General Grant rode up to Sheridan. He inclined his head toward the village and asked, "Is General Lee up there?" Sheridan said, "Yes," and Grant said, "Well, then, let's go up."

THE TERMS OF DEFEAT

They "went up" to that McLean House which, ironically, had brought the war full circle. It was at the home of Wilmer McLean that General Pierre Beauregard made his headquarters during the First Battle of Bull Run. To get away from the war, McLean sold out and moved to Appomattox. Now it was in McLean's front parlor that Grant met Lee.

Grant came in alone and saw Lee with two aides. Taking off his yellow thread gloves, Grant stepped forward to shake Lee's hand. He was aware of his own mud-stained appearance and Lee's splendor, but he gave no sign of it. Both men sat at tables while a half dozen of Grant's generals entered with tinkling spurs and clanking sabers to stand behind their chief. Lee gave no sign of disapproval of their presence.

Grant spoke: "I met you once before, General Lee, while we were serving in Mexico, when you came over from General Scott's headquarters to visit Garland's brigade, to which I then belonged. I have always remembered your appearance, and I think I should have recognized you anywhere."

"Yes," Lee said, "I know I met you on that occasion, and I have often thought of it and tried to recollect how you looked, but I have never been able to recall a single feature."

Grant talked eagerly of Mexico, perhaps to soften the impact of the request that he must make, and Lee, probably anxious to be done with the ordeal of surrender, brought him back gently with the words: "I suppose, General Grant, that the object of our present meeting is fully understood. I asked to see you to ascertain upon what terms you would receive the surrender of my army."

Without changing countenance, with not a hint of exultation or gloating in his voice, Grant quickly outlined his terms: ". . . the officers and men surrendered to be paroled and disqualified from taking up arms again until properly exchanged, and all arms, ammunition and supplies to be delivered up as captured property."

Next Grant set down his terms in writing. Lee read them,

courteously corrected an unintentional oversight, and agreed. There was, however, the matter of the horses, which were the private property of his cavalrymen and artillerists. Would the men be permitted to retain them? At first Grant said that the terms allowed only officers to keep private property, but then, seeing how much this request meant to Lee, he promised "to let all the men who claim to own a horse or mule take the animals home with them to work their little farms."

Lee was relieved and grateful. "This will have the best possible effect on the men," he said. "It will be very gratifying and will do much toward conciliating our people." In Grant's generosity Lee saw not a vindictive but a compassionate conqueror.

THE END OF THE SOUTH

Robert E. Lee knew then that the South had fallen. Even though the army which he formally surrendered a few minutes later was only his own, even though combat might sputter on until May 26, the fighting soul of the South died with Lee's signature on that Palm Sunday of 1865.

After he signed, Lee arose and shook hands with Grant. He bowed to the others in the room and strode silently out the door. On the porch of the McLean House he paused to draw on his gauntlets. He gazed sadly toward the hillside where his little army lay, faithful and fearless to the last. Twice, with slow and savage ruefulness, Lee drove his fist into his palm. Then, crying for Traveller in a hoarse and choking voice, he mounted and rode out of sight.

The Reconstruction Era

CHAPTER 3

President Abraham Lincoln's Assassination

Gideon Welles

In 1865, John Wilkes Booth, a racist and Southern sympathizer, masterminded a conspiracy to assassinate President Abraham Lincoln, Vice President Andrew Johnson, and Secretary of State William Seward. On April 14, Booth shot Lincoln in the back of the head while the president and his wife watched a play at the Ford's Theater just outside Washington, D.C. The president never regained consciousness and died the next day in the Peterson House across the street from the theater. Seward was superficially wounded by one of Booth's accomplices, and no attempt was made on Johnson. The following article is excerpted from the diary of Gideon Welles, who was the secretary of the navy under Lincoln. Welles was present during President Lincoln's final hours, and he describes the confusion and sadness that followed his death.

I had retired to bed about half past-ten on the evening of the 14th of April, and was just getting asleep when Mrs. Welles, my wife, said some one was at our door. Sitting up in bed, I heard a voice twice call to John, my son, whose sleeping-room was on the second floor directly over the front entrance. I arose at once and raised a window, when my messenger, James Smith, called to me that Mr. Abraham Lincoln, the President, had been shot, and said Secretary William Seward and his son, Assistant

Excerpted from *The Diary of Gideon Welles, Volume II* by Gideon Welles (Boston, MA: Houghton Mifflin, 1911).

Secretary Frederick Seward, were assassinated. James was much alarmed and excited. I told him his story was very incoherent and improbable, that he was associating men who were not together and liable to attack at the same time. "Where," I inquired, was the President when shot?" James said he was at Ford's Theatre on 10th Street. "Well," said I, "Secretary Seward is an invalid in bed in his house yonder on 15th Street." James said he had been there, stopped in at the house to make inquiry before alarming me.

I immediately dressed myself, and, against the earnest remonstrance and appeals of my wife, went directly to Mr. Seward's, whose residence was on the east side of the square, mine being on the north. James accompanied me. As we were crossing 15th Street, I saw four or five men in earnest consultation, standing under the lamp on the corner by St. John's Church. Before I had got half across the street, the lamp was suddenly extinguished and the knot of persons rapidly dispersed. For a moment and but a moment I was disconcerted to find myself in darkness, but, recollecting that it was late and about time for the moon to rise, I proceeded on, not having lost five steps, merely making a pause without stopping. Hurrying forward into 15th Street, I found it pretty full of people, especially so near the residence of Secretary Seward, where there were many soldiers as well as citizens already gathered.

THE STUNNED CROWD

Entering the house, I found the lower hall and office full of persons, and among them most of the foreign legations, all anxiously inquiring what truth there was in the horrible rumors afloat. I replied that my object was to ascertain the facts. Proceeding through the hall to the stairs, I found one, and I think two, of the servants there holding the crowd in check. The servants were frightened and appeared relieved to see me. I hastily asked what truth there was in the story that an assassin or assassins had entered the house and assaulted the Secretary. They said it was true, and that Mr. Frederick was also badly injured. They wished me to go up, but no others. At the head of the first stairs I met the elder Mrs. Seward, who was scarcely able to speak but desired me to proceed up to Mr. Seward's room. I met Mrs. Frederick Seward on the third story, who, although in extreme distress, was, under the circumstances, exceedingly composed. I asked for the Secretary's room, which she pointed out,—the southwest room. As I entered, I met Miss Fanny Seward, with whom I exchanged a single word, and proceeded to the foot of the bed. Dr. Verdi and, I think, two others were there. The bed was saturated with blood. The Secretary was lying on his back, the upper part of his head covered by a cloth, which extended down over his eyes. His mouth was open, the lower jaw dropping down. I exchanged a few whispered words with Dr. V. Secretary Stanton, who came after but almost simultaneously with me, made inquiries in a louder tone till admonished by a word from one of the physicians. We almost immediately withdrew and went into the adjoining front room, where lay Frederick Seward. His eyes were open but he did not move them, nor a limb, nor did he speak. Doctor White, who was in attendance, told me he was unconscious and more dangerously injured than his father.

As we descended the stairs, I asked Stanton what he had heard in regard to the President that was reliable. He said the President was shot at Ford's Theatre, that he had seen a man who was present and witnessed the occurrence. I said I would go immediately to the White House. Stanton told me the President was not there but was at the theatre. "Then," said I, "let us go immediately there." He said that was his intention, and asked me, if I had not a carriage, to go with him. In the lower hall we met General Montgomery C. Meigs, whom he requested to take charge of the house, and to clear out all who did not belong there. General Meigs begged Stanton not to go down to 10th Street; others also remonstrated against our going. Stanton, I thought, hesitated. Hurrying forward, I remarked that I should go immediately, and I thought it his duty also. He said he should certainly go, but the remonstrants increased and gathered round him. I said we were wasting time, and, pressing through the crowd, entered the carriage and urged Stanton, who was detained by others after he had placed his foot on the step. I was impatient. Stanton, as soon as he had seated himself, turned round, rose partly, and said the carriage was not his. I said that was no objection. He invited Meigs to go with us, and Judge Harley High Cartter of the Supreme Court mounted with the driver. At this moment Major T.T. Eckert rode up on horseback beside the carriage and protested vehemently against Stanton's going to 10th Street; said he had just come from there, that there were thousands of people of all sorts there, and he considered it very unsafe for the Secretary of War to expose himself. I replied that I knew not where he would be more safe, and that the duty of both of us was to attend the President immediately. Stanton concurred. Meigs called to some soldiers to go with us, and there was one on each side of the carriage. The streets were full of people. Not only the sidewalk but the carriage-way was to some extent occupied, all or nearly all hurrying towards 10th Street. When we entered that street we found it pretty closely packed.

A DYING PRESIDENT

The President had been carried across the street from the theatre, to the house of a Mr. Peterson. We entered by ascending a flight of steps above the basement and passing through a long hall to the rear, where the President lay extended on a bed, breathing heavily. Several surgeons were present, at least six, I should think more. Among them I was glad to observe Dr. Hall, who, however, soon left. I inquired of Dr. H., as I entered, the true condition of the President. He replied the President was dead to all intents, although he might live three hours or perhaps longer.

The giant sufferer lay extended diagonally across the bed, which was not long enough for him. He had been stripped of his clothes. His large arms, which were occasionally exposed, were of a size which one would scarce have expected from his spare appearance. His slow, full respiration lifted the clothes with each breath that he took. His features were calm and striking. I had never seen them appear to better advantage than for the first hour, perhaps, that I was there. After that, his right eye began to swell and that part of his face became discolored.

Senator Charles Sumner was there, I think, when I entered. If not he came in soon after, as did Speaker Schuyler Colfax, Mr. Secretary Hugh McCulloch, and the other members of the Cabinet, with the exception of Mr. Seward. A double guard was stationed at the door and on the sidewalk, to repress the crowd, which was of course highly excited and anxious. The room was small and overcrowded. The surgeons and members of the Cabinet were as many as should have been in the room, but there were many more, and the hall and other rooms in the front or main house were full. One of these rooms was occupied by Mrs. Lincoln and her attendants, with Miss Harris. Mrs. Dixon and Mrs. Kinney came to her about twelve o'clock. About once an hour Mrs. Lincoln would repair to the bedside of her dying husband and with lamentation and tears remain until overcome by emotion.

THE NEXT DAY

[*April 15.*] A door which opened upon a porch or gallery, and also the windows, were kept open for fresh air. The night was dark, cloudy, and damp, and about six it began to rain. I remained in the room until then without sitting or leaving it, when, there being a vacant chair which some one left at the foot of the bed, I occupied it for nearly two hours, listening to the heavy groans, and witnessing the wasting life of the good and great man who was expiring before me.

About 6 A.M. I experienced a feeling of faintness and for the first time after entering the room, a little past eleven, I left it and the house, and took a short walk in the open air. It was a dark and gloomy morning, and rain set in before I returned to the house, some fifteen minutes [later]. Large groups of people were gathered every few rods, all anxious and solicitous. Some one or more from each group stepped forward as I passed, to inquire into the condition of the President, and to ask if there was no hope. Intense grief was on every countenance when I replied that the President could survive but a short time. The colored people especially—and there were at this time more of them, perhaps, than of whites—were overwhelmed with grief.

Returning to the house, I seated myself in the back parlor, where the Attorney-General and others had been engaged in taking evidence concerning the assassination. Stanton, and Attorney General James Speed, and Secretary of the Interior John P. Usher were there, the latter asleep on the bed. There were three or four others also in the room. While I did not feel inclined to sleep, as many did, I was somewhat indisposed. I had been so for several days. The excitement and bad atmosphere from the crowded rooms oppressed me physically.

A little before seven, I went into the room where the dying President was rapidly drawing near the closing moments. His wife soon after made her last visit to him. The death-struggle had begun. Robert, his son, stood with several others at the head of the bed. He bore himself well, but on two occasions gave way to overpowering grief and sobbed aloud, turning his head and leaning on the shoulder of Senator Sumner. The respiration of the President became suspended at intervals, and at last entirely ceased at twenty-two minutes past seven.

LEGAL DUTIES

A prayer followed from Dr. Gurley; and the Cabinet, with the exception of Mr. Seward and Mr. McCulloch, immediately thereafter assembled in the back parlor, from which all other persons were excluded, and there signed a letter which was prepared by Attorney-General Speed to the Vice-President, informing him of the event, and that the government devolved upon him.

Mr. Stanton proposed that Mr. Speed, as the law officer, should communicate the letter to Mr. Andrew Johnson with some other member of the Cabinet. Mr. Postmaster General Dennison named me. I saw that, though all assented, it disconcerted Stanton, who had expected and intended to be the man and to have Speed associated with him. I was disinclined personally to disturb an obvious arrangement, and therefore named Mr. McCulloch as the first in order after the Secretary of State.

I arranged with Speed, with whom I rode home, for a Cabinet-meeting at twelve meridian at the room of the Secretary of the Treasury, in order that the government should experience no detriment, and that prompt and necessary action might be taken to assist the new Chief Magistrate in preserving and promoting the public tranquillity. We accordingly met at noon. Mr. Speed reported that President Andrew Johnson had taken the oath, which was administered by the Chief Justice, and had expressed a desire that the affairs of the government should proceed without interruption. Some discussion took place as to the propriety of an inaugural address, but the general impression was that it would be inexpedient. I was most decidedly of that opinion.

President Johnson, who was invited to be present, deported himself admirably, and on the subject of an inaugural said his acts would best disclose his policy. In all essentials it would, he said, be the same as that of the late President. He desired the members of the Cabinet to go forward with their duties without any change. Mr. Hunter, Chief Clerk of the State Department, was designated to act *ad interim* as Secretary of State. I suggested Mr. Speed, but I saw it was not acceptable in certain quarters. Stanton especially expressed a hope that Hunter should be assigned to the duty.

SITUATING PRESIDENT JOHNSON

A room for the President as an office was proposed until he could occupy the Executive Mansion, and Mr. McCulloch offered the room adjoining his own in the Treasury Building. I named the State Department as appropriate and proper, at least until the Secretary of State recovered, or so long as the President wished, but objections arose at once. The papers of Mr. Seward would, Stanton said, be disturbed; it would be better he should be here, etc., etc. Stanton, I saw, had a purpose; among other things, feared papers would fall under Mr. Johnson's eye which he did not wish to be seen.

On returning to my house this morning, Saturday, I found Mrs. Welles, who had been ill and confined to the house from indisposition for a week, had been twice sent for by Mrs. Lincoln to come to her at Peterson's. The housekeeper, knowing the state of Mrs. W.'s health, had without consultation turned away the messenger, Major French, but Mrs. Welles, on learning the facts when he came the second time, had yielded, and imprudently gone, although the weather was inclement. She remained at the Executive Mansion through the day. For myself, wearied, shocked, exhausted, but not inclined to sleep, the day, when not actually and officially engaged, passed off strangely.

I went after breakfast to the Executive Mansion. There was a cheerless cold rain and everything seemed gloomy. On the Avenue in front of the White House were several hundred colored people, mostly women and children, weeping and wailing their loss. This crowd did not appear to diminish through the whole of that cold, wet day; they seemed not to know what was to be their fate since their great benefactor was dead, and their hopeless grief affected me more than almost anything else, though strong and brave men wept when I met them.

At the White House all was silent and sad. Mrs. W. was with Mrs. L. and came to meet me in the library. Speed came in, and we soon left together. As we were descending the stairs, "Tad," who was looking from the window at the foot, turned and, seeing us, cried aloud in his tears, "Oh, Mr. Welles, who killed my father?" Neither Speed nor myself could restrain our tears, nor give the poor boy any satisfactory answer.

THE FREEDMEN'S BUREAU

JOHN WILLIAM DE FOREST

In March 1865, Congress created the Freedmen's Bureau, which strove to ease the Southern transition from a slave to a free society. It provided food, clothing, and shelter for black and white Southerners. The bureau created schools for freedmen, supervised labor contracts, and helped freedmen settle on confiscated or abandoned lands. The Freedmen's Bureau represented the one attempt by Congress to reduce some of the social and economic strife that Reconstruction brought to the South. John William De Forest (1826–1906), an officer in the Freedmen's Bureau, describes some of the complaints the bureau received and the difficulties of solving them. De Forest, a significant literary figure in the mid–nineteenth century, is best known for his 1867 novel *Miss Ravenel's Conversion from Secession to Loyalty*.

M ost of the difficulties between whites and blacks resulted from the inevitable awkwardness of tyros in the mystery of free labor. Many of the planters seemed to be unable to understand that work could be other than a form of slavery, or that it could be accomplished without some prodigious binding and obligating of the hireling to the employer. Contracts which were brought to me for approval contained all sorts of ludicrous provisions. Negroes must be respectful and polite; if they were not respectful and polite they must pay a fine for each offense; they must admit no one on their premises unless by consent of the landowner; they must have a quiet household and not keep too many dogs; they must not go off the plantation without leave. The idea seemed to be that if the laborer were not bound body and soul he would be of no use. With regard to many freedmen I was obliged to admit that this assumption was only too correct and to sympathize with the desire to limit their noxious liberty, at the same time that I knew such limitation to be impossible. When a darkey frolics all night and thus renders himself worthless for the next day's work; when he takes into his cabin a host of lazy relatives who eat him up, or of thievish ones who steal the neighboring pigs and chickens; when he gets high notions of freedom into his head and feels himself bound to answer his employer's directions with an indifferent whistle, what can the latter do? My advice was to pay weekly wages, if possible, and discharge every man as fast as he got through with his usefulness. But this policy was above the general reach of Southern capital and beyond the usual circle of Southern ideas.

FALLACIES OF AUTHORITY

One prevalent fallacy was the supposition that the farmer could, of his own authority, impose fines; in other words, that he could withhold all or a part of the laborer's pay if he left the farm before the expiration of his contract. The statement, "You can not take your man's wages for July because he has refused to work for you during August," was quite incomprehensible from the old-fashioned, patriarchal point of view.

"But what am I to do with this fellow, who has left me right in the hoeing season?" demands a wrathful planter.

"You have no remedy except to sue him for damages resulting from a failure of contract."

"Sue him! He ha'n't got nothing to collect on."

"Then don't sue him."

Exit planter, in helpless astonishment over the mystery of the new system, and half inclined to believe that I have been making game of him. I could, of course, have sent for the delinquent and ordered him to return to his work; but had I once begun to attend personally to such cases I should have had business enough to kill off a regiment of Bureau officers; and, moreover, I never forgot that my main duty should consist in educating the entire population around me to settle their difficulties by the civil law; in other words, I considered myself an instrument of reconstruction.

INJUSTICES TO BLACKS

The majority of the complaints brought before me came from Negroes. As would naturally happen to an ignorant race, they were liable to many impositions, and they saw their grievances with big eyes. There was magnitude, too, in their manner of statement; it was something like an indictment of the voluminous olden time—the rigmarole which charged a pig thief with stealing ten boars, ten sows, ten shoats, etc. With pomp of manner and of words, with a rotundity of voice and superfluity of detail . . . a Negro would so glorify his little trouble as to give one the impression that humanity had never before suffered the like. Sometimes I was able to cut short these turgid narratives with a few sharp questions; sometimes I found this impossible and had to let them roll on unchecked, like Mississippis. Of course the complaints were immensely various in nature and importance. They might refer to an alleged attempt at assassination or to the discrepancy of a bushel of pea vines in the division of a crop. They might be against brother freedmen, as well as against former slave owners and "Rebs." More than once have I been umpire in the case of a disputed jackknife or petticoat. Priscilly Jones informed me that her "old man was a-

Freed slaves gather in Charleston, South Carolina. The Freedmen's Bureau was established to ease the transition from slavery to freedom.

routin' everybody out of the house an' a-breakin' everything";
then Henry Jones bemoaned himself because his wife Priscilly
was going to strange places along with Tom Lynch; then Tom
Lynch wanted redress and protection because of the disquieting threats of Henry Jones. The next minute Chloe Jackson desired justice on Viney Robinson, who had slapped her face and
torn her clothes. Everybody, guilty or innocent, ran with his or
her griefs to the Bureau officer; and sometimes the Bureau officer, half distracted, longed to subject them all to some huge
punishment. Of the complaints against whites the majority were
because of the retention of wages or of alleged unfairness in the
division of the crops.

If the case brought before me were of little consequence, I usually persuaded the Negro, if possible, to drop it or to "leave it
out" to referees. Without a soldier under my command, and for
months together having no garrison within forty miles, I could
not execute judgment even if I could see to pronounce it; and,
moreover, I had not, speaking with official strictness, any authority to act in matters of property; the provost court having
been abolished before I entered upon my jurisdiction. If the complaint were sufficiently serious to demand attention, I had one
almost invariable method of procedure: I stated the case in a
brief note and addressed it to the magistrate of the "beat" or
magisterial precinct in which the Negro resided. Then, charging
him to deliver the letter in person and explaining to him what
were his actual wrongs and his possibilities of redress, I dismissed him to seek for justice precisely where a white man
would have sought it. Civil law was in force by order of the commanding general of the department; and the civil authorities
were disposed, as I soon learned, to treat Negroes fairly. Such being the case, all that my clients needed in me was a counselor.

"But the square won't pay no sawt 'tention to me," a Negro
would sometimes declare. To which I would reply: "Then come
back and let me know it. If he neglects his duty we will report
him and have him removed."

Of the fifty or sixty magistrates in my district I had occasion
to indicate but one as being unfit for office by reason of political partialities and prejudices of race. New York City would be
fortunate if it could have justice dealt out to it as honestly and
fairly as it was dealt out by the plain, homespun farmers who
filled the square-archates of Greenville, Pickens, and Anderson
[in North Carolina].

ABSENT PLAINTIFFS

But the Negro often lacked confidence in the squire; perhaps, too, he was aware that his case would not bear investigation; and so, instead of delivering my letter in person, he often sent it by a messenger. As the magistrate could not act without the presence of the complainant, nothing was done. A week or fortnight later the Negro would reappear at my office, affirming that "dese yere Rebs wouldn't do nothin' for black folks nohow."

"What did the squire say?" I would ask.

"Didn' say nothin'. Jes took the ticket an' read it, an' put it in his pocket."

"Did you see him?"

"No. I was feared he wouldn' do nothin'; so I sont it roun' to him."

"Now then, go to him. If you have a story to tell, go and tell it to him, and swear to it. I shall do nothing for you till you have done that."

And so the process of education went on, working its way mainly by dint of general laws, without much regard to special cases. As this is the method of universal Providence and of the War Department, I felt that I could not be far wrong in adopting it. But even this seemingly simple and easy style of performing duty had its perplexities. Magistrates rode from ten to thirty miles to ask me how they should dispose of this, that, and the other complaint which had been turned over to them for adjudication. Their chief difficulty was to know where the military orders ended and where civil law began; and here I was little less puzzled than they, for we were acting under a hodgepodge of authorities which no man could master. I had files of orders for 1865, and 1866, and 1867; files from the Commissioner, and from the Assistant Commissioner, and from the general commanding the department; the whole making a duodecimo volume of several hundred closely printed pages. To learn these by heart and to discover the exact point where they ceased to cover and annul the state code was a task which would have bothered not only a brevet major but a chief justice. My method of interpretation was to limit the military order as much as might be, and so give all possible freedom of action to the magistrate.

THE BLACK CODES

Benjamin Grubb Humphreys

According to many white Southerners, emancipation created a population of 4 million free Negroes who lacked the education and skills necessary to lead an independent, productive lives. White Southerners feared that without the discipline of slavery, idle blacks would engage in disorder and lawlessness and wreak more havoc on a society already smarting from the destruction of their social order. Most important, Southern whites wanted to ensure their continued domination of the Negro race. The Black Codes were similar to antebellum laws that controlled the slaves; the codes required blacks to work, controlled where and when they traveled, and regulated marriage. The Mississippi legislature passed one of the most severe codes in 1865. In the following speech, Mississippi governor Benjamin Grubb Humphreys urges the passage of the code and warns the legislature of the threat that three hundred thousand newly freed slaves posed to the Mississippi community.

G ENTLEMEN *of the Senate and House of Representatives:* In view of your resolution to take, at an early day, a recess until after the holidays, I deem it proper to call your attention to a few subjects of vital importance to the welfare of the State.

By the sudden emancipation of over 300,000 slaves, Mississippi has imposed upon her a problem of vast magnitude, upon the proper solution of which depend the hopes and future prosperity of ourselves and our children.

Under the pressure of Federal bayonets, urged on by the misdirected sympathies of the world, in behalf of the enslaved African, the people of Mississippi have abolished the institution

Excerpted from "Governor Humphreys' Message," by Benjamin Grubb Humphreys, *New York Times*, December 3, 1865.

of slavery, and have solemnly declared in their State Constitution that "the Legislature should provide by law for the protection and security of the persons and property of the freedmen of the State against evils that may arise from their sudden emancipation." How this important provision and requirement of the constitution is to be carried into effect is the question now presented for our solution. We must now meet the question as it is, and not as we would like to have it. The rule must be justice. The negro is free, whether we like it or not; we must realize that fact now and forever. To be free, however, does not make him a citizen, or entitle him to political or social equality with the white man. But the constitution and justice do entitle him to protection and security in his person and property, both real and personal.

RECOGNITION IN COURT

In my humble judgment, no man, bond or free, under any form of government, can be assured of protection or security, either in person or property, except through an independent and enlightened judiciary. The courts, then, should be open to the negro. But of what avail is it to open the courts, and invite the negro "to sue and be sued," if he is not permitted to testify himself and introduce such testimony as he or his attorney may deem essential to establish the truth and justice of his case? Whether the witness be white or black, it is the denial of the most common privilege of freedom, an unmeaning delusion, the merest mockery.

As a measure of domestic policy, whether for the protection of the person or property of the freedman, or for the protection of society, the negro should be allowed and required to testify for or against the white and black, according to the truth. There are few men living in the South who have not known many white criminals to go "unwhipped of justice" because negro testimony was not permitted in the courts. And now that the negro is no longer under the restraint or care of his master, he will become the dupe and "cats-paw" of the vile and vicious white man who seeks his association, and will plunder our land with entire security from punishment, unless he can be reached through negro testimony. It is an insult to the intelligence and virtue of our courts, and juries of white men, to say or suspect that they cannot or will not protect the innocent, whether white or black, against the falsehood and perjury of black witnesses.

The question of admitting negro testimony for the protection of their persons and property sinks into insignificance by the side of the other great question of *guarding them and the State* against the evils that may arise from their sudden emancipation. What are the evils that have already arisen against which we are to guard the negro and the State? The answer is patent to all—vagrancy and pauperism, and their inevitable concomitant crime and misery, hang like a dark pall over a once prosperous and happy, but now desolated land.

FAILURE OF THE FREEDMEN'S BUREAU

To the guardian care of the Freedmen's Bureau has been intrusted the emancipated slaves. The civil law, and the white man outside of the bureau, has been deprived of all jurisdiction over them. Look around you and see the result. Idleness and vagrancy has been the rule. Our rich and productive fields have been deserted for the filthy garrets and sickly cellars of our towns and cities. From producers they are converted into consumers, and as Winter approaches their only salvation from starvation and want is Federal rations, plunder and pillage. Four years of cruel war, conducted upon principles of vandalism disgraceful to the civilization of the age was scarcely more blighting and destructive to the homes of the white man, and impoverishing and degrading to the negro, than has resulted in the last six or eight months from the administration of this black incubus. Many of the officers connected with that bureau are gentlemen of honor and integrity, but they seem incapable of protecting the rights and property of the white man against the villainies of the vile and villains with whom they are associated.

How long this hideous course, permitted of Heaven, is to be allowed to rule and ruin our happy people, I regret it is not in my power to give any assurance further than can be gathered from the public and private declarations of President Andrew Johnson that "the troops will be withdrawn from Mississippi, when in the opinion of the government the peace and order and civil authority has been restored and can be maintained without them." In this uncertainty as to what will satisfy the government of our loyalty and ability to maintain order and peace and civil government, our duty under the constitution to guard the negro and the State from the evils arising from sudden emancipation, must not be neglected. Our duty to the State and to the freedmen seems to me to be clear, and I respectfully recommend—

First. That negro testimony should be admitted to our courts, not only for the protection of the person and property of the freedmen, but for the protection of society against the crimes of both races.

Second. That the freedman be encouraged at once to enter in some pursuit of industry for the support of his family and the education of his children, by laws assuring him of friendship and protection. Tax the freedman for the support of the indigent and helpless freedmen, and then, with an iron will and the strong hand of power, take hold of the idler and the vagrant and force him to some profitable employment.

Third. Pass a militia law that will enable the militia to protect our people against insurrection, or any possible combination of vicious white men and negroes.

I deem the passage of these measures, before you take a recess, of vital importance. By them we may secure the withdrawal of the Federal troops, and thus again inspire our people with hope and confidence in the future, and encourage them to engage again in agricultural pursuits, upon which our all depends. If we fail to pass them, the future is all uncertainty, gloom and despondency.

THE FOURTEENTH AMENDMENT

AVERY CRAVEN

In January 1866, Senator Lyman Trumbull proposed his Civil Rights Bill, which granted the newly emancipated slaves the same rights as whites to sue or be sued in court and to hold contracts and personal property, the protection of life and liberty, and other rights. The bill passed in Congress, but was then vetoed by President Andrew Johnson. Johnson claimed that blacks' rights were secure under state and federal laws, and the bill was unnecessary and unconstitutional. Congress overrode the president's veto, but the dissension proved that a constitutional amendment was necessary to protect the rights of the Negro. The Fourteenth Amendment, containing much of the substance of the Civil Rights Bill, passed in late spring of 1866, but it was not ratified by all the states until 1868. In the following article, Avery Craven describes the Fourteenth Amendment and the difficult process of its approval. Craven is a well-known historian, who specializes in mid–nineteenth century American history. He is the author of *Repressible Conflict 1830–1861* and *The Growth of Southern Nationalism 1848–1861*.

N ewspaper editorials in the Reconstruction period reveal that a kind of restlessness had been developing throughout the nation—a weariness of the quarrel between President Andrew Jackson and the Congress, which seemed at times to be largely personal. People were demanding progress toward some solution of the tragic situation into which the nation had drifted. Business was suffering; Congress was so occupied with

Johnson and the South that serious economic problems were being neglected. Johnson had at least done something toward a final settlement, and Congress had evidently decided that this was unsatisfactory. But as yet, in its Freedmen's Bureau and Civil Rights bills, Congress had only dealt with certain specific items. It had not faced the larger problem of "resumption." Even here the result had been only to intensify the quarrel with the President. If the Joint Committee represented Congress at work on the larger problem, it was time for some indication of progress.

THE PEOPLE DEMAND ACTION

The basic issues to be settled were becoming quite clear to all. Even the points of difference were generally understood. They had been revealed in the Freedmen's Bureau debates, more clearly in the Civil Rights debates, and in the President's veto messages. Everyone understood that some decision had to be made regarding the Negro's rights, southern representation, the disenfranchisement of Confederate leaders, and the national and Confederate debts. So insistent had become the demand for action that senators not on the Joint Committee and persons not even in Congress began offering suggestions for action.

On March 16, 1865, Senator William M. Stewart of Nevada introduced a series of resolutions that brought immediate response. He suggested that each southern state, as soon as it had amended its constitution ending all distinctions as to civil rights based on race or color, repudiated all debts incurred in the rebellion, yielded all claims for loss of slaves, and extended the franchise to all persons on the same terms and conditions, would be recognized as having fully resumed its relations to the government. Northern states would also incorporate this same amendment into their constitutions. A general amnesty would then be declared for all who had taken part in the rebellion. Here was a specific proposal for ending the suspense and removing all the difficulties to resumption. Yet both Andrew Johnson and Representative Thaddeus Stevens took a hand in bringing it to nothing.

Then Indiana reformer Robert Dale Owen, ever ready to save the nation, came to Washington to offer his program. He too would end discrimination, extend the right to vote to all, reduce representation for such discrimination before 1876, and void rebel debts and all claims for loss of slaves. He would give Congress the right to enforce these provisions. He too revealed the

basic issues to be faced and offered a solution. His proposal met
the same fate as had Stewart's, Congress could not agree on all
its terms.

Yet these efforts had made action necessary and delay politically dangerous. Democratic approval of these efforts could not
be ignored. The reason for the committee's hesitation and delay
readily became apparent. It had been dominated from the beginning by the Radical element, with what has been called
"social-revolutionary purposes" for reconstructing the South.
However, in the debates on Senator Lyman Trumbull's Civil
Rights Bill, these Radicals had learned that reflection of such
purposes in a report would meet strong opposition. They had
to be constitutionally careful.

RIGHTS TO NATIONAL CITIZENSHIP

Both Thaddeus Stevens and Senator John A. Bingham, who
were to shape the report that was now being demanded from
the committee, had been important figures in the prewar antislavery drive. They had then argued that the Declaration of Independence conferred a national citizenship with a rather comprehensive body of natural rights and civil liberties. They had
found additional support for this philosophy in an earlier decision by Justice Bushrod Washington. In the case of *Corfield vs.
Coryell*, Washington had set forth in detail a long list of civil liberties guaranteed by the comity clause in Article IV of the Constitution. It stated clearly that citizens of each state were to be
entitled to all privileges and immunities of citizens in the several states. From this comes the theory of "equal protection of
the laws." . . . In late 1850s Bingham himself had said in the
House, "It must be apparent that the absolute equality of all,
and the equal protection of each, are principles of our constitution . . . as universal and indestructible as the human race."

To this had gradually been added the "due process clause"
of the Fifth Amendment, protecting persons from loss of life,
liberty, or property without due process of law. Chief Justice
Roger B. Taney had used this in the Dred Scott case, and antislavery advocates Theodore Weld and James G. Birney had
fought the "black laws" of Ohio [that placed severe restrictions
on blacks' civil rights] with the same weapon. It appeared also
in the Free-Soil platforms of 1848 and 1852.

These two constitutional doctrines now became the constitutional ideology of the Radical Republicans on the committee.

They had been the legal weapons against class legislation by race offered by Lyman Trumbull in defending his Civil Rights Bill. They had on that occasion been attacked by the Democrats, who denied, as had Taney, that the Negro could be a citizen or that there was such a thing as national citizenship.

FROM FREEDOM TO CITIZENSHIP

Trumbull, however, had argued that the Thirteenth Amendment endowed the Negro with citizenship "as a necessary incident of freedom" and that Congress had both the power and the duty to guarantee the rights that went with citizenship. Trumbull had then attacked the Black Codes, which of course did not make the Negro a slave but did deprive him of his rights as a free man. His bill was to end these discriminations and to give full meaning to the Thirteenth Amendment. Trumbull had cited as support Bushrod Washington's decision in the Corfield case. He was, he said, only protecting rights already existing.

Democrats and conservatives had seen in this, as they well might, the threat of social revolution. Senator Edgar Cowan of Connecticut, a Conservative Republican, was quick to comment, "Now as I understand the meaning and intent of this [civil rights] bill, it is that there shall be no discrimination between the inhabitants of the several states of this union, none in any way." He then called attention to the segregated schools of his state, and asked whether it was Trumbull's purpose to punish, for violation of a United States statute, the school directors who carried out this state law. He added, "To me it is monstrous."

Others noted the various state laws in the North prohibiting marriage between the races, and asked if the bill would invalidate them. A senator from Kentucky observed that in his state laws for certain crimes varied with the race. Would these be destroyed? Both Trumbull and Fessenden said no, and gave assurance that the bill would leave the two races in the same relationship as before. Yet doubts remained and the words "revolutionary" and "perfect equality" kept cropping up. The question of the constitutionality of such a sweeping act also began to be raised. One said, "It brings the two races upon the same great plane of perfect equality."

At that, Senator Bingham rose to state his belief that civil rights included the entire range of civil privileges and immunities within organized society, excepting only political rights. He accepted the conservatives' objections and interpretations, and agreed that Congress had no power to enact such legislation merely by right derived from the Thirteenth Amendment. The Civil Rights Bill, nevertheless, was aimed to strike down every state law that established any kind of discrimination against Negroes. It did have the revolutionary purpose; and since there was some doubt as to constitutionality and since all discriminatory legislation ought to be wiped out, Bingham thought the proper way would be by an amendment to the Constitution. Yet by eliminating the discrimination clause, the Civil Rights Bill was finally passed with the constitutional uncertainty remaining.

This was the situation that led to the framing of the Fourteenth Amendment. Agreement on the basic issues had not been reached but public pressure for a congressional program could no longer be resisted. The debates in Congress on the various proposals that had been made began to clear the air, and the Joint Committee set to work on the terms to be incorporated into a constitutional amendment. That was an important task and the time was too short to do a sound and enduring job. That would become clear in the years ahead.

THE FIVE SECTIONS OF THE FOURTEENTH AMENDMENT

The Joint Committee amendment, as presented to the Senate and House on April 30, 1865, by Congressman William Pitt Fessenden and Congressman Thaddeus Stevens contained five sections. The first proclaimed a national citizenship and stated that no state could abridge the privileges and immunities of citizens of the United States, or deprive them of life, liberty, or property without due process of law, or deprive them of equal protection of the laws.

The second apportioned representatives among the states according to the whole number of persons in each state, but added the provision that where the right to vote for federal and state officials was denied to any male inhabitant of twenty-one years of age and a citizen [except for participation in rebellion or other crimes], the basis of representation should be reduced in the proportion that the number of such males bear to the total number of eligible males in the state.

The third section barred from voting for representatives in Congress and electors for President and Vice-President, until July 4, 1870, any person connected in any way with the late rebellion. The fourth simply forbade the payment by the United

States or by any state of the debts incurred in support of the rebellion or for loss of slaves. The fifth gave Congress the power to enforce the above articles.

As to the resumption of southern states in the Union, two bills followed. The first stated that when the above amendment became part of the Constitution, and when the southern states had modified their constitutions to conform, their representatives should be admitted to Congress. The only other condition was the payment of their share of the direct tax within a period not exceeding ten years.

The second bill barred from federal office most persons who had held high office in the Confederacy, or those who had left United States service of any kind for service in the Confederacy. This section, generally objectionable to all, was soon dropped.

Neither Johnson nor all of Congress accepted this program without debate and change. The disfranchisement section, especially, met sharp opposition. Some asked for more detailed statements of terms, and a few followed Johnson's attitude of rejecting the whole amendment.

REVISION AND RATIFICATION

At length, a five-man committee began work to make the desired revisions, and produced the final Fourteenth Amendment as it was to be submitted to the states for ratification. The main change from the original suggestion was to drop the punitive section and to add at the very beginning Bingham's definition of citizenship. The question here is whether the section was added merely to remove doubt as to the constitutional status of the Civil Rights Act, or whether the intent was to go beyond the scope of that act and put all civil rights as the Radicals saw them under the protection of the amendments.

Knowing the opinions Bingham had always held and the social revolutionary sweep of his purpose all along, many scholars believe that the purpose was to go well beyond the guarantees of the Civil Rights Act and to place all civil rights, in the expansive Bingham definition, under federal guarantees of equality against state law. They have noted that the very phrases used, by virtue of their history and derivation, are intentionally vague and not capable of precise legal description. The terms are those of prewar days and have a radical, humanitarian, equalitarian quality. They are not the terms of the Civil Rights Bill, which had, in the debate, permitted the states to retain segregation. "Privileges and immunities," "due process of law," and "equal protection" are not derived from the Civil Rights Act, but have a very familiar ring. Radicals were now amending the Constitution as the law of the land, not writing a statute.

Yet, in defending the amendment before the House, Stevens observed, "Some answer, 'Your civil rights bill secures the same things.' That is partly true, but a law is repealable by a majority. And I need hardly say that the first time that the South . . . obtain[s] command of the Congress it will be repealed. . . . This amendment once adopted cannot be amended without two-thirds of Congress. That they will hardly get." Others echoed this idea. As [future president] James A. Garfield said, "The civil rights bill is now a part of the law of this land. But every gentleman knows it will cease to be a part of the law whenever the sad moment arrives when [the Democratic party] comes into power." Others supported the amendment because they thought the Civil Rights Bill was unconstitutional.

PRIVILEGES AND IMMUNITIES

Opposition, however, talked of the revolutionary character of the first section [of the amendment]. As one asked:

> What are privileges and immunities? Why, sir, all the rights we have under the laws of the country are embraced under the definition of privileges and immunities. The right to vote is a privilege. The right to marry is a privilege. The right to contract is a privilege. The right to be a juror is a privilege. The right to be a judge or President of the United States is a privilege. I hold if that ever becomes a part of the fundamental law of the land it will prevent any state from refusing to allow anything to anybody embraced under the terms of privileges and immunities. If the negro is refused the right to be a juror, that will take away from his privileges and immunities as a citizen of the United States, and the Federal Government will step in and interfere. It will result in a revolution worse than that through which we have just passed.

Bingham's reply to this is revealing:

> The necessity for the first section of this amendment to the constitution, Mr. Speaker, is one of the lessons that has been taught to your committee and taught to

all the people of this country by the history of the past four years of terrible conflict . . . that history in which God is, and in which he teaches the profoundest lessons to men and nations . . . that is to protect by national law the privileges and immunities of all the citizens of the Republic and the inborn rights of every person within its jurisdiction whenever the same shall be abridged or denied by the unconstitutional acts of any State.

Then to get back to the Declaration of Independence, Bingham added:

This amendment takes from no state any right that ever pertained to it. No state ever had the right, under the forms of law or otherwise, to deny to any freeman the equal protection of the laws or to abridge the privileges or immunities of any citizen of the Republic, although many of them have assumed and exercised the power, and that without remedy.

Here was both the lawyer and the old antislavery man talking.

The Fourteenth Amendment thus started on its troubled way. The American dream of possible social perfection had become part of the law of the land through those vague and elastic terms "privileges or immunities"—things which "no State shall abridge" in a land where all persons born there or naturalized are citizens.

MULTIPLE PURPOSES

The difficulties that beset the amendment in the days ahead were due in large part to the tangle of purposes that went into its making. Unquestionably the philanthropic motive was present, but the Negro's right to the ballot was not directly granted. The choice to grant or refuse was cleverly left in southern hands. For a price, they could deny the Negro the franchise. The reason for this was that something important even for the Negro's rights was involved—the continued dominance of the Republican party. The amendment had been framed in a way to make certain that if the Negro's vote were restricted or controlled, southern representation, now increased by the fact that the Negro was a citizen, would be reduced in proportion. That would accomplish two things. It would prevent the increase of Democratic power and also appease that large element in the

Republican party which had a positive dislike for the Negro and was opposed to his enfranchisement. It was as important to protect the North from the Negro as to protect the Negro from the South.

An economic interest was also involved. Power in Democratic hands could threaten the Republican interest in public lands, the tariff, financial programs, railroad expansion, and other issues. It is therefore interesting that when southern and Democratic success proved less dangerous, the Fourteenth Amendment and its civil rights' purposes were largely ignored.

THE KU KLUX KLAN

JOSEPH H. RAINEY

The Ku Klux Klan began as an organization of white Southern Democrats who felt that they needed to regain control of a society that was torn from them by the Civil War and Reconstruction. As the Union strove to assimilate the emancipated slaves into Southern society, white Southerners had secret meetings where they planned the attacks and murders of blacks and Republicans. They were notorious for their violent nocturnal raids wearing white robes and masks. The following excerpt from the testimony of Joseph H. Rainey describes the atrocities of the Klansmen and argues that measures against the Klan are necessary to protect the rights to life and liberty of black Southerners and white Republicans. Joseph H. Rainey was the first black Congressman and served from 1870 to 1879.

I need not, Mr. Speaker, recite here the murderous deeds committed both in North and South Carolina. I could touch the feelings of this House by the story of widows and orphans now wandering amid the ravines of the rural counties of my native State seeking protection and maintenance from others who are yet unable, on account of their own poverty, to grant them aid. I could dwell upon the sorrows of poor women, with their helpless infants, cast upon the world, homeless and destitute, deprived of their natural protectors by the red hand of the midnight assassin. I could appeal to you, members upon this floor, as husbands and fathers, to picture to yourselves the desolation of your own happy firesides should you be suddenly snatched away from your loved ones. Think of gray-haired men, whose fourscore years are almost numbered, the venerated heads of peaceful households, without warning murdered

Excerpted from Joseph H. Rainey's testimony before the Forty-Second Congress, First Session, April 1, 1871.

for political opinion's sake. In proof I send to the desk the following article and ask the Clerk to read. It is taken from the Spartanburg (South Carolina) Republican, March 29, 1871.

The Clerk read as follows:

"Horrible Attempt at Murder by Disguised Men.—One of the most cowardly and inhuman attempts at murder known in the annals of crime was made last Wednesday night, the 22d instant, by a band of disguised men upon the person of Dr. J. Winsmith at his home about twelve miles from town. The doctor, a man nearly seventy years of age, had been to town during the day and was seen and talked with by many of our citizens. Returning home late, he soon afterward retired, worn out and exhausted by the labors of the day. A little after midnight he was aroused by some one knocking violently at his front door. The knocking was soon afterward repeated at his chamber door, which opens immediately upon the front yard. The doctor arose, opened the door, and saw two men in disguise standing before him. As soon as he appeared one of the men cried out, 'Come on boys! Here's the damned old rascal.' The doctor immediately stepped back into the room, picked up two single-barreled pistols lying upon the bureau, and returned to the open door. At his reappearance the men retreated behind some cedar trees standing in the yard. The doctor, in his night clothes, boldly stepped out into the yard and followed them. On reaching the trees he fired, but with what effect he does not know. He continued to advance, when twenty or thirty shots were fired at him by men crouched behind an orange hedge. He fired his remaining pistol and then attempted to return to the house. Before reaching it, however, he sank upon the ground exhausted by the loss of blood, and pain, occasioned by seven wounds which he had received in various parts of his body. As soon as he fell the assassins mounted their horses and rode away.

"The doctor was carried into the house upon a quilt, borne by his wife and some colored female servants. The colored men on the premises fled on the approach of the murderers, and the colored women being afraid to venture out, Mrs. Winsmith herself was obliged to walk three quarters of a mile to the house of her nephew, Dr. William Smith, for assistance. The physician has been with Dr. Winsmith day and night since the difficulty occurred, and thinks, we learn, that there is a possible chance of the doctor's recovery.

"The occasion of this terrible outrage can be only the fact that

Dr. Winsmith is a Republican. One of the largest land-holders and tax-payers in the county, courteous in manner, kind in disposition, and upright and just in all his dealings with his fellowmen, he has ever been regarded as one of the leading citizens of the county. For many years prior to the war he represented the people in the Legislature, and immediately after the war he was sent to the senate. Because he has dared become a Republican, believing that in the doctrines of true republicanism only can the State and country find lasting peace and prosperity, he has become the doomed victim of the murderous Ku Klux Klan.

"The tragedy has cast a gloom over the entire community, and while we are glad to say that it has generally been condemned, yet we regret to state that no step has yet been taken to trace out and punish the perpetrators of the act. The judge of this circuit is sitting on his bench; the machinery of justice is in working order; but there can be found no hand bold enough to set it in motion. The courts of justice seem paralyzed when they have to meet such issues as this. Daily reports come to us of men throughout the country being whipped; of schoolhouses for colored children being closed, and of parties being driven from their houses and their families. Even here in town there are some who fear to sleep at their own homes and in their own beds. The law affords no protection for life and property in this county, and the sooner the country knows it and finds a remedy for it, the better it will be. Better a thousand times the rule of the bayonet than the humiliating lash of the Ku Klux and the murderous bullet of a midnight assassin.". . .

PROTECTING UNION SUPPORTERS

It has been asserted that protection for the colored people only has been demanded; and in this there is a certain degree of truth, because they are noted for their steadfastness to the Union and the cause of liberty as guarantied by the Constitution. But, on the other hand, this protection is equally desired for those loyal whites, some to the manner born, others who, in the exercise of their natural rights as American citizens, have seen fit to remove thither from other sections of the States, and who are now undergoing persecution simply on account of their activity in carrying out Union principles and loyal sentiments in the South. Their efforts have contributed largely to further reconstruction and the restoration of the southern States to the old fellowship of the Federal compact. It is indeed hard that

their reward for their well-meant earnestness should be that of
being violently treated, and even forced to flee from the homes
of their choice. It will be a foul stain upon the escutcheon of our
land if such atrocities be tamely suffered longer to continue.

In the dawn of our freedom our young Republic was widely
recognized and proudly proclaimed to the world the refuge, the
safe asylum of the oppressed of all lands. Shall it be said that at
this day, through mere indifference and culpable neglect, this
grand boast of ours is become a mere form of words, an utter
fraud? I earnestly hope not! And yet, if we stand with folded
arms and idle hands, while the cries of our oppressed brethren
sound in our ears, what will it be but a proof to all men that we
are utterly unfit for our glorious mission, unworthy our noble
privileges, as the greatest of republics, the champions of freedom for all men? I would that every individual man in this
whole nation could be aroused to a sense of his own part and
duty in this great question. When we call to mind the fact that
this persecution is waged against men for the simple reason that
they dare to vote with the party which has saved the Union in-
tact by the lavish expenditure of blood and treasure, and has
borne the nation safely through the fearful crisis of these last few
years, our hearts swell with an overwhelming indignation. . . .

I say to the gentlemen of the Opposition, and to the entire
membership of the Democratic party, that upon your hands
rests the blood of the loyal men of the South. Disclaim it as you
will the stain is there to prove your criminality before God and
the world in the day of retribution which will surely come. I
pity the man or party of men who would seek to ride into
power over the dead body of a legitimate opponent.

Andrew Johnson's Impeachment Trial

Douglas O. Linder

When Andrew Johnson assumed the presidency after Abraham Lincoln's death in 1865, he made several decisions that rankled members of Congress. One of the most controversial was his veto of the Civil Rights Act of 1866. Radical Republicans in Congress advocated Negro suffrage and citizenship, which the Civil Rights Act conferred, but Johnson rejected as unnecessary. The final straw was his attempt to oust Secretary of War Edwin Stanton, but Stanton's position was protected by the 1867 Tenure of Office Act. Johnson tried to remove him from office anyway, which fired the smoldering tempers of Republican congressmen. They initiated an Impeachment Resolution of Andrew Johnson in February 1868. The Court acquitted Johnson in May 1868 by a slim margin of one vote. In the following article, Douglas O. Linder describes Johnson's impeachment trial and the events that led up to it. Douglas O. Linder is a professor of law at the University of Missouri at Kansas City.

I n May 1868, the Senate came within a single vote of taking the unprecedented step of removing a president from office. Although the impeachment trial of Andrew Johnson was ostensibly about a violation of the Tenure of Office Act, it was about much more than that. Also on trial in 1868 were Johnson's lenient policies towards Reconstruction and his vetoes of the Freedmen's Bureau Act and the Civil Rights Act. The trial was, above all else, a political trial.

Andrew Johnson was a lifelong Democrat and slave owner

From "A Trial Account," by Douglas O. Linder, www.law.umkc.edu, 1998. Copyright © 1998 by Douglas O. Linder. Reprinted with permission.

who won a place alongside Abraham Lincoln on the 1864 Republican ticket in order to gain the support of pro-war Democrats. Johnson was fiercely pro-Union and had come to national prominence when, as a Senator from the important border state of Tennessee, he denounced secession as "treason."

On April 11, 1865, Abraham Lincoln gave his last major address. Lincoln congratulated Confederate general Robert E. Lee on his surrender, announced that his cabinet was united on a policy of reconstructing the Union, and expressed the hope that the states of the confederacy would extend the vote to literate negroes and those who served as Union soldiers. Then came his tragic assassination at the Ford Theater.

JOHNSON'S PRESIDENCY

When Andrew Johnson became president after the assassination of Abraham Lincoln, some of the Republicans in Congress, most opposed to what they saw as the too-lenient policies of Lincoln toward reconstruction, saw Johnson's ascension as a hopeful sign. One of the radical Republicans of the Senate, Benjamin Wade, expressed his support: "Johnson, we have faith in you. By the gods, there will be no more trouble in running the government." Less than three years later, Wade would cast a vote to convict Johnson in the impeachment trial that nearly made him the next president of the United States.

There were two contending theories in post-war Washington concerning reconstruction. One theory argued that the states of the United States are indestructible by the acts of their own people and state sovereignty cannot be forfeited to the national government. Under this theory, the only task for the federal government was to suppress the insurrection, replace its leaders, and provide an opportunity for free government to re-emerge. Rehabilitation of the state was a job for the state itself. The other theory of reconstruction argued that the Civil War was a struggle between two governments, and that the southern territory was conquered land, without internal borders—much less places with a right to statehood. Under this theory, the federal government might rule this territory as it pleases, admitting places as states under whatever rules it might prescribe.

Andrew Johnson was a proponent of the first, more lenient theory, while the radical Republicans who would so nearly remove him from office were advocates of the second theory. The most radical of the radical Republicans, men like Thaddeus

Stevens and Charles Sumner, believed also in the full political equality of the freed slaves. They believed that black men must be given equal rights to vote, hold office, own land, and enter into contracts, and until southern states made such promises in their laws they had no right to claim membership in the Union. (Republicans also had more practical reasons to worry about Johnson's lenient reconstruction policy: the congressmen elected by white southerners were certain to be overwhelmingly Democrats, reducing if not eliminating the Republican majorities in both houses.)

The first serious conflict over the course of reconstruction concerned the plan drafted by the Johnson Administration for North Carolina. The plan called for residents to elect delegates to a state convention that would frame a new state constitution. The cabinet split 4 to 3 in favor of allowing black residents to vote, but Johnson sided with those who would restrict voters to those qualified to vote under state law at the time of North Carolina's secession—whites only. Secretary of War Edwin Stanton reported that "the opposition of the President to throwing the franchise open to the colored people appeared to be fixed."

THE CIVIL RIGHTS ACT

In January 1866, Senator Lyman Trumbull introduced two bills. One would enlarge the powers of the Freedmen's Bureau while the other would extend basic civil rights to negro citizens. Andrew Johnson surprised many who believed he would postpone confrontation with the radical Republicans by vetoing both bills. Congress was unable to override the Freedmen's Bureau veto, but succeeded in overriding the Civil Rights Act veto on a Senate vote of 33 to 15. Except for veto overrides on two minor pieces of legislation, one in the Franklin Pierce and one in the John Tyler administrations, it was the first successful override in the nation's history and portended serious trouble for the President and his reconstruction policies. By February of 1866, the radicals viewed Johnson as "an outlaw undeserving of quarter."

A summer massacre in New Orleans further fueled the growing animosity between Johnson and the Republican Congress. A mob, including members of the Louisiana police, fired upon whites and blacks gathering for a Republican-backed convention that would frame a new state government. Forty were killed and over one hundred wounded. Only after the killing was over did U.S. troops arrive to place the city under martial law. Republicans angrily denounced Johnson for not anticipating trouble and protecting convention delegates and supporters. Impeachment talk began to swirl around Washington. Complaints against Johnson included his public drunkenness, generous use of the pardon power, and even suggestions that he was a principal in the Lincoln assassination plot.

Johnson, for his part, answered denunciation with denunciation. In a series of combative speeches in cities such as Cleveland and St. Louis, the President lashed out at his congressional critics as "traitors." He accused ultra-radicals Thaddeus Stevens, Wendell Phillips, and Charles Sumner of comparing themselves to "the Savior." Johnson's intemperate speeches would later become the basis for articles of impeachment.

THE FOURTEENTH AMENDMENT

In the spring of 1867, the new Congress passed over Johnson's veto a second Freedmen's Bureau bill and proposed to the states a Fourteenth Amendment to the U.S. Constitution. (The Fourteenth Amendment is best known today for its requirement that states guarantee equal protection and due process of law, but the most controversial provisions of the time concerned the conditions precedent that imposed on states for readmission to the Union.) Johnson announced his opposition to the Fourteenth Amendment and campaigned for its defeat. The Reconstruction Act of 1867, also passed over a presidential veto, wiped out the "pretended state governments" of the ten excluded states and divided them into five military districts, each commanded by an officer of the army. To escape military rule, states were required to assent to the Fourteenth Amendment, frame a new constitution with delegates chosen without regard to color, and submit the new constitution to the Congress for examination. Johnson's message vetoing the Reconstruction Act was angry and accusatory, calling the act "a bill of attainder against nine million people at once" and suggesting that it reduced southerners to "the most abject and degrading slavery." Impeachment efforts in the House intensified, but the doubtfulness of conviction in the Senate, due in part to the knowledge that removal of Johnson would elevate to the presidency the less than universally popular Ben Wade, President Pro Tempore of the Senate, convinced many in the House to hold their fire. Representative James G. Blaine spoke for a number of conservative

Republicans when he said he "would rather have the President than the shallywags of Ben Wade."

The issue that finally turned the tide in favor of impeachment concerned Johnson's alleged violation of the Tenure of Office Act. The Tenure of Office Act, passed in 1867 over yet another presidential veto, prohibited the President from removing from office, without the concurrence of the Senate, those officials whose appointment required Senate approval. The Act was passed primarily to preserve in office as Secretary of War Edwin Stanton, a holdover from the Lincoln Administration, who the radical Republicans regarded "as their trusty outpost in the camp of the enemy." Although Stanton for many months largely acquiesced in Johnson's reconstruction policies, by June of 1867, his opposition was out

Andrew Johnson

in the open. By July, Johnson was close to convinced that Stanton must go, Tenure of Office Act or no Tenure of Office Act. The final straw appears to have been the revelation on August 5, 1867, during an ongoing trial of Lincoln assassination conspirator John Surratt that Stanton two years earlier had deliberately withheld from Johnson a petition from five members of the military commission that convicted Mary Surratt urging that her death sentence be commuted to imprisonment. Stanton, Johnson believed, had hood-winked him into signing the death warrant of a woman who he most likely would have spared. That day Johnson sent Secretary Stanton the following message: "Sir: Public consideration of high character constrain me to say that your resignation as Secretary of War will be accepted." Stanton answered "that public considerations of a high character . . . constrain me not to resign." The Tenure of Office Act allowed the President to "suspend" an officer when the Congress was out of session, as it was at the time, so the President responded by suspending Stanton and replacing him with Union war hero Ulysses S. Grant.

In January of 1868 the returning Senate took up the issue of Johnson's suspension of Secretary Stanton, and voted 35 to 6 not to concur in the action. On January 14, a triumphant Stanton marched to his old office in the War Building as the President considered his next move. Johnson was anxious to challenge the constitutionality of the Tenure of Office Act in court, but to do so he would have to replace Stanton and defy the Senate. This he did on February 21, 1868, naming as the new Secretary of War Major General Lorenzo Thomas. When Stanton notified his Capitol Hill allies of the presidential order to vacate his office, he received from Senator Sumner a one-word telegram: "Stick." Impeachment in the House for violation of the Tenure of Office Act and other "high crimes and misdemeanors" was by now inevitable. On February 24, the House voted to adopt an Impeachment Resolution by a vote of 126 to 47. Five days later, formal articles of impeachment were adopted by the House.

THE IMPEACHMENT TRIAL

On March 30, 1868, Benjamin Butler rose before Chief Justice Salmon Chase and fifty-four senators to deliver the opening argument for the House Managers in the impeachment trial of Salmon Chase. Historians such as David Dewitt have been struck by the improbability of the scene: "The ponderous two-handed engine of impeachment, designed to be kept in cryptic darkness until some crisis of the nation's life cried out for interposition, was being dragged into open day to crush a formidable political antagonist a few months before the appointed time when the people might get rid of him altogether." Butler's three-hour opening argument was "a lawyer's plea with a dash of the demagogue." He contemptuously dismissed arguments that the Tenure of Office Act didn't cover Stanton, read parts of Johnson's 1866 speeches that were the basis of the tenth article of impeachment, and referred to the President as "accidental Chief" and "the elect of an assassin."

House Managers proceeded to introduce documentary evidence and witness testimony supporting the eleven various articles of impeachment. Two witnesses described the confrontation between Edwin Stanton and Lorenzo Thomas in the War Office on the day of Stanton's firing, February 22. One witness brought on torrents of laughter by his description of his meeting with Thomas in the East Room of the White House when he told Thomas "that the eyes of Delaware were upon him." Several witnesses testified as to details concerning speeches by the President delivered in Cleveland and St. Louis in September of 1866. On Thursday, April 9, the Managers closed their case.

Many observers concluded that the testimony added little to the Manager's case, and may have actually hurt their case by emphasizing the President's isolation and powerlessness in the face of a hostile Congress.

The opening argument for the President was delivered by Benjamin Curtis, a former justice of the Supreme Court best known for his dissent in the famous Dred Scott case. Curtis argued that Stanton was not covered by the Tenure of Office Act because the "term" of Lincoln ended with his death, that the President did not in fact violate the Act because he did not succeed in removing Stanton from office, and that the Act itself unconstitutionally infringed upon the powers of the President. As for the article based on Johnson's 1866 speeches, Curtis said "The House of Representatives has erected itself into a school of manners . . . and they desire the judgment of this body whether the President has not been guilty of indecorum." Curtis argued that conviction based on the tenth article of impeachment would violate the free speech clause of the First Amendment.

Counsel for the President called only two witnesses of real consequence. Lorenzo Thomas, Johnson's would-be Secretary of War, was sworn in as a witness for the President and examined by Attorney General Henry Stanbery concerning his encounters with Stanton. According to Thomas's testimony, the two were surprisingly cordial after Stanton had Thomas arrested, at one point sharing a bottle of whiskey together. Secretary Gideon Welles was called for the purpose of testifying to the fact that the Cabinet had advised Johnson that the Tenure of Office Act was unconstitutional, and that Secretaries William Seward and Stanton had agreed to prepare a draft of a veto message. Benjamin Curtis argued that the testimony was relevant because an article of impeachment charged the President with "intending" to violate the Constitution, and that Welles's testimony tended to show that the President honestly believed the law to be unconstitutional. Over the House Managers' objection, Chief Justice Chase ruled the evidence admissible, but was overruled by the Senate 29 to 20, and the testimony was not allowed.

THE FINAL ARGUMENTS

Final arguments in the impeachment trial stretched from April 22 to May 6, with the Managers speaking for six days and counsel for the President speaking for five days. Arguments ranged from the technical to the hyperbolic. Manager Thaddeus Stevens railed against the "wretched man, standing at bay, surrounded by a cordon of living men, each with the axe of an executioner uplifted for his just punishment." Manager John Bingham brought the crowded galleries to its feet with his thunderous closing:

> May God forbid that the future historian shall record of this day's proceedings, that by reason of the failure of the legislative power of the people to triumph over the usurpations of an apostate President, the fabric of American empire fell and perished from the earth! . . . I ask you to consider that we stand this day pleading for the violated majesty of the law, by the graves of half a million of martyred hero-patriots who made death beautiful by the sacrifice of themselves for their country, the Constitution and the laws, and who, by their sublime example, have taught us all to obey the law; that none are above the law; . . . and that position, however high, patronage, however powerful, cannot be permitted to shelter crime to the peril of the republic.

William Groesbeck's peroration for the President offered a spirited defense of Johnson's view of reconstruction:

> He was eager for pacification. He thought that the war was ended. It seemed so. The drums were all silent; the arsenals were all shut; the roar of the cannon had died away to the last reverberations; the army was disbanded; not a single enemy confronted us in the field. Ah, he was too eager, too forgiving, too kind. The hand of reconciliation was stretched out to him and he took it. It may be that he should have put it away, but was it a crime to take it? Kindness, forgiveness a crime? Kindness a crime? Kindness is statesmanship. Kindness is the high statesmanship of heaven itself. The thunders of Sinai do but terrify and distract; alone they accomplish little; it is the kindness of Calvary that subdues and pacifies.

William Everts contended in his closing argument for the President that violation of the Tenure of Office Act did not rise to the level of an impeachable offense:

> They wish to know whether the President has be-

trayed our liberties or our possessions to a foreign state. They wish to know whether he has delivered up a fortress or surrendered a fleet. They wish to know whether he has made merchandise of the public trust and turned the authority to private gain. And when informed that none of these things are charges, imputed, or even declaimed about, they yet seek further information and are told that he has removed a member of his cabinet.

Finally, Attorney General Henry Stanbery's closing for the President compared conviction to a despicable crime:

> But if, Senators, as I cannot believe, but as has been boldly said with almost official sanction, your votes have been canvassed and the doom of the President is sealed, then let that judgment not be pronounced in this Senate Chamber; not here, where our Camillus in the hour of our greatest peril, single-handed, met and baffled the enemies of the Republic; not here, where he stood faithful among the faithless; not here, where he fought the good fight for the Union and the Constitution; not in this Chamber, whose walls echo with that clarion voice that, in the days of our greatest danger, carried hope and comfort to many a desponding heart, strong as an army with banners. No, not here. Seek out rather the darkest and gloomiest chamber in the subterranean recesses of this Capitol, where the cheerful light of day never enters. There erect the altar and immolate the victim.

DOUBT SURFACES

Outwardly, House Managers were confident. Union general Benjamin Butler told a Republican audience on May 4 that "The removal of the great obstruction is certain. Wade and prosperity are sure to come with the apple blossoms." Privately, they were less optimistic. In the week before the vote, much money was being bet by professional gamblers on the outcome of the trial, and the odds favored acquittal. On May 11, from 11 A.M. to midnight, senators debated the merits of the case behind closed doors. The best chance for conviction seemed to rest with the eleventh article that charged the President with attempting to prevent Stanton from resuming his office after the Senate disapproved his suspension. It was obvious that the vote would be very close, depending upon the decisions of two or three undecided Senators. No Senator's vote was more critical than that of Edmund Ross of Kansas, who remained stubbornly silent throughout the trial and discussions.

At noon on May 16, 1868, the High Court of Impeachment was called to order by Chief Justice Chase. The galleries were packed and the House of Representatives was present en mass. A motion was made and adopted to vote first on the eleventh article. The Chief Justice said, "Call the roll." Historian David Dewitt described the tension as the roll call reaches the name of Senator Ross:

> Twenty-four "Guilties" have been pronounced and ten more certain are to come. Willey is almost sure and that will make thirty-five. Thirty-six votes are needed, and with this one vote the grand consummation is attained, Johnson is out and Wade in his place. It is a singular fact that not one of the actors in that high scene was sure in his own mind how his one senator was going to vote, except, perhaps, himself. "Mr. Senator Ross, how say you?" the voice of the Chief Justice rings out over the solemn silence. "Is the respondent, Andrew Johnson, guilty or not guilty of a high misdemeanor as charged in this article?" The Chief Justice bends forward, intense anxiety furrowing his brow. The seated associates of the senator on his feet fix upon him their united gaze. The representatives of the people of the United States watch every movement of his features. The whole audience listens for the coming answer as it would have listened for the crack of doom. And the answer comes, full, distinct, definite, unhesitating and unmistakable. The words "Not Guilty" sweep over the assembly, and, as one man, the hearers fling themselves back into their seats; the strain snaps; the contest ends; impeachment is blown into the air.

THE COMPROMISE OF 1877

ROWLAND CONNOR

The Compromise of 1877 solved not only the contested presidential election of 1876, but also ended Reconstruction in the South. The presidential election pitted Republican Rutherford B. Hayes against Democrat Samuel L. Tilden. The South disputed the claim of the election boards that the popular votes in Louisiana, South Carolina, and Florida were in favor of Hayes. A commission was established to resolve the dispute and settled the election in favor of the Republicans, but it also granted concessions to the South. It stipulated the withdrawal of Republican troops from the South, the appointment of at least one Southerner to Hayes's cabinet, and granted economic benefits to industrialize the South. In the following article, *Nation* editor Rowland Connor describes the South's integration into the Union way of life and the abandonment of the Southern social hierarchy.

The dissolution of the last sham government at the South—an event which we have a right to believe cannot now be long delayed—will place the Southern States, as regards the rest of the nation, in a position which they have not before occupied for almost a generation. Heretofore, in the discussion of nearly all national questions, the most embarrassing and vexatious element at any time to be considered, and frequently an overwhelmingly important one, was "the South." This term designated a number of contiguous States, bound together by mutual interest in the maintenance of a social system which was understood to be inimical to the feelings, at least, if not to the

From "The Political South Hereafter," by Rowland Connor, *Nation*, April 5, 1877.

welfare, of the inhabitants of all other States; and "the South" was always, therefore, a more definite term than "the East" or "the North." Slavery dominated every other interest, and held the Southern States together in political unity. The phrase "the solid South" was a legitimate one before, during, and even after the war, and only recently has it become a political bugbear. But the threefold cord which bound the Southern States together—the defence and perpetuation of slavery, the struggle for the establishment of an independent confederacy, and the trials of reconstruction—no longer exists, and nothing has taken or can take its place. For a time, perhaps, traditions of the dead "institution," war memories, and the possession of a race of freedmen may together do something toward perpetuating a united South, but the union will surely be mostly in appearance, and any little reality which it may possess will speedily give way before opposing and stronger forces.

We believe the proposition to be almost self-evident, indeed, that hereafter there is to be no South; none, that is, in a distinctively political sense. The negro will disappear from the field of national politics. Henceforth the nation, as a nation, will have nothing more to do with him. He will undoubtedly play a part, perhaps an important one, in the development of the national civilization. The philanthropist will have still a great deal to do both with him and for him, and the sociological student will find him, curiously placed as he is in contact and competition with other races, an unfailing source of interest; but as a "ward" of the nation he can no longer be singled out for especial guardianship or peculiar treatment in preference to Irish laborers or Swedish immigrants. There is something distasteful, undeniably, in the idea of one who has played so important a part in our past political history making his final exit in the company of the Carpet-baggers; but for this unfortunate coincidence the negro is not to be blamed.

RAPID SOUTHERN DEVELOPMENT

The disappearance of the factitious interest which made the South politically a unit will permit the rapid development of several natural and obvious disintegrating forces which, indeed, have been already in operation for some time, but the results of which have been obscured by the overshadowing interloper which has just been disposed of. Climate, soil, natural productions, diversity of pursuit, and varieties of race will certainly disintegrate politically the States of the South as well as the States of the North. The "sunny" South, of course, was a fiction, an agreeable convention only, for in the matter of climate the South presents variations comparable at least with any to be found in the North. St. Louis, St. Augustine, and New Orleans, for instance, are as diverse in climate as are any three cities which might be selected in the Northern States. The pecuniary ties, moreover, which unite some Southern States to the North are already stronger than any which bind them to their former political associates. Missouri, for instance, in its commercial relations and sympathies is a Northern State, as, in a modified sense, are Maryland and Delaware; and Florida apparently is set apart already as the winter home of wealthy and invalided Northern men, whose influence upon the tone of its politics begins to be perceptible notwithstanding the hubbub of its recent performances in counting electoral votes. Again, it is evident that the cotton, rice, tobacco, and cane-producing districts of the South will attract very different classes of people, and beget very different manners and opinions from those inevitably associated with mining and manufacturing communities. Thus, South Carolina will soon differ from Missouri even more than Vermont does from Pennsylvania or Minnesota from Massachusetts. Political disintegration at the South may show itself most plainly at first in connection with the discussion of economic questions. There is to-day throughout all the Southern States, probably, a traditional inclination towards free-trade, although the leaning is not a very decided one, and the change from this to an opposing attitude is a process which may be witnessed soon in several of them. Is it not possible, at least, that the cotton and rice States may increase their present leaning towards free-trade, while Louisiana, Virginia, and Kentucky demand protection against Cuban sugar and tobacco? Or, on the other hand, may not South Carolina yearn for Government aid in the establishment of manufactories, and New Orleans sigh for free-trade in Mississippi products? Will the present great poverty of the Southern States, again, incline them to give ear to the jingle of "silver" theories, and make "greenback" delusions easy of belief, or will the memory of their own once plentiful "scrip" be a sufficient protection against indulgence in financial heresies? And will the South look with longing eyes upon visions of canals and railroads until it heedlessly begins the cry for internal improvements at Government expense, or will it be warned by the ghosts of the Crédit Mobilier and Northern Pacific scandals? It is evident, we believe, without lengthening the list of these enumerations or suggestions, that the Southern States may soon be as divided upon the subjects of tariff, currency, *laissez-faire* or paternity in government, etc., as we have been and still are at the North, and if New Hampshire and North Carolina should happen to join hands in defence of some political theory in opposition (say) to Louisiana and New York, "the South" would soon become as vague an expression, from a political point of view, as "the West" is now.

EMPLOYMENT OPPORTUNITIES FOR BLACKS

The future of the freedman will be bound up undoubtedly with that of the white man, and does not now require separate consideration. Great numbers of negroes will certainly remain upon the cotton-fields, rice-swamps, and cane and tobacco plantations, and, being employed as field-hands, their political opinions for a long time to come will inevitably reflect those of their employers. Others will learn to work in factories or become mechanics and small farmers, and, generally, all over the South for a long time, negroes will fill the places now filled at the North by Irish, German, and Chinese laborers. The political influence of the freedman, considered as distinct from that of the white man, will be almost imperceptible. His ultimate influence upon our civilization, as determined by the relative fecundity of the two races, and their action and reaction upon one another as the negro becomes better educated and more independent, is a subject which can be discussed more profitably a generation hence.

Generally speaking, while the political breaking up of the South will do away with a powerful barrier to national advancement, and will bring each State into closer sympathy with the national Government, nevertheless we hardly expect to receive any immediate and valuable aid from the South toward the solution of our present executive, judicial, and legislative problems. In this, however, we may happily be mistaken. It is true that the South has long been more "provincial" than the North, that it is far from possessing similar educational advantages, that it is now almost barren of literary productions or literary and scientific men, and that these facts would seem to indicate a natural soil for the germination and growth of all kinds of crude and coarse theories of society and government; but, on the other hand, it is not easy to imagine the South developing theories more crude than some now cherished in Indiana and Pennsylvania, and which find shelter even in New York and Massachusetts. We are inclined to believe, also, that the average man of the South is a more pliant and enthusiastic follower of his chosen leader than the average man of the North, and [war heroes like] the Gordons, Hills, Lamars, and Hamptons may be depended upon to exert a widespread and, in the main, healthful influence. . . . The important point to be remembered here is the fact that *all* political contributions of the South, of whatever character, will hereafter go towards the upbuilding of a national as distinguished from a "sectional" unity. For the first time in our history we are entitled to assert that there is no danger of national dissolution. Heretofore our chief attention has been given to the saving of national life, and only incidentally have we been able to consider its character or to decide upon the best methods of perfecting it. We can now devote ourselves to legitimate politics—that is, to studies of governmental science—with a fair prospect of being able to throw some light upon many of the unsolved problems of modern life.

The United States and the Native Americans Battle over Land Rights

CHAPTER 4

THE RESERVATION ERA

ARRELL MORGAN GIBSON

When the Civil War ended in 1865, the U.S. military focused on subduing the restive American Indians in the west. The goal was to assimilate the Indian into white culture, and thereby ensure peace and safety for white settlers in former Indian territory. Despite Indian resistance, tribes were ordered off their land and forced onto reservations that occupied the poorest climate and most unproductive soil. The government strove to strip the Indian of his heritage and identity by breaking up tribes, forbidding traditional Indian clothing, and requiring Indian children to attend Christian schools. The United States demanded that the nomadic tribes settle down and farm lands that the whites had abandoned. In spite of numerous uprisings, the sheer numbers of white men successfully beat down the rebels. The following article by Arrell Morgan Gibson describes the injustice of the reservation movement and its effect on the Native American Indians. Gibson was a professor of history and government at Phillips University in Enid and at the University of Oklahoma in Norman.

For many tribes the reservation era covered the period 1867 to 1887. In these twenty years the federal government expected to accomplish the magical transformation of Indians from free, roving hunters and raiders into settled, peaceful, law-abiding wards, made self-sufficient by the adoption of agriculture and stock raising. The reservation was to be the center for tribal management and reformation. However, from the In-

Excerpted from *The American Indian* by Arrell Morgan Gibson (Lexington, MA: D.C. Heath, 1980). Copyright © 1980 by D.C. Heath and Company. Reprinted with permission.

dian viewpoint, the reservation experience matched, and in some cases exceeded, the somber "Trail of Tears" [which forced the Cherokee Indians to migrate from Georgia to Oklahoma in 1838 and 1839 and led to the deaths of about 4,000 Indians] for needless, agonizing want, unthinkable suffering, and personal and group decline to the brink of destruction. Demographers, sociologists, and anthropologists have claimed that the Anglo-American nation exceeded all others in causing native population decline. By 1890 the Indian population of the United States had been reduced from an estimated original 1,500,000 to less than 250,000. Their numbers declined drastically during the reservation era due largely to the unhealthy conditions.

The shock of defeat in battle and loss of territory, of being forcibly required to submit to daily surveillance, and enduring overt and covert pressure to abandon Indianness and become hybrid Americans [Americanization], devastated Native American will. Sudden destitution was traumatic, too, as the tribes went from prosperity to poverty when federal agents concentrated them on reservations. Tribes were deprived of the land base which had provided their economic, political, and military power and strength. To Native Americans the reservation was a prison, a reform institution; the penitentiary aspect of reservations varied from large compounds where only moderate coercion and repression were applied to isolated military prisons with cellblocks. . . .

DETRIBALIZATION

Reformers and bureaucrats who fashioned the aboriginal Americanization program ignored Indian diversity—the fact that on the new reservations were scores of tribal communities with vastly differing life-styles and languages—and applied a monolithic formula, a single transformation model, to all Native Americans. Federal planners observed the so-called melting pot which had transformed millions of European immigrants into American citizens and assumed that it had erased their ethnic quality and differences and that it would work for Indians.

During the last quarter of the nineteenth century, there arose a number of religious and social reform groups committed to Native American betterment, broadly called "Friends of the Indian." All except one followed the same monistic approach and supported federal officials in their Americanization program to erase all sign of Indianness. Only the National Indian Defense

Association, headed by Thomas A. Bland, editor of *Council Fire Magazine*, thought to ask the Indians what their preferences might be in the transformation process. The National Indian Defense Association "opposed rather than encouraged governmental action on the theory that Indians should be left alone." Above all else this group stressed self-determination. Other than it, Native Americans had no public defender; they were captives of the system, of drastic cultural change unilaterally conceived and applied.

As indicated, agents, teachers, and missionaries in applying the detribalization process worked to eradicate Indian religion and life-style, to transform the economy of each Indian family, and to destroy tribal institutions, particularly government. In addition, workers in the Americanization program placed great emphasis upon eliminating external signs of Indianness, including names and personal appearance.

ANGLICIZED INDIAN NAMES

Missionaries had attempted to rename Native Americans since colonial times. Furthermore, mixing of races over the years had produced a large community of mixed bloods with Anglo-American, French, and Spanish surnames in several tribes. However, most Indians placed on reservations during the postwar era had only their aboriginal names. Teachers, missionaries, and agents believed that an essential step in civilization was to eradicate Indian identity. Names of the reservation Indians were derived from nature and descriptive, and some of them were difficult for English-speaking people to pronounce. Most Native Americans on reservations also lacked surnames which made it difficult to organize them in the Americanization program which stressed family surname as basic identity. Teachers and missionaries continued to rename children in their schools, but they stressed first names—Morning Star to Mildred or Stands-in-the-Timber to Stanley. Then during the reservation era and the succeeding allotment-in-severalty era officials made a comprehensive attempt to rename Indians and provide each a surname. Examples of the surnames invented include American Horse to Horse, Spotted Horse to Spotted, All Runner to Runner, Black Wolf to Blackwulf or Blackwell, Brave Bear to Braveber, Big Nose to Bignus, and Black Owl to Blackall.

Another external symbol of Indianness that attracted considerable attention from officers was dress and hair style. Reservation Indians were pressured to abandon tribal attire and take on what agents called "citizen dress." Hair was a vexing problem. Most Indian men wore their hair long for cosmetic effect; it provided a source of the male ego, and some ascribed supernatural significance to long hair. But to agents, long hair was a symbol "of resistance to the civilization process." The Mescalero Apaches were among the last of the reservation tribesmen to submit to the haircut. Their agent first directed members of the reservation Indian police force to cut their hair or face discharge. Slowly, reluctantly, they conformed. The rest of the warriors of the tribe, "gorgeous in paint, feathers, long hair, breechclouts and blankets," ignored the agent's demands until he threatened them with "confinement at hard labor." After six weeks he could report that "every male Indian had been changed into the semblance of a decent man."

Thus, Native Americans, stripped of ethnic pride, humiliated by picayune impositions, and shorn of tribal moorings, eventually complied with repressive reservation routines. For most of them it was surface compliance with a detestable system while they covertly, inventively contrived strategies of evasion. However, some Indians seem to have accepted their fate and seriously attempted to relate to the new order by collaborating with federal agents, serving as reservation police and judges to suppress aboriginal life-style, supporting missionaries and joining reservation churches, and voluntarily enrolling their children in government schools. . . .

GREAT EXPECTATIONS

The reservation system forcibly compressed Native Americans on reservations and subjected them to an intensive Americanization program in an attempt to transform them into dutiful Anglo-American apprentices, poised on the threshold of the dominant society. Its mission was largely a failure due less to Indian cussedness or negativism and more to the strength, resiliency, and attractiveness of Indian culture, its mystical essence which would not expire in spite of intensive, sustained assaults upon it. Another factor, rarely considered, was that Indians possessed natural intelligence, some richly so, which enabled them to observe and to judge the relative merits of the Anglo-American culture which they were expected, even required, to accept. Most adult Indians found it pietistic, legalistic, obsessively materialistic, and downright unattractive. It promised

Native Americans a bland, repressed, puritanical life-style. And many of its advocates were so patently corrupt that most Native Americans scorned this cultural alternative.

But there were other reasons why Indians failed to shape up, to conform to the reservation-derived model. They lacked faith in the system. A chain of duplicity, deceit, exploitation, and opportunism over the centuries had forged a tradition among Indians of distrust of Anglo-American overtures. Talayesva, the Hopi, recalled that he

> grew up believing that whites are wicked, deceitful people. It seemed that most of them were soldiers, government agents, or missionaries, and that quite a few were Two-Hearts. The old people said that the Whites were tough, possessed dangerous weapons, and were better protected than we were from evil spirits. . . . They were known to be big liars too. They . . . tricked our war chiefs to surrender without fighting, and then broke their promises. . . . [The Hopis believed that whites] needed to be reminded daily to tell the truth. I was taught to mistrust them and to give warning whenever I saw one coming.

Federal policy reflecting what the American people expected of Native Americans had frequently changed to the detriment of Indian peoples. Many Indians also refused to subscribe to the Americanization program because they were insulted by the contemptuous, ethnocentric attitudes of federal officials. Intelligent Indians were enraged at congressmen arrogantly demanding that reservation dwellers conform and become self-supporting, and soon, because that body was weary of having "for years footed the bills that maintained them in idleness, filth, immorality, and barbarism," when in fact the United States government presumptively served as trustee for Indian property including proceeds from land cessions. Thus in most cases when congressmen allocated funds to Indians for rations, clothing, education, livestock, and tools, they were simply determining unilaterally what expenditures should be permitted from Indian trust funds.

MAKING FARMERS OUT OF HUNTERS

Congressmen and officials in the Bureau of Indian Affairs were unyielding in their determination to force Indians on reservations to become self-supporting through agriculture. Lack of progress in this regard was a regular cause for denunciation and threats of public abandonment. What federal officials did not understand was that Indians were reluctant to make extensive agricultural improvements on reservation lands for several reasons. A principal deterrent to conscientious application was cultural; it was sociologically unsound to expect rapid transformation of reservation people from hunting to agriculture. Such drastic change in aboriginal life-style required time, patience, and substantive family role change because in many Indian communities farming was regarded as "women's work." Also, in a very short period many of the tribes had been moved from one reservation to another, and talk of further concentration continued.

Rulings by federal officials on the question of tribal title to reservation lands also destroyed incentive among Indians to clear and open fields and perform other laborious tasks required to establish farms on virgin land. These administrative decrees defined Indians on reservations as tenants, having only limited rights to use the land and resources of the area assigned, which compromised absolute title in the tribe. An attorney general's opinion in 1819 held that Indians could not even "alienate the natural productions of the soil, the timber growing on it . . . the use of Lands permitted to the Indians is . . . intended for their subsistence and looking to their personal occupation of it, although they have the right to cultivate and sell the crops which are the production of their own labours, they have no more right to sell the standing timber . . . than they have to sell the soil itself." And during 1885 a ruling by the secretary of the interior held that "the right of the Indians to the reservations ordinarily occupied by them is that of occupancy alone." They were permitted to clear the land for farming and cut wood for fuel but were forbidden to "cut growing timber, open mines, quarry stone, etc. to obtain lumber, coal, building material, etc. solely for the purpose of sale. . . . In short, what a tenant for life may do, upon lands . . . Indians may do on their reservations."

Another deterrent to Indians shaping up and becoming self-supporting yeoman farmers in the pioneer Anglo-American tradition was environmental limitation. Most reservations were located in arid regions of marginal agricultural potential, generally not highly valued by Anglo-American settlers. The unreasonable, unyielding expectation of Congress and the Bureau of Indian Affairs was that they become farmers in spite of all manner of acknowledged natural limitations upon agrarian success. Most of the northern reservations were in a climatic zone of short growing season with perennial threat of crop-killing early frosts and freezes. Many southern reservations were in an arid region where blistering summer droughts were a common occurrence. If this were not enough, there was the deterrent of pervasive poverty. As indicated, most Native Americans, only recently affluent and independent with vast tribal territories, many horses and buffalo robes, and prodigious dried meat stores, were quickly reduced to destitution and dependence by the reservation ordeal. They lacked capital to purchase seed, draft animals, plows, and other farming essentials. Congressional appropriations from tribal funds to purchase some of these needs were siphoned off by agent and contractor graft and only a token distribution was possible. Eventually federal agents relented their agricultural preoccupation by permitting reservation Indians to take up stock raising, for which much of the region containing the reservations was suitable. However, the success of this venture was limited by the perennial shortage of food on reservations. More often than not immediate need for subsistence to survive forced aboriginal stockmen to slaughter their small breeding herds to feed starving Indians. . . .

AN INDIAN VIEW OF RESERVATION LIFE

Most Indians silently endured the reservation experience, their muted thoughts on this ordeal communicated through their haggard faces, their defeated spirits. A few spoke out, and their statements have been translated and preserved. One of the most eloquent was an oration by the Shoshoni head man Washakie, delivered in 1878 to Governor John W. Hoyt of Wyoming Territory.

> I cannot hope to express to you the half that is in our hearts. They are too full for words. Disappointment; then a deep sadness; then a grief inexpressible; then, at times, a bitterness that makes us think of the rifle, the knife and the tomahawk, and kindles in our hearts the fires of desperation—that sir, is the story of our experience, of our wretched lives. The white man, who possesses this whole vast country from sea to sea, who roams over it at pleasure, and lives where he likes, cannot know the cramp we feel in this little spot, with the undying remembrance of the fact, which you

know as well as we, that every foot of what you proudly call America, not very long ago belonged to the redman. The Great Spirit gave it to us. There was room enough for all his many tribes, and all were happy in their freedom. But the white man had, in many ways we know not of, learned some things we had not learned; among them, how to make superior tools and terrible weapons, better for war than bows and arrows; and there seemed no end to the hordes of men that followed them from other lands beyond the sea. And so, at last, our fathers were steadily driven out, or killed, and we, their sons, but sorry remnants of tribes once mighty, are cornered in little spots of the earth all ours of right—cornered like guilty prisoners, and watched by men with guns, who are more than anxious to kill us off. Nor is that all. The white man's government promised that if we, the Shoshones, would be content with the little patch allowed us, would keep us well supplied with everything necessary to comfortable living, and would see that no white man should cross our borders for our game, or for anything that is ours. *But it has not kept its word!* The white man kills our game, captures our furs, and sometimes feeds his herds upon our meadows. And your great and mighty government . . . does not protect us in our rights. It leaves us without the promised seed, without tools for cultivating the land, without implements for harvesting our crops, without breeding animals better than ours, without the food we still lack. . . . I say again, *the government does not keep its word!* And so after all we can get by cultivating the land, and by hunting and fishing, we are sometimes nearly starved, and go half naked, as you see us! Knowing all this, do you wonder, sir, that we have fits of desperation and think to be avenged?

A NON-INDIAN VIEW OF RESERVATION LIFE

Late in the nineteenth century the author Hamlin Garland spent several years visiting western reservations. His observations of the lot of confined Indians confirm Washakie's despair. Garland characterizes reservations as "corrals" or "open air prisons" where the original owners of the continent have been impounded by the white race. Most of the reservations are in the arid parts of the Great Rocky Mountain Plateau; a few are in timbered regions of the older states like Wisconsin and Minnesota. Speaking generally, we may say these lands are relatively the most worthless to be found in the State or Territory whose boundaries enclose the red man's home, and were set aside for his use because he would cumber the earth less there than elsewhere. [However,] scarcely a single one of these minute spots is safe to the red people. Every acre of land is being scrutinized, and plans for securing even these miserable plots are being matured. . . . The Sioux, the Blackfeet, and the Northern Cheyennes live practically the same life. They have small, badly-ventilated log or frame hovels of one or two rooms, into which they closely crowd during cold weather. In summer, they supplement these miserable shacks by canvas tepees and lodges, under which they do their cooking, and in which they sleep. Their home life has lost all its old-time picturesqueness, without acquiring even the comfort of the settler in a dug-out. Consumption is very common among them because of their unsanitary housing during cold weather. They dress in a sad mixture of good old buckskin garments and shoddy clothing, sold by the traders or issued by the government. They are, of course, miserably poor, with very little to do but sit and smoke and wait for ration day. To till the ground is practically useless, and their herds are too small to furnish them support. They are not allowed to leave the reservation to hunt or to seek work, and so they live like reconcentrados [people in concentration camps]. Their ration, which the government by an easy shift now calls a charity, feeds them for a week or ten days and they go hungry till the next ration day comes round. From three to seven days are taken up with going after rations. These words also apply to the Jicarilla Apaches, and to a part of the Southern Utes. Each tribe, whether Sioux, or Navajo, or Hopi, will be found to be divided, like a white village, into two parties, the radicals and the conservatives—those who are willing to change, to walk the white man's way; and those who are deeply, sullenly skeptical of all civilizing measures, are often the strongest and bravest of their tribes, the most dignified and the most intellectual. They represent the spirit that will break but will not bow. And, broadly speaking, they are in the majority. Though in rags, their spirits are unbroken; from the point of view of their sympathizers, they are patriots.

FRIENDS OF THE INDIAN

Anglo-American society, saturated with the Protestant ethic of performance and Darwinian natural selection, was largely desensitized to the Native American's pitiful state on western reservations, although occasionally a critic emerged to challenge the nation's repressive Indian policy. One pioneer voice for better conditions for Indians was John Beeson, an English immigrant who settled in Oregon. He was shocked at Anglo-American settlers and local newspapers which said that Indians "had nothing in common with humanity but the form," and he publicly challenged political candidates who urged "extermination" of the Oregon Indians. In 1855 during the Rogue River Wars Beeson regarded the settlers "aggressors" and took the Indian side in public debates. For this he was bitterly denounced, his life was threatened, and he moved to the eastern United States where, in 1858, he published *A Plea for the Indians.* Beeson continued to urge Indian reform into the 1870s.

Another pioneer critic of Native American management was Henry B. Whipple, Episcopal bishop of Minnesota. Whipple was the strongest and most persistent voice for Indian reform before the Civil War. In the postwar era, many persons previously active in bettering life for blacks and in the abolitionist movement began to voice concern for Native Americans. During the late 1860s author Lydia Maria Child wrote several pamphlets urging humane treatment of Indians. Harriet Beecher Stowe, author of *Uncle Tom's Cabin,* helped found the Connecticut Indian Association, and abolitionist Wendell Phillips actively supported Indian reform until his death in 1884. Samuel F. Tappan, a Boston abolitionist, moved to Colorado Territory in 1860 and developed a strong interest in Indian policy reform.

However, the person who touched the public heart strings and launched a national "Friends of the Indian" movement was Helen Hunt Jackson. She may be regarded as a pioneer muckraker because, like the author-critics of the early 1900s, she used her literary talent to expose a public evil and to urge corrective action. In 1881 she published *A Century of Dishonor,* an emotional treatise which exposed and denounced federal Indian policy and which served the cause of Native American reform in much the same way that *Uncle Tom's Cabin* served the antebellum crusade for blacks. Mrs. Jackson wrote in *A Century of Dishonor* that the purpose of her book was to "show our cause for national shame in the matter of our treatment of the Indians." In 1884 she published *Ramona,* a work of fiction depicting the plight of California Indians, which also had a wide and extended public appeal.

But for exceptions to be noted, the critics who stirred reformers to mount the "Friends of the Indian" movement wholeheartedly supported the federal government's Americanization program. To them Indianness was a base, primitive survival which had to be eradicated before the Native American could be transformed and assimilated. The thrust of their reforms then was that reservations, rather than being a focal point for the transformation process, were really a public disgrace which had to be abolished with alternatives found for transforming the Indians.

Rare were those persons who saw redeeming qualities in aboriginal lifestyle and defended the Indians' right to retain it. Thomas A. Bland and Alfred B. Meacham, lecturers and editors, were champions of self-determination for the Indians and urged that they be consulted in the matter of Americanization. Hamlin Garland was a constant Indian advocate who resented the federal government applying "measures of Saxon virtue" to Native Americans. He respected Indian life-style, urged that it and native crafts be preserved, and he stated that his writing, fiction and nonfiction, was dedicated to "one underlying motive . . . to show the Indian as a human being, a neighbor."

RED CLOUD AND THE FORT LARAMIE TREATY

FRANK WATERS

Red Cloud waged one of the most successful wars on U.S. troops in Native American history. Red Cloud and his band of Oglala Sioux Indians resided near the Platte River in Nebraska. The discovery of gold in Montana brought white men into Sioux territory along a path known as the Bozeman Trail that extended from Nebraska to Wyoming. Red Cloud refused to allow wagons to pass through his territory and ruthlessly attacked U.S. forts along the trail. The warfare persuaded the United States to commission the 1868 Fort Laramie Treaty, which demanded that the military abandon its forts along the Bozeman Trail and guaranteed the Sioux their possession of what is now the western half of South Dakota, including the Black Hills, along with much of Montana and Wyoming. Red Cloud's was the only Indian campaign that forced the United States to relinquish Indian land and accept defeat. In the following article, Frank Waters describes Red Cloud's bloody battle between U.S. troops and the Sioux Indians. Frank Waters, part Cheyenne, is the author of several books about Native Americans, including *Book of the Hopi* and *To Possess the Land*.

S parks of war were flying north from Sand Creek to set the plains of the Sioux on fire. A chief named for the reddened sky at his birth now rose quickly to command.

Red Cloud was an Oglala, the largest band of the Sioux Nation. Born at the forks of the Platte River in Nebraska, he was now forty-three years old. He was not a chief by birth, but rose to prominence by his own force of character. He was not by nature a warrior, although he had counted eighty coups, but a statesman and a general. Quiet and dignified, he exemplified the integrity and pride of his people.

The Teton Sioux was a powerful confederation of seven council fires that extended along the upper Missouri from Dakota into Nebraska, Wyoming, and Montana. Their own name for themselves was Dakota or Lakota. The Chippewas of Wisconsin had given them the name Na-du-Wa-Su, meaning "serpents" or "enemies," which the French corrupted into "Sioux."

GOLD IS DISCOVERED IN MONTANA

The main cause of alarm to the Sioux in that bloody year of 1864 was the discovery of gold in Montana. John M. Bozeman, a prospector, promptly blazed a wagon road from the Platte River north through Wyoming to the gold camps around Virginia City, Montana. Red Cloud just as promptly captured a small detachment of road builders and held them prisoner for two weeks. To the officials of the newly created Territory of Montana he sent word that the Bozeman Trail cut through the buffalo plains of the Sioux. He would not allow any wagons to pass.

The following year government commissioners at Fort Laramie, using threats of force, insisted on Sioux and Cheyenne permission for wagons to pass through their country. Red Cloud refused: "Is this a peace talk, that you threaten to bring soldiers if we do not agree? Why do you pretend to negotiate for land you intend to take by force? Are we children you can frighten with threats? I say you can force us only to fight for the land the Great Spirit has given us."

Stalking out of the tent with Man-Afraid-of-His-Horses, Red Cloud began to unite the Sioux, Brules, Cheyennes, and Arapahos.

The government moved quickly to establish a line of forts to guard the Bozeman Trail. Colonel Henry Carrington with an army of soldiers and civilian workmen garrisoned Fort Reno with 250 men. He then established Fort Phil Kearny with a garrison of 450 men. While a hundred wagons under heavy guard hauled timber from the Bighorn Mountains to build its log stockade, a group of Cheyenne chiefs came to visit Carrington. Among them were Dull Knife, Two Moons, Black Horse, and Red Arm.

"Take your soldiers back to Fort Reno," they begged. "If you do not, we Cheyennes will have to fight with the Sioux."

Colonel Carrington completed the fort, and in 1866 marched north to establish Fort C.F. Smith on the Bighorn River.

The die was cast. Red Cloud's War began.

RED CLOUD PURSUES RELENTLESSLY

In it, new stars appeared among the galaxy of chiefs who were to shine brighter in later years: Sitting Bull, Rain-in-the-Face, Roman Nose, Crazy Horse, a dozen others. Red Cloud, the guiding chief, selected Fort Phil Kearny as his target. He kept it under relentless siege. Not a load of hay, nor a wagon of wood, could be brought in except under a strongly armed guard.

Four mornings before Christmas an armed wagon train left the fort to get wood from the nearby mountains. Pickets on the lookout soon signaled that the train was being attacked. Carrington ordered Colonel W.J. Fetterman to lead seventy-nine cavalrymen to its aid.

"Proceed directly to the train," he instructed. "Keep within sight of the fort. Do not follow the Indians beyond Lodge Trail Ridge."

Fetterman, who had boasted, "Give me eighty men and I'll ride through the whole Sioux Nation," disobeyed orders. Decoyed into ambush by Crazy Horse and a half dozen companions, he took a shortcut over the ridge and out of sight of the fort. Red Cloud's massed warriors then swarmed upon them, killed all eighty men, and butchered their bodies beyond recognition.

The whole nation was shocked. Sherman's telegram to President Grant has been often quoted: "We must act with vindictive earnestness against the Sioux, even to their extermination, men, women and children. Nothing less will reach the root of the cause."

TAKING NO CHANCES

Again that summer a work crew from the fort was sent out with an escort of fifty-one troopers. This time the commanding officer took no chances. He removed the wagon boxes from the running gears, arranging them to form a barricade. Red Cloud attacked as usual. This time, however, the troopers were armed with new breech-loading Springfield rifles and stood off the attack until relief arrived from the fort.

Still another band of Cheyennes attacked a group of soldiers in a hay field outside of Fort C.F. Smith, but was forced to retire.

The Fetterman Massacre and the Wagon Box and Hayfield fights sobered the government commissioners. Another treaty meeting was held at Fort Laramie in 1868. Red Cloud, polite and firm as ever, stated his conditions.

"The Bozeman Trail will be closed," he said. "Every fort will be abandoned. Then only can there be peace."

"We agree," said the commissioners. "Sign the treaty."

"Not until the garrison of all the forts are withdrawn," answered Red Cloud.

It was done. The garrisons of the three forts were removed, and the Cheyennes and Sioux burnt all the forts to the ground. For nine years the Bozeman Trail was closed. Red Cloud was the only Indian chief who had won a war with the United States.

Keeping his word never to fight again, he settled down at the Red Cloud, Nebraska, agency. But his success soured. Younger Indians accused him of selling out to the whites, of living on government handouts, of being a reservation Indian. Red Cloud shrugged off these accusations, and still counseled peace. Later he was moved to the Great Sioux Reservation, where in 1881 the agent V.T. McGillycuddy stripped him of his standing as chief of the Oglalas.

THE BATTLE AT LITTLE BIGHORN

IRON HAWK

In 1875, Sioux and Cheyenne Indians defiantly left their reservations, outraged over the continuous intrusion of whites seeking gold in the Black Hills. They gathered at the Little Bighorn River in Montana with the great warrior and Teton Sioux chief Sitting Bull. On June 25, 1876, General George Custer launched a surprise attack on the Indians, commonly referred to as Custer's Last Stand. The Indians had combined the forces of the Oglala Sioux, the Hunkpapa Sioux, and the Cheyenne, and they outnumbered Custer's men by three to one. In less than an hour, Custer and his 210 men were slaughtered. Although the Sioux and Cheyenne Indians celebrated their victory, it was to be their last. The United States was infuriated over the massacre of so many soldiers and the war hero Custer. Within a year, the Sioux nation was obliterated and the reservation lines were redrawn. The Black Hills were outside the reservation and open to white settlement. The following article is the firsthand account of the Battle of Little Bighorn by Iron Hawk, a fourteen-year-old Hunkpapa Sioux warrior.

I am a Hunkpapa Sioux, and, as I told you before, I was fourteen years old. The sun was overhead and more, but I was eating my first meal that day, because I had been sleeping. While I was eating I heard the crier saying: "The chargers are coming." I jumped up and rushed out to our horses. They were grazing close to camp. I roped one, and the others stampeded, but my older brother had caught his horse already and headed

Excerpted from *Black Elk Speaks* by John G. Neihardt (Lincoln: University of Nebraska Press, 1961). Copyright © 1961 by University of Nebraska Press. Reprinted with permission.

the others off. When I got on my horse with the rope hitched around his nose, the soldiers were shooting up there and people were running and men and boys were catching their horses that were scared because of the shooting and yelling. I saw little children running up from the river where they had been swimming; and all the women and children were running down the valley.

Our horses stampeded down toward the Minneconjous, but we rounded them up again and brought them back. By now warriors were running toward the soldiers, and getting on the ponies, and many of the Hunkpapas were gathering in the brush and timber near the place where the soldiers had stopped and got off their horses. I rode past a very old man who was shouting: "Boys, take courage! Would you see these little children taken away from me like dogs?"

War Paint

I went into our tepee and got dressed for war as fast as I could; but I could hear bullets whizzing outside, and I was so shaky that it took me a long time to braid an eagle feather into my hair. Also, I had to hold my pony's rope all the time, and he kept jerking me and trying to get away. While I was doing this, crowds of warriors on horses were roaring by up stream, yelling: "Hoka hey [Hurry up]!" Then I rubbed red paint all over my face and took my bow and arrows and got on my horse. I did not have a gun, only a bow and arrows.

When I was on my horse, the fight up stream seemed to be over, because everybody was starting back downstream and yelling: "It's a good day to die!" Soldiers were coming at the other end of the village, and nobody knew how many there were down there.

A man by the name of Little Bear rode up to me on a pinto horse, and he had a very pretty saddle blanket. He said: "Take courage, boy! The earth is all that lasts!" So I rode fast with him and the others downstream, and many of us Hunkpapas gathered on the east side of the river at the foot of a gulch that led back up the hill where General George Custer's second soldier band was. There was a very brave Shyela [Cheyenne] with us, and I heard someone say: "He is going!" I looked, and it was this Shyela. He had on a spotted war bonnet and a spotted robe made of some animal's skin and this was fastened with a spotted belt. He was going up the hill alone and we all followed part way. There were soldiers along the ridge up there and they were on foot holding their horses. The Shyela rode right close to them in a circle several times and all the soldiers shot at him. Then he rode back to where we had stopped at the head of the gulch. He was saying: "Ah, ah!" Someone said: "Shyela friend, what is the matter?" He began undoing his spotted belt, and when he shook it, bullets dropped out. He was very sacred and the soldiers could not hurt him. He was a fine looking man.

BROTHER-FRIEND DUTY

We stayed there awhile waiting for something and there was shooting everywhere. Then I heard a voice crying: "Now they are going, they are going!" We looked up and saw the cavalry horses stampeding. These were all gray horses.

I saw Little Bear's horse rear and race up hill toward the soldiers. When he got close, his horse was shot out from under him, and he got up limping because the bullet went through his leg; and he started hobbling back to us with the soldiers shooting at him. His brother-friend, Elk Nation, went up there on his horse and took Little Bear behind him and rode back safe with bullets striking all around him. It was his duty to go to his brother-friend even if he knew he would be killed.

By now a big cry was going up all around the soldiers up

The Battle of Little Bighorn, also referred to as Custer's Last Stand, is considered one of the worst American military disasters.

there and the warriors were coming from everywhere and it was getting dark with dust and smoke.

We saw soldiers start running down hill right towards us. Nearly all of them were afoot, and I think they were so scared that they didn't know what they were doing. They were making their arms go as though they were running very fast, but they were only walking. Some of them shot their guns in the air. We all yelled "Hoka hey!" and charged toward them, riding all around them in the twilight that had fallen on us.

Ruthless Bloodshed

I met a soldier on horseback, and I let him have it. The arrow went through from side to side under his ribs and it stuck out on both sides. He screamed and took hold of his saddle horn and hung on, wobbling, with his head hanging down. I kept along beside him, and I took my heavy bow and struck him across the back of the neck. He fell from his saddle, and I got off and beat him to death with my bow. I kept on beating him awhile after he was dead, and every time I hit him I said "Hownh!" I was mad, because I was thinking of the women and little children running down there, all scared and out of breath. These Wasichus [whites] wanted it, and they came to get it, and we gave it to them. I did not see much more. I saw Brings Plenty kill a soldier with a war club. I saw Red Horn Buffalo fall. There was a Lakota [Sioux] riding along the edge of the gulch, and he was yelling to look out, that there was a soldier hiding in there. I saw him charge in and kill the soldier and begin slashing him with a knife.

Then we began to go towards the river, and the dust was lifting so that we could see the women and children coming over to us from across the river. The soldiers were all rubbed out there and scattered around.

The women swarmed up the hill and began stripping the soldiers. They were yelling and laughing and singing now. I saw something funny. Two fat old women were stripping a soldier, who was wounded and playing dead. When they had him naked, they began to cut something off that he had, and he jumped up and began fighting with the two fat women. He was swinging one of them around, while the other was trying to stab him with her knife. After awhile, another woman rushed up and shoved her knife into him and he died really dead. It was funny to see the naked Wasichu fighting with the fat women.

By now we saw that our warriors were all charging on some soldiers that had come from the hill up river to help the second band that we had rubbed out. They ran back and we followed, chasing them up on their hill again where they had their pack mules. We could not hurt them much there, because they had been digging to hide themselves and they were lying behind saddles and other things. I was down by the river and I saw some soldiers come down there with buckets. They had no guns, just buckets. Some boys were down there, and they came out of the brush and threw mud and rocks in the soldiers' faces and chased them into the river. I guess they got enough to drink, for they are drinking yet. We killed them in the water.

Afterwhile it was nearly sundown, and I went home with many others to eat, while some others stayed to watch the soldiers on the hill. I hadn't eaten all day, because the trouble started just when I was beginning to eat my first meal.

THE SURRENDER OF CHIEF JOSEPH AND THE NEZ PERCÉ

CHIEF JOSEPH

The Nez Percé was a peaceful tribe located in the Wallowa Valley in eastern Oregon. In 1863, Old Chief Joseph refused to sign a treaty that significantly reduced the ancestral landholdings of his people. His refusal paved the way for more than fourteen years of dissension between the Nez Percé and the U.S. military. In 1877, General John Howard demanded that Young Chief Joseph, Old Joseph's son, remove his people from their native land to a reservation or prepare for war. A four-month-long battle ensued, and Joseph boldly fought four different U.S. armies with only two hundred warriors. He and his band brought nearly 500 women and children over 1,500 miles of mountainous terrain before they were finally stopped by General Nelson A. Miles. In the following excerpt from Joseph's narrative of the battle, he maintains that he surrendered partly to relieve his people of their weakness and fatigue, and also because General Miles promised him that he and his tribe could return to the Nez Percé homelands. After his surrender, Joseph tried every possible appeal to return to the Wallowa Valley, but he and his people were denied and forced onto a reservation.

T
hrough all the years since the white men came to Wallowa we have been threatened and taunted by them and the [unauthorized] treaty Nez Percés [that severely reduced

Excerpted from "An Indian's Views of Indian Affairs," by Chief Joseph, *North American Review*, April 1879.

Nez Percé landholdings]. They have given us no rest. We have had a few good friends among white men, and they have always advised my people to bear these taunts without fighting. Our young men were quick-tempered, and I have had great trouble in keeping them from doing rash things. I have carried a heavy load on my back ever since I was a boy. I learned then that we were but few, while the white men were many, and that we could not hold our own with them. We were like deer. They were like grizzly bears. We had a small country. Their country was large. We were contented to let things remain as the Great Spirit Chief made them. They were not; and would change the rivers and mountains if they did not suit them.

Year after year we have been threatened, but no war was made upon my people until General Oliver Howard came to our country in 1877 and told us that he was the white war-chief of all that country. He said: "I have a great many soldiers at my back. I am going to bring them up here, and then I will talk to you again. I will not let white men laugh at me the next time I come. The country belongs to the Government, and I intend to make you go upon the reservation.". . .

The General Casts an Ultimatum

In the council, next day, General Howard informed me, in a haughty spirit, that he would give my people *thirty days* to go back home, collect all their stock, and move on to the reservation, saying, "If you are not here in that time, I shall consider that you want to fight, and will send my soldiers to drive you on."

I said: "War can be avoided, and it ought to be avoided. I want no war. My people have always been the friends of the white man. Why are you in such a hurry? I can not get ready to move in thirty days. Our stock is scattered, and Snake River is very high. Let us wait until fall, then the river will be low. We want time to hunt up our stock and gather supplies for winter."

General Howard replied, "If you let the time run over one day, the soldiers will be there to drive you on to the reservation, and all your cattle and horses outside of the reservation at that time will fall into the hands of the white men."

I knew I had never sold my country, and that I had no land in Lapwai; but I did not want bloodshed. I did not want my people killed. I did not want anybody killed. Some of my people had been murdered by white men, and the white murderers were never punished for it. I told General Howard about this, and again said I wanted no war. I wanted the people who lived upon the lands I was to occupy at Lapwai to have time to gather their harvest.

I said in my heart that, rather than have war, I would give up my country. I would give up my father's grave. I would give up everything rather than have the blood of white men upon the hands of my people.

General Howard refused to allow me more than thirty days to move my people and their stock. I am sure that he began to prepare for war at once. . . .

THE FIRST BATTLE

My friends among white men have blamed me for the war. I am not to blame. When my young men began the killing, my heart was hurt. Although I did not justify them, I remembered all the insults I had endured, and my blood was on fire. Still I would have taken my people to the buffalo country without fighting, if possible.

I could see no other way to avoid a war. We moved over to White Bird Creek, sixteen miles away, and there encamped, intending to collect our stock before leaving; but the soldiers attacked us, and the first battle was fought. We numbered in that battle sixty men, and the soldiers a hundred. The fight lasted but a few minutes, when the soldiers retreated before us for twelve miles. They lost thirty-three killed, and had seven wounded. When an Indian fights, he only shoots to kill; but soldiers shoot at random. None of the soldiers were scalped. We do not believe in scalping, nor in killing wounded men. Soldiers do not kill many Indians unless they are wounded and left upon the battle-field. Then they kill Indians.

Seven days after the first battle, General Howard arrived in the Nez Percés country, bringing seven hundred more soldiers. It was now war in earnest. We crossed over Salmon River, hoping General Howard would follow. We were not disappointed. He did follow us, and we got back between him and his supplies, and cut him off for three days. He sent out two companies to open the way. We attacked them, killing one officer, two guides, and ten men.

We withdrew, hoping the soldiers would follow, but they had got fighting enough for that day. They intrenched themselves, and next day we attacked them again. The battle lasted all day, and was renewed next morning. We killed four and wounded seven or eight.

About this time General Howard found out that we were in his rear. Five days later he attacked us with three hundred and fifty soldiers and settlers. We had two hundred and fifty warriors. The fight lasted twenty-seven hours. We lost four killed and several wounded. General Howard's loss was twenty-nine men killed and sixty wounded.

The following day the soldiers charged upon us, and we retreated with our families and stock a few miles, leaving eighty lodges to fall into General Howard's hands.

RETREAT TO BITTER ROOT VALLEY

Finding that we were outnumbered, we retreated to Bitter Root Valley. Here another body of soldiers came upon us and demanded our surrender. We refused. They said, "You can not get by us." We answered, "We are going by you without fighting if you will let us, but we are going by you anyhow." We then made a treaty with these soldiers. We agreed not to molest any one, and they agreed that we might pass through the Bitter Root country in peace. We bought provisions and traded stock with white men there.

We understood that there was to be no more war. We intended to go peaceably to the buffalo country, and leave the question of returning to our country to be settled afterward.

With this understanding we traveled on for four days, and, thinking that the trouble was all over, we stopped and prepared tent-poles to take with us. We started again, and at the end of two days we saw three white men passing our camp. Thinking that peace had been made, we did not molest them. We could have killed or taken them prisoners, but we did not suspect them of being spies, which they were.

That night the soldiers surrounded our camp. About daybreak one of my men went out to look after his horses. The soldiers saw him and shot him down like a coyote. I have since learned that these soldiers were not those we had left behind. They had come upon us from another direction. The new white war-chief's name was General John Gibbon. He charged upon us while some of my people were still asleep. We had a hard fight. Some of my men crept around and attacked the soldiers from the rear. In this battle we lost nearly all our lodges, but we finally drove General Gibbon back.

COWARDLY TACTICS

Finding that he was not able to capture us, he sent to his camp a few miles away for his big guns (cannons), but my men had captured them and all the ammunition. We damaged the big guns all we could, and carried away the powder and lead. In the fight with General Gibbon we lost fifty women and children and thirty fighting men. We remained long enough to bury our dead. The Nez Percés never make war on women and children; we could have killed a great many women and children while the war lasted, but we would feel ashamed to do so cowardly an act.

We never scalp our enemies, but when General Howard came up and joined General Gibbon, their Indian scouts dug up our dead and scalped them. I have been told that General Howard did not order this great shame to be done.

We retreated as rapidly as we could toward the buffalo country. After six days General Howard came close to us, and we went out and attacked him, and captured nearly all his horses and mules (about two hundred and fifty head). We then marched on to the Yellowstone Basin.

On the way we captured one white man and two white women. We released them at the end of three days. They were treated kindly. The women were not insulted. Can the white soldiers tell of one time when Indian women were taken prisoners, and held three days and then released without being insulted? Were the Nez Percés women who fell into the hands of General Howard's soldiers treated with as much respect? I deny that a Nez Percé was ever guilty of such a crime.

A few days later we captured two more white men. One of them stole a horse and escaped. We gave the other a poor horse and told him he was free.

Nine days' march brought us to the mouth of Clarke's Fork of the Yellowstone. We did not know what had become of General Howard, but we supposed that he had sent for more horses and mules. He did not come up, but another new war-chief (General Samuel D. Sturgis) attacked us. We held him in check while we moved all our women and children and stock out of danger, leaving a few men to cover our retreat.

A FOURTH ARMY

Several days passed, and we heard nothing of General Howard, or Gibbon, or Sturgis. We had repulsed each in turn, and began to feel secure, when another army, under General Nelson A.

Miles, struck us. This was the fourth army, each of which outnumbered our fighting force, that we had encountered within
sixty days.

We had no knowledge of General Miles's army until a short
time before he made a charge upon us, cutting our camp in two,
and capturing nearly all of our horses. About seventy men, myself among them, were cut off. My little daughter, twelve years
of age, was with me. I gave her a rope, and told her to catch a
horse and join the others who were cut off from the camp. I have
not seen her since, but I have learned that she is alive and well.

I thought of my wife and children, who were now surrounded by soldiers, and I resolved to go to them or die. With
a prayer in my mouth to the Great Spirit Chief who rules above,
I dashed unarmed through the line of soldiers. It seemed to me
that there were guns on every side, before and behind me. My
clothes were cut to pieces and my horse was wounded, but I
was not hurt. As I reached the door of my lodge, my wife
handed me my rifle, saying: "Here's your gun. Fight!"

The soldiers kept up a continuous fire. Six of my men were
killed in one spot near me. Ten or twelve soldiers charged into
our camp and got possession of two lodges, killing three Nez
Percés and losing three of their men, who fell inside our lines. I
called my men to drive them back. We fought at close range, not
more than twenty steps apart, and drove the soldiers back upon
their main line, leaving their dead in our hands. We secured
their arms and ammunition. We lost, the first day and night,
eighteen men and three women. General Miles lost twenty-six
killed and forty wounded. The following day General Miles
sent a messenger into my camp under protection of a white flag.
I sent my friend Yellow Bull to meet him.

A MEETING WITH GENERAL MILES

Yellow Bull understood the messenger to say that General Miles
wished me to consider the situation; that he did not want to kill
my people unnecessarily. Yellow Bull understood this to be a
demand for me to surrender and save blood. Upon reporting
this message to me, Yellow Bull said he wondered whether
General Miles was in earnest. I sent him back with my answer,
that I had not made up my mind, but would think about it and
send word soon. A little later he sent some Cheyenne scouts
with another message. I went out to meet them. They said they
believed that General Miles was sincere and really wanted

peace. I walked on to General Miles's tent. He met me and we shook hands. He said, "Come, let us sit down by the fire and talk this matter over." I remained with him all night; next morning Yellow Bull came over to see if I was alive, and why I did not return.

General Miles would not let me leave the tent to see my friend alone.

Yellow Bull said to me: "They have got you in their power, and I am afraid they will never let you go again. I have an officer in our camp, and I will hold him until they let you go free."

I said: "I do not know what they mean to do with me, but if they kill me you must not kill the officer. It will do no good to avenge my death by killing him."

Yellow Bull returned to my camp. I did not make any agreement that day with General Miles. The battle was renewed while I was with him. I was very anxious about my people. I knew that we were near Sitting Bull's camp in King George's land, and I thought maybe the Nez Percés who had escaped would return with assistance. No great damage was done to either party during the night.

On the following morning I returned to my camp by agreement, meeting the officer who had been held a prisoner in my camp at the flag of truce. My people were divided about surrendering. We could have escaped from Bear Paw Mountain if we had left our wounded, old women, and children behind. We were unwilling to do this. We had never heard of a wounded Indian recovering while in the hands of white men.

THE SURRENDER

On the evening of the fourth day General Howard came in with a small escort, together with my friend Chapman. We could now talk understandingly. General Miles said to me in plain words, "If you will come out and give up your arms, I will spare your lives and send you to your reservation." I do not know what passed between General Miles and General Howard.

I could not bear to see my wounded men and women suffer any longer; we had lost enough already. General Miles had promised that we might return to our own country with what stock we had left. I thought we could start again. I believed General Miles, or *I never would have surrendered*. I have heard that he has been censured for making the promise to return us to Lapwai. He could not have made any other terms with me at that time. I would have held him in check until my friends came to my assistance, and then neither of the generals nor their soldiers would have ever left Bear Paw Mountain alive.

On the fifth day I went to General Miles and gave up my gun, and said, "From where the sun now stands I will fight no more." My people needed rest—we wanted peace.

THE SURRENDER OF GERONIMO AND THE APACHE

JOHN EDWARD WEEMS

In the following article, John Edward Weems describes the final surrender of Chiricahua Apache leader Geronimo and his band. Geronimo was not a chief by birth; he was a shaman, or medicine man, who rose to power by his determination and forceful personality. In the 1870s, Geronimo led a revolt of four thousand Apaches who had been forcibly removed by U.S. authorities to a small, barren reservation in southeast Arizona. After years of turmoil and bloodshed, Geronimo finally surrendered in 1884 and was sentenced to hard labor in a Florida prison. He died in 1909 on a reservation with his tribe in Oklahoma. John Edward Weems is the author of several historical books, including *To Conquer a Peace* and *Dream of Empire*.

M uch of the trouble [between the Arizona Apaches and the United States] stemmed specifically from governmental selection (about 1876) of a reservation on which to concentrate large numbers of Apaches from many groups and bands. The chosen site—San Carlos, in southeastern Arizona (at the junction of the San Carlos and Gila rivers)—became known immediately for its hot, sickly climate, for its crowded conditions (by Indian standards, anyway), and for its inadequate ration issue. An army officer left this description of the place:

A gravelly flat rose some thirty feet or so above the

river bottoms and was dotted here and there by the drab adobe buildings of the agency. Scrawny, dejected lines of scattered cottonwoods, shrunken, almost leafless, marked the course of the streams. Rain was so infrequent that it took on the semblance of a phenomenon when it came at all. Almost continuously dry, hot, dust-and-gravel laden winds swept the plain, denuding it of every vestige of vegetation.

In addition to having been cursed by a dreadful climate the location was plagued by hordes of insects. Yet this was the place the government expected Apaches to inhabit in large numbers, and on which they were to learn farming. Worse (at least for governmental integrity) several bands had been promised reservations in other locations. Now they were collected and taken to San Carlos, invariably against their wishes. There some were forced to live near other bands with whom they had developed mutual animosities.

GERONIMO'S HIDEOUT

Before the days of San Carlos the reservation system had meant little to Geronimo [the Arizona Chiricahuan Apache shaman] and to a cohort (and cousin) named Juh, a Nedni Apache chief who accompanied him on many raids. They and their warriors would sneak off for raids into Mexico, remain away as long as they were successful, then return for brief periods—if only to escape the Mexicans. But when Geronimo learned he was to be moved to San Carlos he asked for a few days' delay (ostensibly to prepare kinfolk for the move), then he and Juh broke camp and took their people to Mexico and into the depths of the Sierra Madre. They divided into small groups under various leaders, as customary, and supported themselves by raiding—occasionally even into the United States. For months no one knew Geronimo's exact location until he struck, always unexpectedly. . . .

In 1880 Geronimo and Juh came back across the border and agreed to go back to San Carlos, where meals came in handouts and nights passed without the interruption of sleep due to a variety of strange noises.

For a year or so the new tranquillity lasted—blissfully at first, then with less and less ecstasy. The usual complaints about skimpy rations began coming; the usual restlessness returned to old roamers. When soldiers shot a medicine man said to have been fomenting San Carlos Indians, Geronimo became jumpy as well as restless. When a strong cavalry force one day appeared in the vicinity he and Juh and other leaders collected their people and again raced for the Mexican border and the comparative safety of the Sierra Madre, using the darkness of a starlit night to get a head start on the troopers they knew would pursue them. "We thought it more manly to die on the warpath than to be killed in prison," Geronimo explained later.

The fleeing Apaches reached the Sierra Madre, then a few months afterward sneaked back across the border, returned to San Carlos, killed a white police chief and one of his Indian scouts, and "rescued" as many kin previously left behind as they could round up. They forced these people to go with them to Mexico, regardless of individual desires.

Most of the Indians thus redeemed would have preferred to remain in peace at San Carlos. They realized that their absences would in effect convict them as followers of Geronimo and of his uncompromising colleagues. Now they could not return to San Carlos without convincing authorities of their innocence in those two slayings—something they realized would be difficult, or impossible. They could only keep quiet and accompany their tribesmen into Mexico. One young Apache caught in this predicament wondered, "What had we done to be treated so cruelly by members of our own race?". . .

AN INDIAN DEFECTOR

On March 21, 1883, a band of Sierra Madre Apaches led by a warrior named Chato ("Flat-nosed") killed three men near Tombstone while on a foray northward to capture fresh supplies of ammunition needed for their American-made weapons. Later they veered eastward, into New Mexico, killed a federal judge from Lordsburg and his wife, and took with them into Mexico the couple's six-year-old son.

During the raid, however, they lost a defector who was war-weary and angry at having been "rescued" from the San Carlos Reservation against his will [by Geronimo]: a man named Tso-ay, later nicknamed "Peaches" by army personnel because of his surprisingly light complexion. This gave General George Crook an opportunity. He persuaded Peaches to agree to guide soldiers to those Sierra Madre hideouts. Next, Crook visited Mexican officials and received their approval for sending his troopers into the country to get Geronimo. . . .

Peaches led the expedition to a place deep in the mountains

where a main camp had been located when he was with the Apaches. The site resembled a natural amphitheater. It was watered by a clear stream and shaded by pines, oaks, cedars. But now the occupants obviously had retreated farther into the rugged wilderness.

Crook's Apaches proposed (on May 10) going ahead alone. Mules and soldiers were proving to be a hindrance. Crook approved, first emphasizing to them that they should do everything possible to persuade their fellow tribesmen to surrender. The General wanted no fighting in this wild, unfamiliar region. But when the scouts (on May 15) encountered the first "hostiles"—two warriors and a woman—they fired immediately and missed. The three Indians fled, but the scouts surprised and attacked a main camp nearby. They killed nine occupants and captured five others.

Held captive in this camp was the six-year-old son of the slain Lordsburg couple, and some Indian frustrated and infuriated by the unexpected attack seized stones and beat the boy to death before fleeing with the others.

Crook's scouts burned the village and rounded up the livestock. A woman captured in the attack volunteered information that many of the holdouts wanted to return to reservation security, no matter how distasteful it had been once, and promised to solicit surrenders if her captors would release her.

The scouts let her go, then waited. In time the soldiers and pack animals came up and encamped with the scouts.

Just as the woman had foreseen, Apaches began coming in— a few at first, then more. Within a few days Crook could count 121 Indians who preferred reservation existence to the dangers of life in the Sierra Madre. . . .

CHASING GERONIMO

Now Crook had another military campaign to launch. Once more troopers guided by Apache scouts followed hostile Indians through ravines and canyons, over and around giant rocks, across mountain streams awash with runoff from heavy, late-spring rains (which also helped to hide trails). Ahead, the fleeing Chiricahuas [Geronimo's band of Apaches] left the usual mementos of their visits: murdered and sometimes mutilated settlers, stolen stock, goods seized to sustain Indian life. Further, the Apaches this time tried a new trick. Whenever pursuers came uncomfortably close they would throw them off by making "false camps"—starting small camp fires at some selected location, leaving one or two worn-out horses tethered in the vicinity, then dashing on while pursuers halted and prepared an ambush.

An army officer later described the difficulty of chasing Geronimo.

> It is laid down in our army tactics . . . that twenty-five miles a day is the maximum that cavalry can stand. Bear this in mind, and also that here is an enemy with a thousand miles of hilly and sandy country to run over, and each brave provided with from three to five ponies trained like dogs. They carry almost nothing but arms and ammunition; they can live on the cactus; they can go more than forty-eight hours without water; they know every water hole and every foot of ground in this vast . . . country; they have incredible powers of endurance; they run in small bands scattering at the first indications of pursuit. What can the United States soldier, mounted on his heavy American horse, with the necessary forage, rations, and camp equipage, do . . . against this supple, untiring foe? Nothing, absolutely nothing. It is no exaggeration to say that these fiends can travel . . . at the rate of seventy miles a day . . . over the most barren and desolate country imaginable. One week of such work will kill the average soldier and his horse.

Crook's solution, as it had been earlier, was to rely on those Apache scouts. Now he sent two columns of them after Geronimo—one along the eastern slope of the Sierra Madre, the other along the western side. Whenever they found trails leading into the mountains they were to follow them.

One group located a camp and attacked (capturing fifteen women and children), but they did not find Geronimo. The hostile Apaches countered this, whether or not intentionally, by sending a small party of warriors northward past Crook's sentinels to the border country, where their raids terrorized settlers again and once more brought the collective wrath of Arizona settlers down on Crook. Meanwhile, the Apache scouts had found more camps and had attacked, taking prisoners, but Geronimo continued to elude them.

Then (in January 1886) the scouts came upon a main camp

and after a surprise attack that caused few human casualties captured most of the Indians' horses and supplies. Such loss disheartened even Geronimo. After a chance battle between Mexican troops nearby and Crook's Apaches, commenced when identities were mistaken and ended when communication finally was established, the end began to grow near for the freewheeling Apache leader.

GERONIMO TALKS PEACE

Geronimo's band had dwindled since coming into Mexico. Some of his people had been killed. Many had been captured (including Geronimo's entire family, with the exception of an eldest son). Others had gone with the raiding party northward and had not returned. . . . Against their scant numbers was arrayed a large military force of Americans and Mexicans, and the Sierra Madre no longer terrified outsiders. "Our scouts had reported bands of United States and Mexican troops at many points in the mountains," Geronimo said later. "We estimated that about two thousand soldiers were ranging these mountains seeking to capture us." He also made an observation that typified his entire career: "It is senseless to fight when you cannot hope to win."

The time had come again, sadly, to talk about peace.

Captain John Bourke, with Crook, heard of Geronimo's desire to confer with the General. "Geronimo sent word that he would come in . . . at a spot he would designate. This was the Cañon de los Embudos, in the northeast corner of Sonora, on the Arizona line." Already encamped near that canyon was an American army detachment under the command of a Lieutenant Marion Maus, through whom Geronimo had sent his request to meet Crook.

Bourke accompanied Crook to the site, although the General wisely left most of his army behind. The sight of so many soldiers moving toward them would have sent the Apaches running again.

> The rancheria of the hostile Chiricahuas was in a lava bed [Bourke observed], on top of a small conical hill surrounded by steep ravines, not five hundred yards in direct line from [Lieutenant Maus's camp], but having between the two positions two or three steep and rugged gulches which served as scarps and counterscarps. The whole ravine was . . . beautiful: shading

the rippling water were smooth, white-trunked, long, and slender sycamores, dark gnarly ash, rough-barked cottonwoods, pliant willows, briery buck-thorn, and much of the more tropical vegetation already enumerated.

GERONIMO'S FINAL SURRENDER

Bourke saw Geronimo . . . and a number of warriors approach Crook's camp, after some delay. Not all of them entered at once. They came in groups of four, five, or six—"all on the *qui vive,* apprehensive of treachery, and ready to meet it."

Crook's talk with Geronimo was held in a shady grove of cottonwoods and sycamores. Bourke and twenty or so others, including interpreters and a photographer, also attended. The Captain kept notes of what was said at the historic meeting, which ended (after some subsequent talks) with the surrender of Geronimo and all other hostile Apaches. Bourke heard with pleasure Geronimo's words, directed to Crook: "Once I moved about like the wind. Now I surrender to you and that is all.". . .

Years later Geronimo would add his own lament, tempered with a few well-greased words calculated to appeal to his white civilizers.

At least partly because of his previous failure to admit reality his Apaches had been moved far from home. This saddened him enormously.

> I know that if my people were placed in that mountainous region lying around the headwaters of the Gila River they would live in peace and act according to the will of the President [Geronimo would say near the end of his life]. They would be prosperous and happy in tilling the soil and learning the civilization of the white men, whom they now respect. Could I but see this accomplished, I think I could forget all the wrongs that I have ever received, and die a contented and happy old man. . . . If this cannot be done during my lifetime—if I must die in bondage—I hope that the remnant of the Apache tribe may, when I am gone, be granted the one privilege which they request—to return to Arizona.

THE DAWES ACT

FRANCIS PAUL PRUCHA

The Dawes Act, or General Allotment Act, was passed in February 1887 and allotted individual Indians, rather than tribal communities, pieces of land on which they were expected to learn to become farmers. The philosophy behind the act was that individual property ownership would subdue the nomadic nature of the Indians and break up the nucleus of their culture—the tribe. Supporters of the act hoped that smaller landholdings would improve Indian civilization by introducing them to Christian culture. The Indians protested against the act not only because it severely reduced their landholdings, but also because their hunter-gatherer lifestyle would change to an agrarian one. Decades after the enactment of the Dawes Act, most of what had been tribal land was occupied by white settlers. In the following article, Francis Paul Prucha explains the components of the law and how it affected the Indians. Prucha is professor emeritus of history at Marquette University. Among his many books are *The Indians in American Society: From the Revolutionary War to the Present* and *The History of a Political Anomaly*.

N o panacea for the Indian problem was more persistently proposed than allotment of land to the Indians in severalty. It was an article of faith with the reformers that civilization was impossible without the incentive to work that came only from individual ownership of a piece of property. The upsurge of humanitarian concern for Indian reform in the post–Civil War era gave a new impetus to the severalty principle, which was almost universally accepted and aggressively promoted, until Congress finally passed a general allotment law.

Allotment of land in severalty, however, was part of the drive to individualize the Indian that became the obsession of the late-nineteenth-century Christian reformers and did not stand by itself. The breakup of tribalism, a major goal of this Indian policy, had been moved forward by the abolition of the treaty system and would be carried on by a government educational system and by the extension of American law over the Indian communities. Yet for many years the dissolution of communal lands by allotment, together with the citizenship attached to private landowning, was the central issue.

A GENERAL ALLOTMENT LAW

The advocates of change wanted general legislation that would permit or require the allotment of lands in severalty for all the Indians on reservations. Early in 1879, Commissioner of Indian Affairs Ezra Hayt drew up a draft of such legislation. He criticized past allotment provisions for failure to protect the Indian allotments adequately from imprudent alienation, and his own proposal prohibited alienation for a period of twenty-five years. The inefficiency of the old system of common title and of the treaties that granted land in severalty with a title in fee had been demonstrated, he thought, and he believed that his plan with delayed title would solve the problem. By such a measure, he was convinced that "the race can be led in a few years to a condition where they may be clothed with citizenship and left to their own resources to maintain themselves as citizens of the republic."

The measure was considered by Congress in the form of a bill drawn up by Senator Richard Coke of Texas, which had tremendous support from many sides, most importantly, perhaps, from Major General Carl Schurz, who again and again urged its passage. Schurz spoke of the Coke bill as "the most essential step in the solution of the Indian problem," and his statement of the advantages that would accrue summed up the views of the reformers generally:

> It will inspire the Indians with a feeling of assurance as to the permanency of their ownership of the lands they occupy and cultivate; it will give them a clear and legal standing as landed proprietors in the courts of law; it will secure to them for the first time fixed homes under the protection of the same law under which white men own theirs; it will eventually open to settlement by white men the large tracts of land

now belonging to the reservations, but not used by
the Indians. It will thus put the relations between the
Indians and their white neighbors in the Western
country upon a new basis, by gradually doing away
with the system of large reservations, which has so
frequently provoked those encroachments which in
the past have led to so much cruel injustice and so
many disastrous collisions. It will also by the sale,
with their consent, of reservation lands not used by
the Indians, create for the benefit of the Indians a
fund, which will gradually relieve the government of
those expenditures which have now to be provided
for by appropriations. It will be the most effective
measure to place the Indians and white men upon an
equal footing as to the protection and restraints of law
common to both.

ALLOTMENT DISSENTERS

There were, to be sure, some who spoke out against allotment
and who criticized the humanitarians' arguments. By far the
strongest of these was Senator Henry Teller, who criticized the
reformers' desire for a universal and uniform measure, which
did not take into account the tremendous diversity among the
Indian tribes, and he flatly denied the claims of the advocates
of severalty that the Indians were clamoring for allotments in
fee simple [complete personal ownership]. In Teller's view, the
friends of severalty had the whole matter turned around, mis-
taking the end for the means. Once the Indians were civilized
and Christianized and knew the value of property and the
value of a home, then give them an allotment of their own, he
argued. But do not expect the allotment to civilize and Chris-
tianize and transform the Indians.

Early attempts to pass the bill failed in the House, and when
the severalty bill came up again in December 1885, it was introduced by Senator Henry L. Dawes, now chairman of the
Committee on Indian Affairs. His name stuck to the final act, although he had been relatively late in climbing on the allotment
bandwagon, and Senator Coke was soon forgotten. Dawes, perhaps because he despaired of any other answer, became one of
the most active supporters of the individualization of the Indian
through private property, answering questions in public meetings about the details of the proposal and ultimately pushing

the measure through Congress. His bill became law on February 8, 1887.

The Dawes Act dealt primarily with ownership of the land. It authorized but did not require the president to survey the reservations or selected parts of them and to allot the land to individual Indians. The amounts to be allotted reflected the strong tradition of a quarter-section homestead for the yeoman farmer. One-quarter of a section (160 acres) was to be allotted to each head of family and smaller parcels to single persons and minors. In cases where lands were suitable only for grazing, the allotments would be doubled, and if prior treaty provisions specified larger allotments, the treaty would govern. If anyone entitled to an allotment did not make the selection within four years after the president had directed allotment, the law authorized the secretary of the interior to order the agent of the tribe or a special agent to make such selection.

When the secretary of the interior approved the allotments, he would issue to each Indian a patent, which declared that the United States would hold the allotted lands in trust for twenty-five years for the Indian and for his sole benefit or that of his heirs. At the expiration of the trust period, the Indian would receive the land in fee simple. Any conveyance or contract touching the land during the trust period was null and void, and the president at his discretion could extend the period. Once an Indian had received his allotment, he would become a citizen of the United States.

SURPLUS LANDS

After the lands had been allotted on a reservation, or sooner if the president thought it was in the best interests of the tribe, the secretary of the interior could negotiate with the tribe for the purchase of the remaining or surplus lands, the purchase to be ratified by Congress before becoming effective. The money paid to the Indians for the surplus lands was to be held in the Treasury for the sole use of the tribes to whom the reservation belonged, and the funds were subject to appropriation by Congress for the education and civilization of the Indians concerned. Excluded from the provisions of the act were the Five Civilized Tribes [Cherokee, Creek, Choctaw, Chickasaw, and Seminole], the Osages, Miamis, Peorias, and Sacs and Foxes in the Indian Territory, the Seneca Indians in New York, and the strip of Sioux lands in Nebraska.

The Dawes Act, as one historian of the measure observed, was "an act of faith." It was an act pushed through Congress, not by western interests greedy for Indian lands, but by eastern humanitarians who deeply believed that communal landholding was an obstacle to the civilization they wanted the Indians to acquire and who were convinced that they had the history of human experience on their side.

The passage of the Dawes Act caused great exultation among the reformers who had fought so persistently for the proposal. "In securing the passage of this law the Indian Rights Association achieved the greatest success in its history," the executive committee of the association declared, "and its enactment was the most important step forward ever taken by the national Government in its methods of dealing with the Indians." Secretary of the Interior L.Q.C. Lamar described it as "the most important measure of legislation ever enacted in this country affecting our Indian affairs . . . [and] practically a general naturalization law for the American Indians." It was to his mind "the only escape open to these people from the dire alternative of impending extirpation." Merrill E. Gates, president of the Lake Mohonk Conference, said in 1900 that the act was "a mighty pulverizing engine for breaking up the tribal mass."

Year by year the process of allotment moved ahead, and the surplus lands were rapidly transferred to the whites. The Indians held 155,632,312 acres in 1881; by 1890 they had 104,314,349, and by 1900 only 77,865,373, of which 5,409,530 had been allotted. So successful did the process seem that the reformers looked forward to the day when government supervision over the Indians would disappear entirely and the Indians would all be absorbed into American society.

PROBLEMS WITH INDIAN FARMERS

Dissatisfaction with the Dawes Act soon arose, however, when it was realized that the allotment of a homestead to an Indian did not automatically turn him into a practical farmer. The provisions of the act that prohibited the leasing or other such conveyance of the allotments—wisely intended to protect the Indian holdings for an extended period—actually seemed to work a hardship on many Indians. Women and children and Indians who were in some way disabled could not reap the benefits of the allotments because they were unable to farm them. Moreover, lands belonging to students who were away at school lay fallow or were used illegally by whites with no benefit to the Indians. If leasing were allowed for these needy persons, an income from the land could be provided for them. Other Indians, it turned out, did not have the work animals or agricultural implements indispensable for effective use of their allotments. If a portion of their land could be rented, the income could be used to provide the tools needed to farm the rest.

There was in addition the question of advancing the Indians toward full participation in American society by letting them assume the full responsibility for their own property. To hedge their ownership around with all kinds of restrictions in its use hardly was conducive to Indian growth in maturity, and the interspersing of white farmers among the Indians, it was argued, would furnish object lessons of great value in teaching the Indians how to farm.

It is strange how readily the reformers accepted these arguments—the same men and women who had championed allotment in severalty as the way to move the Indians from idleness to hard work on their own land. Only a few voices were raised against the proposals to make leasing legal under set conditions, and the opposition was too slight to stem the movement.

By a law of February 28, 1891, Congress made leasing possible. It allowed Indians who "by reason of age or other disability" were personally unable to occupy and improve their allotments to lease their lands for set periods, subject to the approval of the secretary of the interior. Although the Indian Office moved slowly at first in applying the leasing law, the program soon gained a momentum that swept away the restrictions the advocates had intended, and the wording of the law was loosened in 1894 by adding "inability" to age and disability as a reason for leasing allotments and by extending the period of lease. The number of leases climbed steadily.

There is no doubt that the leasing policy ate deeply into the goals envisaged by reformers for the allotment policy, for many Indians came to look upon the land as a source of revenue from the labor of a tenant, not as a homestead to be worked personally by an independent small farmer. The leasing, furthermore, was a step toward complete alienation of the allotments by sale, a process that soon began to appear as a break in the dike of protection erected around the allotments.

THE BATTLE AT WOUNDED KNEE

JOHN TEBBEL AND KEITH JENNISON

The Battle at Wounded Knee in December 1890 was the last major Native American uprising. The battle was inspired by the Ghost Dance movement, which began as a peaceful religious philosophy that offered the Indians hope for an existence free of white oppression. Lakota, or Sioux, Indians had suffered from mistreatment and dishonesty from soldiers and Indian agents, and they soon perverted the peaceful message into a bloody vendetta against whites. On the morning of December 29, an accidental shot fired in the air sparked the resentment the soldiers had harbored against the Indians since the massacre of Custer at Little Bighorn. About 500 soldiers swarmed upon 350 Lakotas, many of whom were women and children fleeing the battle. The Indians lost between 150 and 300 members, and the battle marked the end of the Indian resistance movement. In the following article, John Tebbel and Keith Jennison describe the events of the battle at Wounded Knee and how it transpired. John Tebbel is the author of *George Washington's America* and *An American Dynasty*; Keith Jennison authored *The Boys and Their Mother* and *The Maine Idea*.

"W hen the sun died I went up to Heaven and saw God and all the people who had died a long time ago. God told me to come back and tell my people they must be good and love one another, and not fight, or steal, or lie. He gave me this dance to give to my people."

With these words a young Piute named Wovoka launched in Nevada, sometime in 1888, a new religion, and from this unlikely beginning developed the last Indian uprising in America.

Wovoka, who was also known as Jack Wilson, his Christian name, had been influenced by the theology he had heard in the missions and only half understood. The doctrine he preached was a pathetic attempt—all the more poignant because it was grasped with such desperation—to convert the white man's religion into a message of hope for the Indians.

As doctrine alone, it was a philosophy of peace. Wovoka told his followers of a vision in which the Great Spirit revealed to him that he, Wovoka, was the Messiah, returned to earth as an Indian because the first Messiah had been crucified by white men, a logical view in Indian eyes. He, the Messiah, would bring vast changes to the earth, Wovoka said. The dead among the Indians would rise again and return to their lands. The slain buffalo would rise too and populate the plains once more in their dense, black flocks. Out of a blazing volcano would come pouring a flood tide of lava that would wipe the earth clean of white men and spare the Indians, except for those among them who were unbelievers.

THE GHOST DANCE

Any Indian could be saved, however, by dancing the sacred Ghost Dance, which Wovoka showed them. The dance was simplicity itself; the dancers joined hands in a circle and shuffled slowly to the left. They wore special shirts that Wovoka asserted would stop a white man's bullet.

The Messiah issued specific instructions to the faithful: "Do not harm anyone. Do right always. Do not tell lies. Do not fight. When your friends die you must not cry."

A religious revival swept the Indians of the Far West, much like the one that gripped the Kentucky and Tennessee frontier in 1800. This was authentic mass hysteria, still seen in the old-fashioned fundamentalist camp meetings that survive today. Visions were seen, squaws and warriors worked themselves to a pitch of ecstasy and fell into trances, and frenzy overtook the shuffling bodies of the Ghost Dancers.

The cult of the Ghost Dance might have been harmless enough, and would certainly have disappeared in time, but unfortunately it spread over the mountains to the Indians of the Plains, whose affairs were in a much worse state. Here dwelt the bitter survivors of the last great war, near starvation, mistreated by the agents, disillusioned by the white man's promises, defeated, and confined to reservations. Life for them was hopeless, and they could not see which way to turn until the ritual of the Ghost Dance and its illusory promises was brought back to them by the delegates they sent to investigate the new teaching.

WITH WAR IN MIND

In transit, however, it took on new meanings. The peaceful basis of the religion was lost. When the Plains people danced the Ghost Dance, war against the whites was in their minds and in the doctrine as their medicine men expounded it. Worse, the magic of the ritual was believed to make them proof against bullets, against death itself. These ideas were accepted whole, with pathetic eagerness, by the Sioux, Arapahos, Cheyennes, and Kiowas, the principal victims of the government. These Indians soon worked themselves into an excitable state, claiming they had seen the reborn buffalo and talked to relatives long dead who were now returning. They believed sincerely that the millennium was at hand.

There were also Ghost Dancers who professed to be caught up in the new faith who actually saw in it a means of reviving the ancient struggle. One of them may well have been Sitting Bull, a practiced manipulator of sacred medicine, who quite naturally saw in Ghost Dancing a means to the end he had almost given up hoping would ever be accomplished.

Tension began to rise on the Sioux reservations of Pine Ridge and Rosebud during the late autumn of 1890, and by December the electric crackle of danger was in the air. Indians were disappearing off the reservation to practice secretly the rites of the Ghost Dance, and it was rumored that Sitting Bull and his supporters meant to follow them.

Still the crisis might have passed if Benjamin Harrison had not been elected president in 1888, and on assuming office the following year, swept out the Indian agents along with the rest of former president Grover Cleveland's Democratic officeholders, and installed new and inexperienced men to take their place.

The new Indian agent at Pine Ridge, a green hand named Daniel Royer, grew alarmed by the defection of the Ghost Dancers and the rumors about Sitting Bull, and notwithstanding that a great majority of the Indians on the reservation were obviously peaceful, he called on the Army for protection. John R. Brooke, the general who responded, was no more familiar with Indians than Royer. He arrived at Pine Ridge on November 19,

1890, which was the date a large company of Ghost Dancers fled to the Badlands, burning their own houses behind them.

THE MURDER OF SITTING BULL

Apparently Brooke and other army officers were afraid that if Sitting Bull joined the Dancers, they might have a war on their hands, consequently the order was sent to Standing Rock Agency to arrest the old chief. An Indian lieutenant named Bull-head led a native police force to Sitting Bull's log cabin on the morning of December 15 and pulled him out of bed.

Before they could lead him away, the chief's angry followers gathered around, and Catch-the-Bear, an old enemy of Bull-head's who was devoted to Sitting Bull, took the opportunity to shoot the Indian lieutenant. As he fell, Bullhead contrived to raise his pistol and fire a slug into the chief's body, while at the same time another policeman, Red Tomahawk, put a bullet into Sitting Bull's head, which killed him instantly.

The whole village erupted. In a few minutes a dozen men lay dead and three others were wounded. Only the arrival of white troops prevented an intramural massacre.

Panic engulfed the Sioux as the news of Sitting Bull's death traveled across the Plains with the speed of wind. No one knew what it meant. Was it the signal for the war the Messiah had prophesied? Or did it mean that the white men had determined to exterminate the Sioux before a war could start? Families fled to their relatives; others came to the agency for protection.

To restore order, the army sent out detachments to bring all Indians back to the reservation. Although nothing was said about it, the implication was that those who remained hostile would be shown little mercy. It was denied later, but there can be no doubt that the memory of General George Custer burned in many of these soldiers, some of whom had served with him.

TENSION AND MISTRUST

One of the vagrant chiefs the troops sought was Big Foot, whose arrest had been ordered. When he heard about it, Big Foot started toward the Pine Ridge Agency with 356 men, women, and children. Thirteen days after Sitting Bull's murder, he encountered Major S.M. Whitside, with eight troops of the Seventh Cavalry and a party of scouts, 470 men all told. Whitside demanded Big Foot's unconditional surrender. The chief complied, and the Indians were escorted to Wounded Knee Creek, twenty miles from the agency. There they camped on the evening of December 28, while the jittery Whitside sent out for reinforcements, which came at once under command of Colonel James Forsyth, the hardy veteran of many Sioux campaigns.

Both sides were deeply suspicious of each other. Dark rumors raced through the Sioux encampment that the white men meant to kill their horses and ship the whole tribe off to Florida in chains. Forsyth, on his part, suspected the Sioux of treachery, as he did all Indians.

Next morning, on the 29th, Forsyth set up his men in an arc around the camp, trained his battery of Hotchkiss guns on the tepees, and prepared to disarm the Indians. There are wildly conflicting reports about what followed. Some authorities say that Big Foot's warriors were, in fact, plotting a treacherous coup and had rifles concealed beneath their blankets which they whipped out when a medicine man named Yellow Bird threw a handful of dust as a signal.

There is good reason to doubt this version. Big Foot was leading his people back to the reservation; if he had been planning war, he would scarcely have gone about it in that way. Moreover, his village was completely surrounded by a superior force which possessed the decisive weapon, howitzers, and there can be little doubt that the Indians from Big Foot on down were thoroughly frightened by what might happen to them.

The more likely account of what triggered the subsequent disaster is that Forsyth's men began to search the Indians roughly for concealed weapons, always a dangerous procedure with the proud Plains Indians, and that a scuffle developed between two soldiers who were trying to take the gun away from a brave. The gun was discharged and Forsyth's men perpetrated within a few minutes what was one of the worst massacres in the whole history of the Indian wars.

THE BLOODY MASSACRE

A government investigator, who could certainly not be charged as a partisan of the Indians, reported later: "The terrible effect may be judged from the fact that one woman survivor, Blue Whirlwind, with whom the author conversed, received fourteen wounds, while each of her two little boys were also wounded by her side. In a few minutes two hundred Indian men, women and children, with sixty soldiers, were lying dead and wounded on the ground, the tepees had been torn down by the shells and some of them were burning above the helpless wounded, and the surviving handful of Indians were flying in wild panic to the shelter of the ravine, pursued by hundreds of maddened soldiers and followed up by a raking fire from the Hotchkiss guns, which had been moved into position to sweep the ravine. There can be no question that the pursuit was simply a massacre, where fleeing women, with infants in their arms, were shot down after resistance had ceased and when almost every warrior was stretched dead or dying on the ground."

The Seventh Cavalry was at last revenged for Custer. But it was typical of the white man, as Oliver La Farge [president of the Association on American Indian Affairs] has pointed out, that the affair on the Little Big Horn came to be known as the Custer Massacre while the shameful slaughter by Forsyth's men was officially labeled the Battle of Wounded Knee.

In the old days, such an atrocity would have touched off a furious Indian reprisal, and Colonel Forsyth quickly learned that the old days were not quite dead. Almost frantic with rage, the Brulé Sioux, under Two Strike, attacked the agency, while another band struck savagely at the Wounded Knee camp on the 30th. Forsyth had to call for reinforcements, which came up just in time to save him from annihilation.

THE FINAL SURRENDER

The sporadic battle raged at first one place and then the other for thirty-two days, and then abruptly it ended. The Indians surrendered and the last uprising was over, burning and dying like a strayed Fourth of July rocket against the bleak winter night.

Back in Nevada, the prophet who had started the dismal chain of events was aghast and utterly dismayed at what had become of the Ghost Dance religion. The round-faced Messiah took off the large-brimmed black hat he wore habitually above his white man's suit and covered his head with a blanket, in the old way. The Sioux had "twisted things," he mourned; it was better to "drop the whole business."

A forlorn, bent figure, Wovoka walked among his people and cried out to them: "Hoo-oo! My children, my children. In days behind many times I called you to travel the hunting trail or to follow the war trail. Now those trails are choked with sand; they are covered with grass, the young men cannot find them. My children, today I call upon you to travel a new trail, the only trail now open—the White Man's Road. . . ."

The Gilded Age

| CHAPTER 5 |

THE INDUSTRIAL REVOLUTION

JOHN E. FINDLING AND FRANK W. THACKERAY

In the following article, John E. Findling and Frank W. Thackeray discuss events in the second half of the nineteenth century that transformed America from an agricultural society to an industrial society. Prior to the Gilded Age, most of America's production and manufacturing took place in individual homes or farms in a system known as the cottage industry. Cottage industries result in few products at extraordinarily high prices. After the Civil War, discoveries of natural resources, technological advances, and a cheap labor supply combined to produce more efficient and affordable methods of manufacture. Products were cheaper and of better quality than those formed in a cottage industry. Production moved from the home into factories, and large, monopolistic companies, such as John D. Rockefeller's Standard Oil, were born. The Industrial Revolution changed America's economic system from agriculture to industrial capitalism and competition. Findling and Thackeray are history professors at Indiana University, Southeast, at New Albany.

T he industrial revolution in the United States, usually thought of as a phenomenon of the Gilded Age (1877–1901), had its origins in the early years of the nineteenth century with the development of textile mills in New England. By the 1830s, farm machinery was being manufactured in considerable quantity, and railroads were beginning to replace canals as the country's principal means of transportation.

Excerpted from *Events That Changed America in the Nineteenth Century* by John E. Findling and Frank W. Thackeray (Westport, CT: Greenwood, 1997). Copyright © 1997 by John E. Findling and Frank W. Thackeray. Reprinted by permission of the publisher.

The census of 1850 showed for the first time that the value of all industrial products was greater than that of agricultural products, although the figures were close and agricultural products regained their lead in the 1860 census. By the 1860s, the beginnings of the North's industrial revolution were quite clear. Abundant natural resources, growing numbers of immigrants, an inventive people, and a flow of investment capital contributed to this transformation of the northern economy, a transformation accelerated by the demands of the Civil War. Still, in 1860, most of the richest men in America were merchants, not industrialists, and the relative weakness of U.S. industry was shown at the beginning of the war by the urgent missions abroad to buy arms and woolen cloth for uniforms, paid for with the proceeds from agricultural exports.

The factory system had become firmly established after the War of 1812 with New England's textile manufacturing. This, along with shoemaking, iron, and lumber, were the major industries, and by 1860, factory employment had risen to over 1.3 million, not including construction workers, who, when added, drove the total industrial force to around 2 million workers.

The first few miles of American railroad service began in 1830; by 1840, there were 2,808 miles of track, by 1850, 9,029 miles, and by 1860, 30,626 miles. Chicago and St. Louis were connected by rail with the Atlantic coast by the 1850s, and Chicago was the nation's rail center by 1856. The great majority of track mileage was in the North, although by 1860, rail lines connected Memphis, New Orleans, Atlanta, and Charleston with the major cities of the North and, except for New Orleans, with each other.

INDUSTRY TAKES THE LEAD

After the Civil War, the pace of industrialization rapidly picked up, fueled by the convergence of a number of important factors. Further discoveries of natural resources, particularly iron ore, coal, and oil, provided the raw materials needed in the factories. Technological advances, from Thomas Edison's brilliant inventions to subtle changes in machine tools, greatly increased production. More and more immigrants arrived every year and provided a cheap labor supply, and more and more money, earned during the Civil War or drawn from real estate holdings, provided investment capital. Finally, aid from a friendly federal government in the form of protective tariffs, railroad subsidies, and an unwillingness to regulate industrial abuses did its part in helping pave the way for unparalleled industrial growth.

The period was also marked by the emergence of several important new industries that had never existed before on a national scale. Among these was the petroleum industry, which developed quickly after the first producing oil well was drilled in Pennsylvania in 1859. Oil was valuable first as an illuminant and lubricant; gasoline for automobiles was not a factor until the end of the century. John D. Rockefeller founded the Standard Oil Company in 1867 and led the way in the formation of large monopolistic businesses. Another important new industry was meat packing, which came about with the rise of beef cattle raising on the Great Plains and the growth of railroads in that region. In the 1870s, Kansas City, St. Louis, and Chicago became centers of the meat-packing industry, from where meat products could be safely shipped east in newly invented refrigerator cars. In some ways, the steel industry may have been the most important new industry of the age because of the many applications of steel, from railroad tracks to machine tools. This industry developed because of the development of both the open-hearth and Bessemer processes during the 1860s, both of which greatly increased the supply and decreased the price of steel.

The steel industry had an important impact on the railroad industry, perhaps its largest customer. Track mileage increased by a factor of six during the last third of the nineteenth century, from 30,000 miles to 180,000 miles, and the nation's coasts were linked by the completion of several transcontinental routes. Other technological improvements played a large role in railroad expansion. The safety coupler allowed trains to be much longer and thus carry more goods. The air brake enabled trains to stop more quickly, and the Pullman sleeping car made passenger travel over long distances bearable by creating a hotel-like atmosphere for travelers. The federal government helped railroads through land grants, loans, and subsidies, and state and local governments, aware of the importance of rail routes for economic survival, plied railroad officials with stock purchases and various kinds of financial inducements, including outright bribes, to persuade them to route their lines through a particular state or locality.

Accompanying the expansion of America's industrial production was the growth of big business, the administrative arm of industry. Fundamental to all ambitious businessmen was the belief that combination and consolidation (and the consequent elimination of competition) were essential to success and the prosperity that came with success. Thus most American industrialists engaged in a ruthless struggle for existence, battling their competitors for dominance of their industry. Although this period has been called the era of trusts, a trust was only one of several different methods by which business combination and the reduction or elimination of competition could take place. These methods ranged from very simple, informal gentlemen's agreements, wherein two businessmen would agree to share a market or divide a territory, to more formal arrangements called pools, in which a written, specific set of rules were made among a number of people in the same line of business to govern their production or market share. A trust was a still more sophisticated arrangement, whereby a number of corporations would agree to place control of their stock into the hands of a board of trustees (hence the name), which would make decisions for all the corporations as if they were one. Trusts often controlled a large proportion of trade in their field and could easily force smaller companies out of business (or into the trust) by undercutting their prices or harassing them in other ways. Toward the end of the century, some business managers moved in the direction of outright amalgamation or merger, wherein the total structures of two (or more) companies were combined into a single new company.

Although business combinations brought many advantages to the successful business manager, they often brought higher prices and limited choices to the consumer. Yet the general public accepted business combinations, at least early in the Gilded Age, because of a preference for laissez-faire economics, which mandated no governmental interference into what were thought to be the natural laws of economics and because of a sense that the rich and powerful were so because God had intended for them to be so, and that the reward of the poorer classes would come in heaven.

PROBLEMS WITH LABOR

Public acceptance of big business organization did not extend to labor organization. When labor activists, often with experience in the radical politics of their European homelands, tried to create labor unions in the years following the Civil War, they ran into great resistance from the public and politicians alike.

As a consequence, most of the earliest labor unions tried to be secret organizations, a tactic that never worked very well. The most prominent of the early labor unions was the Knights of Labor, organized in 1869 to combat the poor pay and working conditions that were the hallmarks of America's industrial revolution. At the end of the 1880s, for example, only 45 percent of industrial workers earned more than $500 per year, then considered the poverty line, and the average day worker earned $1.50 for up to 12 hours of work. Working conditions too were often atrocious. On the railroads, 72,000 workers were killed on the tracks and another 158,000 were killed in shops and roundhouses between 1890 and 1917. Similar casualty rates existed in the steel and coal industries, and few factories of any description paid much heed to worker safety issues.

Workers tried to attract the attention of their employers about these issues through strikes, often accompanied by violence, and through unions such as the Knights of Labor. Although strikes seldom accomplished anything constructive, the union showed some promise, as when the Knights blossomed in the 1880s under the leadership of Terence V. Powderly. With 700,000 members in 1886, the Knights were potentially a significant political force, but the organization dissipated its energy on marginal political issues such as an income tax and then bore the brunt of the blame for the Haymarket Square "massacre" [Chicago], in which a number of policemen were killed or injured by a bomb thrown while they attempted to break up a labor rally in 1886. Seven anarchists, four of them members of the Knights, were convicted and given death penalties, and the incident was a virtual death penalty for the Knights, whose membership declined sharply after the affair.

Far more successful was the American Federation of Labor (AFL), created in 1886, which limited its membership to skilled workers (the Knights took in anybody) and focused its efforts on the much narrower goals of better pay and working conditions for its members. Strong leadership and disciplined members enabled the AFL to survive the depression years of the 1890s with a steady core of 550,000 members and move into the twentieth century as the most important labor union in the United States.

THE GRANGE MOVEMENT

By the 1870s, farmers in the Plains states and the rest of the Midwest began to express their discontent with what they perceived as unfair and discriminatory treatment at the hands of the railroads. For example, railroad companies usually controlled warehouses where farmers stored their crops and charged extremely high prices for the service, knowing that the farmers had no alternative. This unrest led to the formation of the Grange, a widespread political movement in the 1870s that had some success in persuading state legislatures to adopt state regulatory laws against the railroads. Although the Supreme Court initially upheld the constitutionality of these laws, it reversed itself in the early 1880s, leading to calls for a federal effort at railroad regulation. In the mid-1880s, the Cullom Committee, named for Senator Shelby Cullom, a Republican from Illinois, investigated the railroads and uncovered many malpractices. The Cullom Committee report resulted in the passage by Congress of the Interstate Commerce Act (1887), a landmark act that established the first great regulatory agency, the Interstate Commerce Commission (ICC). Under the law, the ICC could require that railroad rates be "reasonable and just," with no pooling, no rebates, and no discriminatory practices. But enforcement of the law was left up to the courts, and the understaffed commission found it difficult to prove its allegations. Farmers' dissatisfaction with their treatment at the hands of the railroads continued, however, and helped lead to the creation in the early 1890s of the Populist movement, a rural-based political movement that brought a number of reforms to national attention for the first time.

Businesses apart from railroads began to come under criticism in the 1880s, led by some well-known literary figures. Henry George wrote *Progress and Poverty* (1879), a best-seller that pointed out the great contrast between the rich and the poor, and advocated a "single tax" on land values, which George felt increased because of social evolution and not the efforts of the landowner. Although the single tax never came into being, the book raised the consciousness of many Americans about the way in which the industrial revolution was shaping society. Other books, such as Edward Bellamy's *Looking Backward, 2000–1887* (1887), which painted a utopian picture of a future America, and Henry D. Lloyd's *Wealth against Commonwealth* (1884), which attacked monopolies, added to public concern.

In 1890, Congress responded by passing the Sherman Anti-Trust Act, which declared any business combination "in restraint of trade" to be a misdemeanor. Theoretically designed to outlaw trusts and other nefarious kinds of business combinations, the Sherman Anti-Trust Act was ineffective during the 1890s. Unlike the Interstate Commerce Act, no agency was created to investigate business malpractices, and the government was reluctant to bring cases to court. Indeed, the only times the act was enforced during the 1890s was against labor unions, which on a number of occasions were declared to be combinations "in restraint of trade."

Despite the ineffectiveness of early reform measures such as the Interstate Commerce Act and the Sherman Anti-Trust Act, the attention surrounding them kept the important issues in the public arena, and when the progressive movement matured after 1900, during the presidency of Theodore Roosevelt, a suitable climate for constructive reform was at hand.

CAPITALISM AND SOCIAL DARWINISM

ANDREW CARNEGIE

The Gilded Age was characterized by big businesses, monopolies, and trusts. The growth of the railroad, steel, and oil industries generated millions of dollars for entrepreneurs, while unskilled workers found extremely low-paying jobs in factories. The discrepancy between the rich and the poor widened considerably, and businesses competed fiercely with each other. A part of Charles Darwin's theory of evolution, the idea of "survival of the fittest," was appropriated and applied to competition and success in business and termed "social Darwinism." In the following article, Andrew Carnegie, founder of Carnegie Steel, describes the theory of social Darwinism, and argues that society has benefited from competition and individualism.

T he price which society pays for the law of competition . . . is great; but the advantages of this law are also greater still, for it is to this law that we owe our wonderful material development, which brings improved conditions in its train. But, whether the law be benign or not, we must say of it, as we say of the change in the conditions of men to which we have referred: It is here; we cannot evade it; no substitutes for it have been found; and while the law may be sometimes hard for the individual, it is best for the race, because it insures the survival of the fittest in every department. We accept and welcome, therefore, as conditions to which we must accommodate ourselves, great inequality of environment, the concentration of business, industrial and commercial, in the hands of a few, and

From "Wealth," by Andrew Carnegie, *North American Review,* June 1889.

the law of competition between these, as being not only beneficial, but essential for the future progress of the race. Having accepted these, it follows that there must be great scope for the exercise of special ability in the merchant and in the manufacturer
who has to conduct affairs upon a great scale. (That this talent
for organization and management is rare among men is proved
by the fact that it invariably secures for its possessor enormous
rewards, no matter where or under what laws or conditions.)
The experienced in affairs always rate the MAN whose services
can be obtained as a partner as not only the first consideration,
but such as to render the question of his capital scarcely worth
considering, for such men soon create capital; while, without
the special talent required, capital soon takes wings. Such men
become interested in firms or corporations using millions; and
estimating only simple interest to be made upon the capital in-
vested, it is inevitable that their income must exceed their expenditures, and that they must accumulate wealth. Nor is there
any middle ground which such men can occupy, because the
great manufacturing or commercial concern which does not
earn at least interest upon its capital soon becomes bankrupt. It
must either go forward or fall behind: to stand still is impossible. It is a condition essential for its successful operation that it
should be thus far profitable, and even that, in addition to interest on capital, it should make profit. It is a law, as certain as
any of the others named, that men possessed of this peculiar talent for affairs, under the free play of economic forces, must, of
necessity, soon be in receipt of more revenue than can be judi-
ciously expended upon themselves; and this law is as beneficial
for the race as the others.

CONDITIONS HAVE IMPROVED

Objections to the foundations upon which society is based are
not in order, because the condition of the race is better with
these than it has been with any others which have been tried.
Of the effect of any new substitutes proposed we cannot be
sure. The Socialist or Anarchist who seeks to overturn present
conditions is to be regarded as attacking the foundation upon
which civilization itself rests, for civilization took its start from
the day that the capable, industrious workman said to his in-
competent and lazy fellow, "If thou dost not sow, thou shalt not
reap," and thus ended primitive Communism by separating the
drones from the bees. One who studies this subject will soon be

brought face to face with the conclusion that upon the sacred-
ness of property civilization itself depends—the right of the laborer to his hundred dollars in the savings bank, and equally
the legal right of the millionaire to his millions. To those who
propose to substitute Communism for this intense Individualism the answer, therefore, is: The race has tried that. All progress
from that barbarous day to the present time has resulted from
its displacement. Not evil, but good, has come to the race from
the accumulation of wealth by those who have the ability and
energy that produce it. But even if we admit for a moment that
it might be better for the race to discard its present foundation,
Individualism,—that it is a nobler ideal that man should labor,
not for himself alone, but in and for a brotherhood of his fel-
lows, and share with them all in common, realizing [theologian
Emanuel] Swedenborg's idea of Heaven, where, as he says, the
angels derive their happiness, not from laboring for self, but for
each other,—even admit all this, and a sufficient answer is, This
is not evolution, but revolution. It necessitates the changing of
human nature itself—a work of æons, even if it were good to
change it, which we cannot know. It is not practicable in our day
or in our age. Even if desirable theoretically, it belongs to another and long-succeeding sociological stratum. Our duty is
with what is practicable now; with the next step possible in our
day and generation. It is criminal to waste our energies in en-
deavoring to uproot, when all we can profitably or possibly accomplish is to bend the universal tree of humanity a little in the
direction most favorable to the production of good fruit under
existing circumstances. We might as well urge the destruction
of the highest existing type of man because he failed to reach
our ideal as to favor the destruction of Individualism, Private
Property, the Law of Accumulation of Wealth, and the Law of
Competition; for these are the highest results of human experience, the soil in which society so far has produced the best fruit.
Unequally or unjustly, perhaps, as these laws sometimes oper-
ate, and imperfect as they appear to the Idealist, they are, nevertheless, like the highest type of man, the best and most valuable of all that humanity has yet accomplished.

THE GROWTH OF THE RAILROADS

GEORGE ROGERS TAYLOR AND IRENE D. NEU

The growth of the railroads in the Gilded Age was an enormous boon for the job market, new industries, and the economy. The expansion of the job market was fueled by the hundreds of jobs created by the construction of the first transcontinental railroad, completed in 1869, and subsequent railroads. The railroad industry stimulated the economy by requiring enormous quantities of manufactured goods, such as iron and steel. New jobs created more capital for investing and fueled the growth of the market economy. In the following article, George Rogers Taylor and Irene D. Neu describe the growth of the railroads and the impact they had on American society and economy. Taylor and Neu are coauthors of *The American Railroad Network, 1861–1890*.

T he American economy, already expanding rapidly before the Civil War, continued growing with almost explosive force during the following decades. In 1860 the United States was a secondary industrial nation among the nations of the world. Before the end of the century it had achieved a position of preëminence. Its pig iron production just prior to the war was only a small fraction of that of Great Britain, and steelmaking had hardly begun. Before the end of the century the American output of both products exceeded that of any other country. It has been estimated that in 1860 the value of manufactured goods in each of the three leading countries, the United Kingdom, France, and Germany, was greater than in the United States. By 1890 the United States had not only moved into first place, but the value of its manufactures nearly equaled the combined output of the three former leaders.

TECHNOLOGICAL IMPROVEMENTS

Fundamental improvements in railroad transportation were among the major factors making possible the post–Civil War expansion. . . . Technological improvements in rails, roadbed, motive power, and rolling stock came in rapid succession. Steel rails, first used in this country during the Civil War, replaced the much less satisfactory iron ones. Stronger rails, roadbed, and bridges made possible the use of heavier engines and cars. In 1860 locomotives seldom weighed more than about 30 tons whereas by 1890 they might weigh as much as 85 tons. Standard capacity for freight cars, about 10 tons in 1860, had doubled by the early eighties, while a few cars of even greater capacity were already in use. A host of other developments facilitated railroad operations: the automatic coupler, the air brake, improved terminal facilities, increased use of the telegraph, and the adoption of the block system for controlling traffic. Freight locomotives on the Pennsylvania Railroad hauled on the average 2,100,000 ton miles of freight in 1870, but were handling 5,100,000 such units per annum eleven years later.

This was the period of most rapid construction of new track. In 1860 there were 30,626 miles of railway in operation in the United States and 2,065 miles in Canada. The total for the two countries combined grew to about 175,000 in 1890. Before the war only one railroad had reached the Missouri River. During the following three decades transcontinental lines were completed in both the United States and Canada, and a great network had been constructed not only in the Mississippi Valley west of the river, but also in Texas, in the Mountain States, and on the Pacific coast. Even in the older area east of the Mississippi and the Great Lakes, track mileage continued to grow as gaps were filled in, bridges built, and roads constructed parallel to existing ones.

RAILROAD EMPIRES

This was the period also when smaller companies were consolidated into extensive railroad systems, and when such men as Cornelius Vanderbilt, Jay Gould, and Collis P. Huntington were building their great railroad empires. Cutthroat competition put heavy pressure on railroad rates, especially in trunk-line territory. In 1858 the rate for shipping wheat by rail from Chicago to New York was 38.61 cents a bushel; in 1870 it had fallen to 26.11 cents; and in 1890 to 14.3. The average rate per ton mile charged by United States railroads just after the Civil War was 1.925 cents. This had fallen to .941 in 1890. But the decline was far from uniform, for rates tended to remain relatively high where there was little competition from other rail lines or from waterways. Where parallel roads competed for traffic, as between Chicago and New York, rates were at times kept up by interline agreements. When these broke down, charges fell drastically, sometimes well below operating costs. Railroad competition proved a crushing blow to most inland water routes. Though traffic continued to grow on the Great Lakes and the Sault Canal, the weaker canals had succumbed to railroad competition during the forties and fifties. Before the eighties were over, the tonnage carried had reached its high point even on such major water routes as the Mississippi River and the Erie Canal.

Tremendous popular enthusiasm for the railroads led to grants of millions of acres of public land and extensive financial aid by federal, state, and local governments. But following the Civil

Railroad workers and officials celebrate the completion of the first transcontinental railroad on May 10, 1869, in Promontory, Utah.

War, and especially after 1873, public opinion gradually turned against the railroads. Stock watering, secret rebates, pooling agreements, political bribery, scandals like the Credit Mobilier exposé, and the public-be-damned attitude of railroad magnates gave rise to anti-railroad agitation by farmers, merchants, and investor groups. Criticism of the railroads took political form in the Granger [a coalition of farmers that protested monopolistic grain transport practices] and Anti-Monopoly movements. Efforts at state regulation were followed in 1887 by the adoption of the federal Interstate Commerce Commission Act [which made the railroads the first industry subject to federal legislation].

The very importance of the railroad in the development of the American economy has tended to obscure the fact that it was itself affected at every stage by the economic environment in which it grew. While no general survey of these environmental factors will be attempted, this study does seek to identify the influences which were active first in erecting and then in removing barriers to the creation of a physically integrated system of national railroad transportation. First, the condition of the uncoördinated railroad net of 1861 will be examined; then, some of the important steps by which during the following three decades it evolved into a truly integrated work will be traced.

THE DOMINANCE OF LOCAL INTERESTS TO 1861

During the nineteenth century there took place in this country a gradual transition from merchant to industrial and finance capitalism. This was a development which profoundly altered the practices and the outlook of the business community. On the one hand the railroads helped to effect this change; on the other their growth was significantly affected by it.

While the merchant-dominated capitalism of the eighteenth century was a decaying institution during the early decades of the following century, the parochial viewpoint which it engendered in the business leaders of the day toward transportation development prevailed until about the time of the Civil War. While merchants ruled the American economy they constituted a business and social elite. From their counting houses they organized and directed the exchange of goods and services in both domestic and foreign trade. Largely unspecialized in function, they brought together and arranged into an effective pattern the threads of an increasingly complex exchange economy. The great merchants not only bought and sold goods in large and small quantities on their own account or for others in the capacity of brokers, factors, or agents, but also performed a host of other services. They were bankers and dealers in foreign trade; they owned ships, docks, and warehouses; they bought and sold marine insurance; they held title to and sometimes operated fishing, mining, or manufacturing ventures; and they became the chief real-estate owners and speculators of their day.

The prosperity of the merchant depended in large part upon the volume of the commerce in his home port and upon the trade carried by his ships and distributed from his own warehouses. The leaders were located in the great ports of the Atlantic coast, which had become in the Colonial period important centers of world trade. Here the products of Europe, Africa, and the East, as well as those from the many smaller coastal towns on the Atlantic and the Gulf of Mexico, were assembled, and then in considerable part reëxported to foreign and domestic markets. This trade expanded greatly during the Napoleonic Wars, when, not infrequently, more than half the commerce of New York, Philadelphia, and Boston consisted of reëxports to foreign markets.

Following the defeat of Napoleon in 1815, the relative importance of the foreign reëxport trade declined. But coastwise commerce greatly expanded and trade with the interior grew as the frontier was pushed outward. There ensued a competitive struggle among the merchants of rival cities who were striving to capture as large a share as possible of the rapidly expanding trade of the hinterland. This intercity competition to dominate the inland trade was an important factor in the early decades of railroad development.

THE FIRST RAILROADS

The first railroads in the United States were built, as were most of the early turnpikes and canals, to serve nearby and local needs. Such was the purpose of the early lines radiating from Boston. The Boston and Worcester, for instance, was designed primarily to secure for Boston the trade of the Worcester area and to divert it from the Blackstone Canal which led to Providence. The little railroads strung out along the Mohawk Valley in New York were constructed for the most part with local capital to provide local transportation for nearby merchants and farmers. The early railroads of eastern Pennsylvania were financed and built largely by owners of coal lands who sought to make possible the movement of anthracite to New York and Pennsylvania markets. The 4½-mile Pontchartrain Railroad, completed in Louisiana in 1831, was designed merely to facilitate movement between New Orleans and the lake of that name.

As the possibilities of railway transportation became more clearly recognized, the roads were looked upon by the business groups in each large city chiefly as devices for forwarding their own interests. Rival groups therefore encouraged the building of lines which widened their own market areas, while they carefully avoided any development which might benefit the merchants of another city. New York and Boston were competitors for the commerce of the Great Lakes and the Erie Canal, as were Troy and Albany on a smaller scale. Charleston sought to divert the cotton trade from Savannah, and Chicago and St. Louis fought for the rich commerce of the upper Mississippi.

A report of a special committee of the Select and Common Council of Philadelphia, urging that the city government invest generously in the stock of the proposed Pennsylvania Railroad, is illustrative of the competition among merchant groups in the pre–Civil War period. The committee declared, in part:

> No one can shut his eyes to the fact, that the enterprise involves, for weal or for woe, the future prospects of Philadelphia. The trade of this city, already retarded by improvements on the North and the South, will be so curtailed by the Baltimore and Ohio Railroad at Pittsburg, and the completion of the railway from New York to Lake Erie, as to drain the public works, and impoverish the city and state. Labour among us will want its reward, business will stagnate, capital will desert our borders, and following this desertion of trade, the interest of the debt of the commonwealth will be unpaid! On the other hand, we have the means, by furnishing the nearest and best route to and from the West, of securing an unexampled prosperity to this city. Our *citizens* will not only be enriched, but the real estate and property of the *corporation* will be enhanced beyond the amount of the proposed subscription.

THE INTEGRATION OF THE RAILROAD NET, 1861–1890

During and following the Civil War, the railroads came to be regarded less as agencies designed to serve the exclusive needs of a particular city or its immediate back country and more as a coördinated network whose primary function was to facilitate transportation. Though parochial interests lingered on and have, indeed, persisted to the present time, they came to be over-shadowed by larger, national considerations.

The Civil War itself brought a changed view of the role of the railroads. The need for through movement of troops and supplies focused attention on variations in gauge and on the lack of connections between railroads in the leading cities of both the North and the South. The exigencies of war highlighted the advantages which could be had from a standardized and interconnected railroad system. But military requirements merely reënforced a movement which was gathering momentum in any case.

As long as population and agricultural production remained centered largely in the seaboard states, pressure for a more integrated railway system and better interstate rail connections was not great. But as the rapid settlement of the frontier continued and when, with the onset of the Civil War, the West began sending a veritable flood of food and animal products eastward and importing manufactured products in exchange, the demand for cheap and expeditious through shipment by rail over long distances became irresistible. Shippers of western products sought favorable rates without preference for particular cities or their captive railroads. Similarly, producers and distributers of manufactured products outgrew the nearby market and began to see the prospects of a national outlet for their products. Isolated railroads which had seemed earlier to offer the advantage of a protected market, now came to be regarded as barriers to profitable commercial relations with more distant areas.

INVESTING IN RAILROADS

At the same time that the market was expanding so prodigiously, the attitude toward railroads as an investment underwent a substantial change. At least until some time in the fifties, funds for railroad development, as we have seen, had come chiefly from local sources, whether private or public. The incentive for investment was less the hope of direct returns from the railroads themselves than a belief that indirect benefits would inure to local producers, property owners, and merchants. During the fifties and increasingly thereafter, the motive for investment shifted more and more to a desire for direct returns: for profits derived from the issue or purchase of railroad securities and from railroad promotion, consolidation, and security manipulation. This development was accompanied by the rise of strong financial interests, especially in Boston and New York, the growth of stock exchanges and specialized banking institutions, and the emergence of so-called "finance capitalism." Both investors and promoters, now looking far beyond the local market areas, sought the profits to be gained from the railroad lines which benefited any part of the continent. . . .

In the age of limited markets before the Civil War the forces of competition led to the building of railroads designed to serve the exclusive needs of each of the great market cities. The result was an uncoördinated railroad patchwork. Later, this patchwork was converted into a well-integrated network. Under the leadership of financiers and promoters whose interests transcended local loyalties, there emerged a national economy which, on the one hand, was made possible by the railroads, and which, on the other, moulded the railroads themselves into a unified transportation system.

IMMIGRATION

MARK WAHLGREN SUMMERS

In the following article, history professor Mark Wahlgren Summers describes the massive immigration that took place during the Gilded Age and its impact on American society. Between 1865 and 1890 nearly 10 million immigrants settled permanently in the United States. Although most of the immigrants were from northwestern Europe, many of them hailed from China. Most immigrants were drawn to America because of tales of streets paved with gold and immense potential for wealth. Although most of the tales were exaggerated, America did offer foreigners more opportunities than their homelands did. America offered the possibility of landownership to peasants who had spent their lives working and tilling other men's farms. With the growth of industry came hundreds of jobs for immigrants who had known famine and starvation. However, many immigrants lived in poverty-stricken shanties and experienced racism and xenophobia from Americans who were born in the United States. Although most newcomers benefited from immigration, issues of poverty and racism delayed their assimilation into American society.

America could not escape from the world but there were times when it seemed that the world was escaping to America. As the nineteenth century's last decade began, 42 percent of New York City's people were foreign-born, as were 41 percent of Chicago's, and 37 percent of Minneapolis's. More than one Minnesotan in three was born abroad, 29 percent of Massachusetts residents, and 22 percent of Illinois's. By 1910, one American in seven was of foreign birth. It was not surprising that the Statue of Liberty standing in New York's harbor

Excerpted from *The Gilded Age* by Mark Wahlgren Summers (Upper Saddle River, NJ: Prentice-Hall, 1997). Copyright © 1997 by Prentice-Hall, Inc. Reprinted with permission.

should have been, from its completion in 1886, less a symbol of the open society than of the open door, nor that even those who were immigrants themselves should feel misgivings over their perception of the door as being too widely ajar. "Give me your tired, your poor," read Emma Lazarus's poem inscribed on the base of the statue,

> Your huddled masses yearning to breathe free,
> The wretched refuse of your teeming shore;
> Send the homeless, tempest tost to me,
> I lift my hand beside the golden door.

The "wretched refuse" themselves might have appreciated the sentiment more than the description, even from a poet only six weeks in this country.

WHY THEY CAME

Two things made this great migration unsettling to those already here. The first was its size. Between 1877 and 1890, more than 6.3 million people immigrated to America, and between 1900 and 1906, nearly as many again. In forty years, fully 23 million Europeans came across the seas. The second was the newcomers' place of origin. Until 1896, most of the immigrants either shared the English language or Protestant religion of those already here. Out of the British Isles they came, out of Germany and Scandinavia. The so-called "Old Immigration" kept coming, but after 1880, their ranks were mixed with a breed more alien in language and religion: laborers from southern Italy, as well as refugees from the empires of Turkey and Russia that stretched from the Baltic to the Black Sea and westward to the Aegean. Many of the "New Immigration" were Jewish or Eastern Orthodox. Even the Catholics of Lithuania and Poland practiced their faith in ways unfamiliar to the clergy already here. In 1880, immigrants from southern and eastern Europe numbered less than a quarter of a million; in the thirty years that followed, 8.4 million more of them emigrated. By 1907, they counted for five of every six who came.

Why did they come? For many, an intensifying bigotry at home made them look abroad for refuge. The nationalism uniting Germany and Italy in the midcentury affected the great Russian empire in quite a different way. There, the czars presided over "Russification," to impose one culture on a multitude of subject peoples. In the Polish provinces, Russian authorities attacked the Catholic church, on the steppes, the Mennonites, but everywhere they gave special attention to the Jews. Lawbooks bulged with restrictions on their rights: 650, by one count. Mobs sacked the Jewish *shtetls*, raped the women, killed the children, burned the temples of Israel, and shredded the word of the Lord. While the pogrom raged, police simply watched. Afterwards, they might escort the rioters to the next ghetto to continue their work. Czarist officials wrote and published as fact the Protocols of the Elders of Zion, a supposed Jewish blueprint for world conquest. Two years of violence left some thousand Jews killed and many more wounded. The message was plain: the Russian empire had no place for keepers of the faith.

New nations needed armies. They did more than recruit— they drafted. When the conscription officer's knock on the door could mean twenty-five years' service in Russia, twelve in Austria-Hungary, residents had the strongest incentives to run for their lives.

NEW FREEDOMS AND OPPORTUNITIES

At the same time, new freedoms made emigration more possible than before. Until 1860, the empires of southern and eastern Europe, and the Far East, forbade their subjects to leave. The birth of Italy brought the death of restrictive laws down the peninsula. In 1867, the Austro-Hungarian authorities loosened the bonds, and with the Russo-Turkish War of 1877, the Turks lost their grip on most of the Balkans, and the gates lay open to them.

Want uprooted the settled peasants of Europe, a want, curiously enough, brought about because, in so many ways, life at home had never been better. More children than ever lived past their infancy. But more people meant less land for the father to divide among his sons and less food on the table. Between 1860 and 1910, population in eastern central Europe grew more than 75 percent. Farmland did not increase anywhere near as much. If work was to be found for all, some must be ready to go wherever else in the world it was being offered.

For consumers, the industrial revolution had brought a new plenty, but it plunged many producers into crisis. Grain from Kansas could undersell the produce of Italy, even in Calabria. The landlord of central Europe found that with the latest threshers and reapers, he could do the work of a dozen tenant families, at a fraction of the cost. Why leave them on the land at all? When steam-driven engines in Boston could turn out shoes so cheaply,

Kiev's Jewish cobbler might have trouble finding buyers.

Old ties loosened less because of hardship than from a new sense of possibilities. Before, a peasant might endure anything, convinced that suffering was the lot of man and work simply a duty ordained by God. It was too much to expect that labor would lead to landownership or savings, or a rise in social class. With the industrial revolution and the end of serfdom in central Europe, the situation changed. Now, bettering oneself *did* seem possible. Especially for those already on the move seeking work, that sense of possibilities must have been particularly strong. If a day's journey would turn up a job with a better income to it than anything the local village could provide, what could a week's journey produce—or two week's, to the New World? That know-how to which Americans contributed so much, that capitalism which Americans liked to see as their special way of thinking, both uprooted the Europeans and set them on the road. . . .

HARSH REALITIES

To [many immigrants], the New World proved a hard, demanding land, and the promise one paid in clipped coin. Those raised in villages must have found city life a harsh adjustment. "My disappointment was unspeakable," a Galician later recalled of his arrival at Johnstown: "squalid and ugly, with those congested shabby houses, blackened with soot from the factory chimneys—this was the America I saw." The smell alone was an unwelcome novelty, enough, as a New Yorker said, "to knock you down." Urban space was too valuable to allot much of it to working-class apartments; there were sure to be too many wedged into too small an area. So in the poorer section of town, one might find four, five, even six-story walkups, the "block of flats" accommodating dozens of families. Overcrowding could be overwhelming. Along Cherry Street in New York, experts estimated the population at 5.6 per apartment. In Boston's North End, where Italians lived in squalor, three or four shared a bed. Neither there nor elsewhere was there privacy to be found. Naturally, with epidemics carried so easily, the death rates in the tenements were appalling. At their worst, New York's slums had a mortality rate 80 percent higher than the national average of 20 per thousand. For slum children, it was 136 per thousand. In Chicago, one child in two died before reaching a fifth birthday. Parts of New York City were known as "lung blocks" because of the sweatshops and tuberculosis that were rampant.

Immigrants were welcomed as cheap labor and used against each other. Each new wave served as strikebreakers against the wave before. So many foreigners came that, in some industries, they drove the wages down below the level of subsistence. A semiskilled worker in the garment trade made fifteen dollars a week in 1883, and less than half that in 1885. Women earned as little as three dollars. The unskilled suffered most of the occupational death and injury, and newcomers stood a better chance of finding jobs in the unskilled labor force than did the skilled. As a result, the roster of those killed on the job in Steelton in 1907 read like the rolls of an eastern European village: Tesak, Pajolic, Stifko, Szep, Susic. "Before I came to America," an Italian joke ran, "I was told that the streets were paved with gold. When I got here, I found out three things. First, the streets were not paved with gold. Second, they were not paved at all. Third, they expected me to pave them."

America required adjustments. Parents and children, wives and husbands, ended years of separation to discover themselves strangers. Occasionally, marriages dissolved, sometimes in divorce and sometimes with no more than another notice in one immigrant paper's "Gallery of Vanished Men." Peasants accustomed to barter found themselves at a loss in stores where prices were fixed. Those wanting to honor the Jewish Sabbath usually could not find jobs that gave them Saturdays off. Religious life that had centered on the synagogue now shifted to the home, with greater obligations on family members to keep the faith. "The whole American life was strange to me," one woman lamented. From knowing everything back at school in Russia, she had come to a place where everyone understood more than she. "All the wrong side up," immigrants grumbled. "The children are fathers to their fathers. The fathers children to their children."

Under the circumstances, it would not have been surprising had many of the immigrants gone home in despair, and not just as commuters having earned their pay. Some did. Would he emigrate from Ireland again, given the chance, someone asked a miner in the Pennsylvania coal fields. Bitter words flew back: "I would buy a ticket for hell rather than here." Yet most immigrants who came planning to stay did so, and not simply because, like the Russian Jews, there was nothing to go back to.

Hardship or no, America offered a chance. The more modest the newcomer's dreams, the more likely they were to be fulfilled. A Swedish farmhand just after the Civil War could make thirty cents a day at home. For the same work, he might make seventy cents in Minnesota, and in harvest season, four dollars. Hungarians and Slovaks compared their modest gains—an acre or two of land, "city" food and readymade clothing—to the comforts of home and were well content. "We had very little," a Pole remembered, "but there was more of this bread here than there, and something on this bread, too." Even the wooden floor of a tenement beat the dirt floor of a shanty. Newcomers knew poverty, not famine. If those left behind had any doubt, they found conviction in a second migration, the migration of money into central Europe. In 1906, the postmaster of Centinje saw thirty thousand dollars in money orders pass through his hands. Other immigrants simply stuffed cash into the envelopes; nearly forty million dollars passed back to Croatia in twelve years. . . .

AMERICANIZATION

Immigrants were Americanizing, sometimes without being aware of it. The first signs were the most obvious. Immigration officials, unable to spell the names given to them, made Wahlgrens into Greens, Lapiscarellas into Carrells. To fit in, foreigners adapted their names as well. Francesco became Frank, Rivka Ruth. Making an Old World name into its English equivalent (for example, Piccolo into Little) was no great step, but some immigrants went further, as a Cincinnati shop sign attested: "Kelley and Ryan, Italian bakers.". . .

The newcomers to America *had* to change. The land itself required it, and American capitalism—with its glistening shops, its consumer culture, its celebration of technology—transformed foreigners as inexorably as it did the country's native sons. Scandinavian loggers headed for Minnesota's forests, while her farmers headed for the state's pastureland. But the hardscrabble life on Scandinavian mountain farms gave newcomers no preparation for the prairie. Everything differed, said one newcomer, except the fleas. Back home, farmers grew cabbages, not corn, barley, or wheat. Penniless Scandinavians hired themselves out to Yankee farmers at a pittance, not just to raise the down payment on land, but to learn American methods for growing an American crop. Wives may have been equal partners in making a living back in Norway, but with the adoption of American machinery, tasks once done by women, such as haying, became a manly prerogative. So did milking and tending the animals, to the disgust of husbands, many of whom had difficulties keeping the milk from going out of the udder and up their sleeves. If women resented losing the privilege of serving as field hands or being restricted to more middle-class and motherly tasks, they kept complaints to themselves. Jewish wives, accustomed to working while their husbands pursued scholarship in Old World communities, found themselves ready and able to work—and their husbands ever more determined to keep them at home like American wives (even if this meant sewing and pressing piecework around the kitchen table rather than earning a wage in the factory).

Even the most commonplace tasks were made anew. Everything from cooking to cleaning changed when peasants moved from farmhouses to tenements. Windows and wood floors were there to be washed; instead of taking food out of the garden, there were trips to the market. There was no root cellar, no storage space for foods in the city. Milk, bread, and virtually everything else had to be bought every day. . . .

Americanization must keep going on, if the foreign-born wanted to advance in the society around them. The only questions were, how much, and on whose terms? From within the immigrant community itself came the pressure to learn enough about the land of their adoption to get along. Mothers set in the old ways wanted their daughters to learn American habits. Some parents even forbade the children to bring home any books but those in English. Institutions helped families assimilate on their own terms. Jews on the Lower East Side of New York turned to Isidor Straus's Educational Alliance. They could take classes in English, or attend lectures on American government taught in Yiddish. If they read the Yiddish press, they might study the features on the geography, education, and government of the United States. From 1897 on, the New York *Tageblatt* provided a page in English that translated the most difficult words into Yiddish equivalents. Yet the forces resisting immediate change were strong, and as long as immigrant communities had thriving institutions, they added to the resistance. A Yiddish newspaper and a Yiddish theater helped keep separate those people not eager to fit in on the terms that their fellow believers "uptown" had arranged. Differences over how far to change the traditional rituals to adapt to city life gave rise to Conservative and Reformed branches of Judaism, just as it splintered Swedish Lutherans. But perhaps the greatest encouragement toward keeping separate from America was the "golden door" that Emma Lazarus immortalized. For most foreigners, it stood wide open. Immigrants knew they could go home, and many planned to do so. Newcomers kept coming. As long as those conditions held, Old World customs would be worth holding onto, and would get a constant refreshing from the latest arrivals. Just possibly, full assimilation would never have happened without immigration restriction. . . .

ENEMIES WITHIN THE GATES?

Immigration changed Americans' lives for the better in many ways, and for the worse in some, but on any terms, change added more disturbance to a world already being transformed by the machine makers and money getters. As natives of the old Protestant stock saw it, the republic needed more than a common set of laws. It depended on a shared cultural heritage: widely held values and an understanding of American traditions. With neither language, religion, nor blood in common, a nation of immigrants would turn into a federation of ethnic enclaves, just made for strife and demagoguery. By the mid-1880s, dark fears were being voiced. "Crime and ignorance and superstition" seemed to land by the boatload—the "dregs of all foreign countries." Businessmen blamed labor violence on newcomers; workers blamed them for low wages. Prejudice dogged all newcomers from beyond the British Isles. Some of it was gentle stereotyping: Italians all ate macaroni, had dark eyes, hot passions, and an inextinguishable love for song. But the stereotypes got darker very quickly as the number of Italians increased. Stiletto—vendetta—brigand—Mafia—such words summed up the entire culture to those who kept the real newcomer at arm's distance. Ignorance could be seen as stupidity. One joke explained why all Italians were called Tony: because when they got to this country, their caps always had a card in them to guide them to their destination, labeled "To NY."

A new, more virulent streak of anti-Semitism surfaced, but showed itself mostly as contempt. Catholics, by contrast, inspired terror. To Protestants, the religion conjured images of tyranny and persecution across the ages, and of voters marching in lockstep to the tune that the Pope played in Rome. Talemongers spread whoppers, all of which found believers: that 72 percent of all desertions in the Civil War were Catholic, for example. The Inquisition already had set up its courts and black-hooded judges in America, one author warned. "For the present it 'tolerates'; it will burn whenever it will be safe to burn." Starting in 1887, the American Protective Association claimed a million members by the mid-1890s. Across the Midwest, it harassed Catholics as far as it dared. Members promised never to hire Catholic employees or join them on a picket line. Crowds stoned Catholic picnickers, petitioners forced school boards to fire Catholic teachers. Phony documents circulated, pretending to be Papal decrees setting the time for worshippers to rise up and kill their Protestant neighbors. So tense were relations in Toledo that the mayor bought Winchester rifles with which to arm Protestants.

Fear of foreigners set second-generation immigrants against the newer arrivals, and against each other. The very Catholic religion that Irish and Italians shared split them apart, right down to their taste in cathedral architecture. As the two immigrant groups vied for day-laborers' jobs, antagonism turned to open war, brawls in the streets, and fistfights in the alleys. Italian chestnut vendors were driven out of business, and the "dago" or "wop" who passed through the doors of an Irish-American saloon was just asking for it. German Jews greeted the first Russian Jews with distrust, even contempt, and dubbed them "kikes," because so many of their names ended in -ky or -ki. "What can we do with those wild Asiatics?" the *American Hebrew* asked.

Not every prejudice turns into a pogrom, and the nativism that stigmatized did not destroy foreigners. One Russian Jew remembered first seeing Manhattan decked in Christmas lights, and felt nothing but wonder. Here was a Christian's holiday, "and people were going in the streets and nothing happening and you didn't have to be afraid. And nobody told you that you killed their God." Still, the sting was there, in the cartoons of shrugging Jewish old-clothes dealers, planning to burn their business for the insurance, or wearing noses big enough to carry in a wheelbarrow. . . .

End, then, not with Emma Lazarus, but with a native poet, Thomas Bailey Aldrich. Not for him the lifted hand beside the golden door:

> Wide open and unguarded stand our gates,
> And through them presses a wild motley throng—

Men from the Volga and the Tartar steppes,
Featureless figures of the Hoang-Ho,
Malayan, Scythian, Teuton, Kelt, and Slav,
Flying the Old World's poverty and scorn;
These bringing with them unknown gods and rites,
Those tiger passions, here to stretch their claws.
In street and alley what strange tongues are loud,
Accents of menace alien to our air,
Voices that once the Tower of Babel knew!

O, Liberty, white Goddess! is it well
To leave the gates unguarded?

. . .

   Have a care
Lest from thy brow the clustered stars be torn
And trampled in the dust. For so of old
The thronging Goth and Vandal trampled Rome,
And where the temples of the Caesars stood
The lean wolf unmolested made her lair.

THE CHINESE EXCLUSION ACT

ANONYMOUS

The large wave of immigration that occurred in the years 1865 to 1890, termed the New Immigration, brought intense racism and xenophobia to the coasts of the United States. At the time of the gold rush in 1849, China suffered economic hardship and poverty, and thousands of Chinese workers immigrated to America as "coolies," or indentured servants who settled in California. They inspired racism in Americans because they were strangers, they kept to themselves, they worked hard, and they were successful. Because the Chinese worked for low wages, American laborers and miners thought that the Chinese threatened their jobs. After thirty years of progressively worsening racism, Congress passed the Chinese Exclusion Act of 1882. The act suspended Chinese immigration for ten years, and prohibited Chinese laborers from remaining in the United States for more than ninety days. In 1892, the Geary Act extended the Chinese Exclusion Act for another ten years, and the Extension Act of 1904 made the exclusion of the Chinese from the United States permanent. The act was not repealed until 1943. The following article is an anonymous editorial published in *Harper's Weekly* that denounces the Chinese Exclusion Act as unconstitutional and unfair to the Chinese.

R epresentative Zachary Taylor, the successor in the House of General James A. Garfield, made an admirable speech against the Chinese bill during the late debate, in which he exposed the singular inconsistency of the arguments ad-

From "The Chinese Bill," by Anonymous, *Harper's Weekly*, April 1, 1882.

vanced to sustain it. The Chinese are represented in one breath as a rotten race, the victims of hideous immorality, and in the next as a people who are going to drive intelligent and sturdy American laborers out of the field. At one moment every man, woman, and child on the Pacific coast loathes and detests the leprous interlopers, and the next the same protesting people neglect the honest American and intrust the care of their homes and of their children to the leprous pariahs because they can be hired more cheaply. They are alleged to be a class of persons who will never assimilate with us like other foreigners. But those who assert this forget to state that our laws prevent assimilation by making the Chinese incapable of naturalization. Moreover, if they are so disreputable and dangerous and degrading, and if the Pacific population is so unanimously opposed to their coming, that population has an obvious and easy remedy in its own hands. It has only to refuse to hire the lepers, and they will come no longer. Part of the complaint is that they do not wish to stay longer than will enable them to pick up a little money. The hope of wages alone unwillingly brings them. If they can get no wages, they will be only too glad to stay at home.

MOTIVES OF EXCLUSION

The only ground upon which the bill prohibiting the voluntary immigration of free laborers into this country can be sustained is self-defense. Every nation may justly decide for itself what foreigners it will tolerate, and upon what terms. But the honor and character of the nation will be tested by the motives of exclusion. Thus in 1803 a bill passed Congress which prohibited bringing to the country certain negro and mulatto immigrants. But it was a bill which sprang from the fears of slave-holders, and which was intended to protect slavery. In the same year South Carolina repealed her State law prohibiting the slave-trade. The objection was to black freemen, not to black slaves; and it is not legislation to which an American can recur with pride, because it was an inhuman abuse of an undoubted national right. We may, unquestionably, determine who shall come, and upon what conditions, as we may decide upon what terms the new-comers shall be naturalized. Against a palpable peril arising from the advent of foreigners, we may justly defend ourselves. Now [from 1857 to 1882] the Chinese immigration—and a large part of it was cooly [indentured servant] traffic—amounted to 228,000 persons, of which more than a hundred thousand have returned, so that by the census of 1880 the Chinese population in the country was 105,000. "All the Chinese in California," says Senator George Hoar, "hardly surpass the number which is easily governed in Shanghai by a police of a hundred men." Considering the traditional declaration of our pride and patriotism that America is the home for the oppressed of every clime and race, considering the spirit of our constitutional provision that neither race, color, nor previous condition of servitude shall bar a citizen from voting, is it not both monstrous and ludicrous to decree that American civilization is endangered by the "Mongolian invasion?"

For the Republican party, which is responsible for national legislation, the simple question is, whether a free laborer who wishes to come to this country for a time and work honestly for honest wages shall be prohibited from coming, lest China should be precipitated upon Western America and overwhelm the New World. Can any such peril or the chance of it be inferred from the facts? Senator John Jones, of Nevada, speaks of the colored race. But that race was brought here by force and fraud. It is not a migratory race. So the Mongolians are not migratory. The coming of 230,000 or 240,000 Chinese in a quarter of a century, and the presence of 100,000 in the country at the end of that time, are not the precursor of an overwhelming invasion. The bill is founded on race hatred and panic. These are both familiar facts even in this country. It is not a very long time since one of the most familiar objections to the antislavery movement was that the fanatics wanted to free the "nay-gurs," who would immediately overrun the North and supplant the Irish. It was mere panic. We have always invited everybody to come and settle among us, because the chance of bettering his condition was fairer here than anywhere else in the world. If we now exercise our right to select new-comers, not upon great public considerations the truth of which is demonstrated, but because of race hatred, or of honest labor competition, or fear of local disorder, the movement will not stop there. The native American crusade of twenty-five years ago was another form of the same spirit. Senator James George was logical in his implication that if a whole race may be excluded from the national domain because of a local desire, a whole enfranchised class may be excluded from the suffrage for the same reason. Mr. Taylor said of the Chinese bill: "It revolutionizes our traditions. I would deem the new country we will have after this bill becomes law as changed from the old country we have to-day as our country would have been changed if the rebellion of 1861 had succeeded." The exclusion bill has passed Congress by a large majority. Public opinion seems to favor it, as it has often favored unwise legislation. Even the amendment to try the experiment of exclusion for ten years failed. It is not probable that there will be a veto, and the only benefit to be anticipated is that, as we have now decided to regulate immigration, we shall exclude every class whose coming can not be considered to be advantageous to the national welfare.

THE KNIGHTS OF LABOR

TERENCE V. POWDERLY

The Industrial Revolution in the Gilded Age fostered the growth of factories and hundreds of new jobs. This, in turn, brought more efficient and cheaper means of production. Unskilled and assembly line workers were poorly paid and easily replaceable. Because unskilled workers were so numerous and expendable, employers wielded considerable control over the hours, wages, benefits, and personal lives of their employees. In response to unfavorable working conditions, many workers formed labor unions and lobbied for eight-hour workdays, higher wages, and safer working environments. The following article is the Preamble adopted by the Knights of Labor, the first major labor organization in the United States. The author, Terence V. Powderly, was the founder of the Knights of Labor.

The recent alarming development and aggression of aggregated wealth, which, unless checked, will inevitably lead to the pauperization and hopeless degradation of the toiling masses, render it imperative, if we desire to enjoy the blessings of life, that a check should be placed upon its power and upon unjust accumulation, and a system adopted which will secure to the laborer the fruits of his toil; and as this much-desired object can only be accomplished by the thorough unification of labor, and the united efforts of those who obey the divine injunction that "In the sweat of thy brow shalt thou eat bread," we have formed the * * * * * [Knights of Labor] with a view of securing the organization and direction, by co-operative

Excerpted from *Thirty Years of Labor* by Terence V. Powderly (New York: Augustus M. Kelley, 1967).

effort, of the power of the industrial classes; and we submit to the world the objects sought to be accomplished by our organization, calling upon all who believe in securing "the greatest good to the greatest number" to aid and assist us:

I. To bring within the folds of organization every department of productive industry, making knowledge a standpoint for action, and industrial and moral worth, not wealth, the true standard of individual and national greatness.

II. To secure to the toilers a proper share of the wealth that they create; more of the leisure that rightfully belongs to them; more societary advantages; more of the benefits, privileges and emoluments of the world; in a word, all those rights and privileges necessary to make them capable of enjoying, appreciating, defending and perpetuating the blessings of good government.

III. To arrive at the true condition of the producing masses in their educational, moral and financial condition, by demanding from the various governments the establishment of Bureaus of Labor Statistics.

IV. The establishment of co-operative institutions, productive and distributive.

V. The reserving of the public lands—the heritage of the people—for the actual settler; not another acre for railroads or speculators.

VI. The abrogation of all laws that do not bear equally upon capital and labor, the removal of unjust technicalities, delays and discriminations in the administration of justice, and the adopting of measures providing for the health and safety of those engaged in mining, manufacturing or building pursuits.

VII. The enactment of laws to compel chartered corporations to pay their employes weekly, in full, for labor performed during the preceding week, in the lawful money of the country.

VIII. The enactment of laws giving mechanics and laborers a first lien on their work for their full wages.

IX. The abolishment of the contract system on national, State and municipal work.

X. The substitution of arbitration for strikes, whenever and wherever employers and employees are willing to meet on equitable grounds.

XI. The prohibition of the employment of children in workshops, mines and factories before attaining their fourteenth year.

XII. To abolish the system of letting out by contract the labor of convicts in our prisons and reformatory institutions.

XIII. To secure for both sexes equal pay for equal work.

XIV. The reduction of the hours of labor to eight per day, so that the laborers may have more time for social enjoyment and intellectual improvement, and be enabled to reap the advantages conferred by the labor-saving machinery which their brains have created.

XV. To prevail upon governments to establish a purely national circulating medium, based upon the faith and resources of the nation, and issued directly to the people, without the intervention of any system of banking corporations, which money shall be a legal tender in payment of all debts, public or private.

WOMEN'S SUFFRAGE

The women's suffrage movement began in the mid–nineteenth century and gained momentum in the Gilded Age. Radical feminists such as Susan B. Anthony and Elizabeth Cady Stanton lectured, lobbied, marched, wrote, and practiced civil disobedience in efforts to attain the vote for women. Susan B. Anthony voted in the presidential election of 1872 and was arrested for ignoring the law denying women the vote. In the following article, written in 1870, feminist Frances Power Cobbe argues that women must dispose of affectations of helplessness to achieve suffrage, and men must accept that women are capable and independent.

There is an instructive story, told by Herodotus, of an African nation which went to war with the South Wind. The wind had greatly annoyed these Psyllians by drying up their cisterns, so they organized a campaign and set off to attack the enemy at head-quarters—somewhere, I presume, about the Sahara. The army was admirably equipped with all the military engines of those days—swords and spears, darts and javelins, battering rams and catapults. It happened that the South Wind did not, however, suffer much from these weapons, but got up one fine morning and blew!—The sands of the desert have lain for a great many ages over those unfortunate Psyllians; and, as Herodotus placidly concludes the story, "The Nasamones possess the territory of those who thus perished."

It seems to me that we women who have been fighting for the Suffrage with logical arguments—syllogisms, analogies, demonstrations, and reductions-to-the-absurd of our antagonists' position, in short, all the weapons of ratiocinative warfare—have been behaving very much like those poor Psyllians,

From *Our Policy: An Address to Women Concerning the Suffrage* by Frances Power Cobbe (London: London National Society for Women's Suffrage, 1870).

who imagined that darts, and swords, and catapults would avail against the Simoon. The obvious truth is, that it is Sentiment we have to contend against, not Reason; Feeling and Prepossession, not intellectual Conviction. Had Logic been the only obstacle in our way, we should long ago have been polling our votes for Parliamentary as well as for Municipal and School Board elections. To those who hold that Property is the thing intended to be represented by the Constitution of England, we have shown that we possess such property. To those who say that Tax-paying and Representation should go together, we have pointed to the tax-gatherers' papers, which, alas! lie on our hall-tables wholly irrespective of the touching fact that we belong to the "protected sex." Where Intelligence, Education, and freedom from crime are considered enough to confer rights of citizenship, we have remarked that we are quite ready to challenge rivalry in such particulars with those Illiterates for whose exercise of political functions our Senate has taken such exemplary care. Finally, to the ever-recurring charge that we cannot fight, and therefore ought not to vote, we have replied that the logic of the exclusion will be manifest when all the men too weak, too short, or too old for the military standard be likewise disfranchised, and when the actual soldiers of our army are accorded the suffrage.

But, as I began by remarking, it is Sentiment, not Logic, against which we have to struggle; and we shall best do so, I think, by endeavouring to understand and make full allowance for it; and they by steadily working shoulder to shoulder so as to conquer, or rather win it over to our side. There is nothing astonishing or blameworthy in the fact that both men and women (women even more than men), when they first hear of the proposal that political action should be shared by both sexes, are startled and shocked. The wonder would be if, after witnessing women's inaction for thousands of years, the set of our brains were not to see them for ever "suckling fools and chronicling small beer." The "hereditary transmission of psychical habits," which Dr. Carpenter talks of, could not fail to leave such an impression; nay, a very short period of seclusion would have sufficed to stamp a prejudice against our ever taking part in public affairs. I had myself the misfortune at one time to consult fourteen eminent surgeons concerning a sprained ankle, and, as a result of that gross imprudence, to pass four of the best years of my life as a miserable cripple upon crutches. At the end of that period, when my friends saw me once more walking erect and free, they unanimously exclaimed, "Oh, do not attempt it! For pity's sake do not go into the street!" One of the tenderest of them even added, almost in tears, "I cannot endure to see you going about without your crutches!" Of course I had much difficulty in persuading these kind people that there was really nothing indecent, or even unladylike, in making use of the limbs wherewith nature had provided me. But I succeeded at last; and so I think women in general will eventually succeed in converting the world to the notion that the faculties bestowed on us by Providence—whether they be great or small—ought all to be used. Humanity might very properly be represented by a man who has all his life used his right hand vigorously, but has kept his left in a sling. Whether the limb were originally weaker than the right, and could not have done as good work, it is not easy to say. It is quite certainly now a poor sinister arm, soft, tender, and without muscular force, and so long accustomed to hang from the neck, that when by chance it is set to work it begins to move in a very nervous and unpractised fashion. Nevertheless, unless any one be prepared to maintain that a man is the better for keeping his left hand tied up, and doing his work with his right alone, it must, I think, be obvious, that this same Humanity will be considerably more happy, and perform its labour more satisfactorily, with two free arms than one.

Releasing the Left Hand

To over the public Sentiment now opposed to it, to this great and portentous emancipation of the Left Hand from its sling, very many different sagacious methods will, I am sure, suggest themselves to my readers. I shall venture merely to offer a few hints, which appear to me most important, regarding, first, the things which we women ought to stop doing and being, and, secondly, the things we ought to begin to do and to be.

For the first, we decidedly ought (as we can) to cease to be silly. It is very tempting, I understand, to be silly, when silliness is obviously infinitely more attractive than sense, and when a sweet little piece of utter folly is received as "so charming" by all who are privileged to hear it. The lady who said (or perhaps did not say) to one of our eminent senators, that "if she had a vote she would sell it directly to the candidate who would give her a pair of diamond ear-rings"—that sweet young thing (if she ever had existence) was no doubt rewarded by the cordial and gallant approbation of the representative of the masculine gender to whom she confided her elevated views. Nevertheless, her silly speech, and the tens of thousands of speeches in the same vein, made in every ball-room in the kingdom, serve, like so many flakes of snow, to hide the ground. The woman who makes one of them with an ingenious simper, generally has her reward in a rapturous smile; but she has done in that moment of folly all that lay in her power to defer a measure of justice on which hangs, more or less directly, the moral and physical welfare of thousands of women.

Nor is it only, or chiefly, by directly scoffing at the demand for Woman Suffrage that silly women hurt our cause. They hurt us much more by showing themselves unfit for it; by perpetuating the delusion that women are so many kittens—charming to play with, but no more fit to be given political rights than [ancient Roman emperor] Caligula's horse to be made a Consul. In looking over an American journal devoted to our interests, I have just fallen on three names in succession, which alone seem (very unjustly no doubt) to place the ladies who are willing to bear them through this serious mortal life, rather in the kittenish than the womanly category. Think of gravely demanding political influence, and then signing oneself as Miss "Mettie" Wauchop, Miss "Lulu" Wilkinson, or Miss "Vinnie" Ream! Silly Dress is a subject so portentous, and on which I feel so little competent to speak, that I shall only remark that, while true taste in attire must always add a pleasant prepossession in favour of everything a woman may ask of right or respect, the style which betrays that hours have been devoted to devising it, is absolutely prohibitive of such consideration. The human soul which has been occupied for an entire morning, like one of poet Alexander Pope's sprites, striving—

> Invention to bestow,
> To change a flounce, or add a furbelow,

has, by the hypothesis, neither leisure nor inclination for the graver and nobler pursuits of a rational being.

FEMININE COURAGE

Another point on which it behooves us women to mend our ways, is the matter of Courage. Men give courage the first place among the virtues, because, without it, there is no guarantee for any other virtue. Assuredly this principle applies no less to women, who, if they be cowards, may be bullied or coerced into every kind of falsehood and baseness, like [humorist Thomas] Ingoldsby's Duchess of Cleves, when her husband pinched her to make her betray her friends—

> His hard iron gauntlet, the flesh went an inch in,
> She didn't mind death, but she couldn't stand pinching.

If we cannot "stand pinching," in more ways than one, slaves we are and slaves we must ever be, whether civil and political rights are given to us or not. When I hear a woman say, with a complacent smile, as if she were announcing an ornament of her reputation, "O, I am such a coward!" I always feel inclined to say, "Indeed? And, may I ask, do you ever go about boasting—'O, I am such a liar?' If you are really a coward you will become a liar any day." Because we have more sensitive nervous systems than men is no reason why honour, and conscience, and self-respect should not teach us to dominate them. I have no doubt there are some virtues, like Temperance, which cost a man more self-control to exercise than they cost a woman, but we do not hold him exonerated on that account if he fail to exert such self-government. We may pity a woman who cannot stop herself from shrieking if a horse runs away, or a boat tosses on the waves; but assuredly we do not feel she is a person to be trusted with an important charge. On the other hand, the sight of a weak, and perhaps sickly or aged woman, calm, silent, and resolute in the face of peril, is a thing never to be forgotten; and the veriest jackanapes alive who expresses his sublime horror of a "strong-minded female" will bless his good fortune that it is in her carriage or boat he is sitting, and not in that of the shrieking Angelina.

There are many more things which we ought to refrain from doing if we desire to conquer public Sentiment to our side; but I must hasten to the second part of my subject—the things which we Ought to Do for that end. In the first place, we ought to perform our present share in the world's work—the house-keeping, the house-adorning, the child-educating—so as to prove that, before we go a step further, we can and will at least do this. Before Political Economy comes the Economy of the Kitchen, the Larder, and the Coal-cellar; and before the national Budget the household weekly bills. I do not say that the wife, daughter, and sister who manages a house with perfect order and frugality, to the comfort of all in-dwellers, will thereby convince them of her right to the Suffrage; but I am quite sure, that if she neglect so to manage the house, or live in a despicable muddle of eternal strife with her servants, she will very completely prove her unfitness for any higher functions.

Next, we should, as much as possible, seek for employments of the kind for which we are suited, but which have been hitherto monopolized by men; and when we have chanced to obtain one, we should take good care not to lose it by fitful, irregular attendance, slovenly work, or any appeal whatever to special consideration as women. Secretaryships, clerkships, telegraph and post-office work, and especially work on the public press (wherein our influence can be direct, as well as indirect), are all objects of concern. I rejoiced much recently to see thirty charming young ladies, the daughters of professional men, at work in the Prudential Insurance Office on Ludgate Hill; and as many more painting porcelain for Messrs. Minton at South Kensington. Mr. Stansfeld's generous appointment of Mrs. Nassau Senior, to report to Government on the condition of pauper girls in London, and that lady's admirable performance of her task, will, I trust, lead ere long to the regular employment, by the State, of Female Inspectors of workhouses, schools, and asylums of all kinds wherein either women or children find refuge. I do not hesitate to say that one woman who does such work as this— even the humblest of those I have named—steadily and thoroughly, does at the same time more for the cause of Woman Suffrage than one who clamours for it most vehemently, but does nothing to prove the fitness of her sex for any public function.

Lastly, we must avail ourselves with the utmost care and conscientiousness of every fragment of Civil Rights which have hitherto been conceded to us. Not the election of a Poor Law Guardian or a parish Churchwarden, still less a municipal election, ought to pass without all the female ratepayers giving their votes, and showing that they do so intelligently, and after due enquiry. If it were possible for us to act in each locality mainly in concert—a committee of the more leisurely obtaining and transmitting the information needed—and everywhere upholding the best candidates, our action would in time come to be felt throughout the country. As to the School Board elections, had they been devised expressly as a prelude and preparation for women's entrance into political life, we could not have had anything better, and we must need regret that, as yet, they have been very inadequately utilized for such purpose. The ladies who have fought the good fight, and their generous male supporters, deserve from us the heartiest thanks, whether they have or have not proved successful.

CHANGING THE SENTIMENTS OF MEN

The sentiments of men about women must necessarily be formed on the characters of those with whom they associate. If a man's mother be a fool, and his sisters "Girls of the Period," and if he select for himself the society of ladies of the *demi-monde* [social class of dubious repute], or of that section of the *grand monde* [high society] which emulates the *demi-monde* as closely as it dares, it is quite obvious that when the abstract idea "Woman" is suggested to him, he will think of a creature in paint, powder, and chignon, whose breath of life is the admiration of men like himself, and who has no more heart, mind, or conscience than a broomstick. He will tell you, and tell you truly, that a woman—such as he knows the creature—loves nobody in earnest, but is ready to pretend to love anybody who will marry her and make her rich; that she is envious of all her female friends, especially the pretty ones; and that she has neither fixed religious nor political opinions, but only pretends ardently to adopt those which she thinks will commend her to the man whom she desires to attract. When I hear a man talk in a mode which implies that this is, at bottom, his idea of a woman, I always make a private memorandum regarding the quarter whence he must have directed his models; just as when I was a [student] of the Roman studios I knew precisely from which old beggarman on the steps of the Basilica Disanta [a Roman church built from 1172–1175] *Trinità* one painter had taken his "Jupiter," and from which damsel of uncertain morals another had copied his "Madonna Immacolata." Of course I am not afterwards surprised when such a man answers the demand for Woman Suffrage by such laughs as resound through the House of Commons when the subject is broached.

> Who would care for a doll, though its ringlets were
> curled
> And its petticoats cut in the fashion?

If women be dolls, none but children would play the farce of giving them political rights—in a Baby-house State. The only question is, Are they toys? Or is the opinion of the men who find (or make) them so, the one to be acted upon?

On the other hand, if a man's mother be a wise and loving woman, if his sisters be innocent-hearted and intelligent girls, and if he have associated in manhood from preference with good and sensible women, the notion which he forms of the other sex is absolutely the reverse of all I have described. He knows that a woman is capable of love—motherly, conjugal, sisterly—the purest, most disinterested, and most tender. He knows that, so far from being without fixed opinions, she is apt to hold those which she has early acquired with too rigid and narrow a prejudice; and that the ideas of duty and religion occupy commonly a far larger space in her mind than in those of the majority of his male companions. Lastly, by one curious test, his view of woman may always be discriminated from that of the man who has perferred to associate with the *Hetaira* [superior class of courtesans] order of female. He will know that, instead of being jealous of her associates, the true woman generally carries her loving admiration for the gifts and graces of her female friends to the verge of exaggeration, and glories in their achievements in educational competitions, in literature, and art, with a generous enthusiasm not often found among masculine rivals. He will take, for example, the letters published in [author Mary] Somerville's "Recollections," which passed between that lady and [her friends] Mrs. Marcet, Miss Edgworth, Miss Berry, and Mrs. Joanna Baillie—each expressing her warm delight in the other's gifts and successes—as precisely the most natural outcome of the feelings of woman of their class for one another.

To a man trained to think thus of women, the proposal that they should begin to take a part in public affairs, may indeed, at first seem startling, even offensive; but it will be because he has thought so highly of them, not so lowly. By degrees, perhaps, he will come to learn that the Niche does not make a Saint, and that Idleness is not the root of all good for women, while it is that of all evil for men. Possibly, at last, he will think as the devout [physician Jabez Baxter] Upham said at the close of his life—that, "since the coming of Christ, no event has promised so much for the virtue and happiness of the human race as the admission of Woman into a share of public duty.". . .

IDLE WOMEN

The great obstacle to the concession of the claims of women does not lie with men, for even those most opposed to them might be won over. Still less is it with busy women, for it has never happened to me yet to meet a woman who had done much work in the world as a philanthropist, artist, litterateur, or landed proprietor, who did not emphatically endorse the demand for the removal of those political disabilities which she had surely found at one point or another clog her steps. But the great obstacle lies with idle women, and nearly exclusively with those for whom nobody dreams of asking for the franchise—for the wives of rich men who have never known a want unsupplied, who have been surrounded by tenderness and homage from their cradles, and have lived all their days like little birds in a downy nest, with nothing to do but to open their beaks and find food dropped into them. It is to the eternal disgrace of such women that, instead of feeling burning shame and indignation at the wrongs and hardships which (as every newspaper shows them) their poorer sisters undergo, they think that, because the world is easy for them, it is "the best of all possible worlds," and that nothing ought to be changed in it. Like [executed French queen] Marie Antoinette, they tell those who want bread to live on buns; and they extol the advantages of the "chivalry" of men as ample compensation for the lack of every right, without once troubling themselves even to inquire whether the same "chivalrous" gentleman, who hands them so courteously into a carriage, will not rudely brush past the shabby old governess, or call up the poor work-girl's blushes by his insolent address. When the time comes . . . when the doors of the Constitution will be opened once more to welcome a new and still lower horde of Illiterates, by the assimilation of the County with the Borough Franchise, we shall, doubtless, again hear the oft-repeated assertion, that our legislators would gladly extend the privilege to women if they believed they really desired it; but that all the ladies whose opinions they have asked, vehemently repudiate the proposal. They might as well offer bread to an alderman at the end of a feast, and, because he declines it, refuse it to a pauper begging at the gate.

But, in spite of the rich and idle wives; and in spite of the men who think the archetypal woman was—not a Monkey—but a Doll; in spite of every obstacle, public Sentiment is unquestionably slowly veering round, and it depends on women themselves to bring it altogether to their favour. In this, as in all other things, however, to be is a much more important matter than to do. The walls of modern Jerichos [city destroyed by Israelites around 1400 B.C.] do not fall down by any trumpeting outside, and the more women shriek for the franchise, or for anything else, the less will men be disposed to open their ears to that extremely unpleasant sound. Let us cease to be silly, and affected, and idle. When we are ignorant, let us cultivate the grace of silence; and when we adorn ourselves, let us do so by the light of the "Lamps" of Truth and Simplicity. This achieved in the first place, let us become steady, diligent sharers in the world's work, creeping up by degrees as we prove our fitness for one higher task after another; never for a moment asking or wishing to have allowance made for our defects, or over-estimation of our success "because we are women." When a sufficient number of us have taken this method of gaining public Sentiment to favour the claims of our sex, the victory will be assured. We may lay by our darts and catapults. The Simoon will blow quite in the opposite direction.

THE SHERMAN ANTITRUST ACT

JOHN A. GARRATY

The growth of big businesses in the Gilded Age—loosely defined as 1866 to 1901—such as John D. Rockefeller's Standard Oil, led to the adoption by Congress in 1890 of the Sherman Antitrust Act. Sponsored by Senator John Sherman, the act was the first U.S. legislation created to curb concentrations of economic power, called trusts or monopolies, that restricted trade and reduced competition. Trusts and monopolies are considered injurious to the public and individuals because they minimize, if not eradicate, normal marketplace competition and produce outrageously high prices. In the following article, John A. Garraty discusses the Sherman Antitrust Act and its impact on American society and economy. Garraty is a lecturer at Columbia University in New York.

I n dealing with the big new manufacturing combinations, most Americans, and certainly most congressmen, continued to postulate that so long as competition existed, the economy would inevitably regulate itself in the public interest. Paradoxically, they exaggerated the extent to which "the trusts" had destroyed competition, and minimized the extent to which large-scale industry had ceased to respond in the old-fashioned way to competitive forces. Most critics interpreted the growth of large manufacturing combinations like [John D. Rockefeller's] Standard Oil Trust as a threat to competition and therefore to a self-regulating economy, not as a response to the changing character of the economic system. Their attack on trusts—profoundly conservative in motivation and philosophy—sought to restore competition on the theory that competition still worked in the simple, automatic way that the classical economists had described. This was at least partially untrue.

STATES TRY TO RESTORE COMPETITION

Although some early state constitutions prohibited business practices that restricted competition, important state antitrust activity began only in the late 1880's. When the public became aware of the trend toward industrial combination at this time, it demanded that the trend be reversed. This demand, however, while pervasive, was not especially intense. Most people had mixed feelings about big business; they took pride in its efficiency and grandeur, even admired the wealth, energy, and ingenuity of the great industrialists. The danger of monopoly remained largely hypothetical, since prices were not going up significantly at any time during the eighties. Most Americans objected to trusts in principle, just as they revered competition in the abstract, but few were suffering noticeably or directly. They wanted action but did not know exactly what they wanted done. By 1890, as a result of this situation, twenty-one states had attempted to "restore" competition either by incorporating antitrust clauses in their constitutions or by statute. These measures ranged from vague denunciations of monopoly to detailed laws spelling out illegal practices and imposing specific penalties upon violators. The Texas antitrust act of 1889 was among the most comprehensive, a "dragnet of great sweep and close mesh" outlawing combinations designed to restrict trade, control production or prices, and prevent competition.

These laws seldom had much effect, however, first because the states which enacted them were mostly in the South and West where few large industrial concerns existed, and second because they were laxly administered and extremely difficult to enforce. Since most combinations were engaged in interstate commerce, often, as in the case of Standard Oil, with facilities scattered over wide regions, state legislation could have only limited success at best.

BRINGING IN THE FEDS

The failure of state laws to reverse the trend toward consolidation, together with the evidence of trust malpractices uncovered by private researchers and by a number of legislative investigations, soon produced a movement for federal action. In 1884 the Republican party had ignored the trust problem and the Democrats had spoken only vaguely and without emphasis of the "prevention of monopoly" and the curbing of "corporate abuses." A national Antimonopoly party polled only 173,000 votes in the presidential election of that year. Four years later, however, the Republicans declared themselves opposed to "all combinations of capital organized in trusts" and the Democrats were equally outspoken. President Grover Cleveland claimed in 1888 that the people were being "trampled to death beneath [the] iron heel" of the trusts, and the next year his Republican successor, Benjamin Harrison, called trusts "dangerous conspiracies against the public good." Of course, these modest examples of the hyperbolic political rhetoric of the eighties do not prove that the voters were clamoring for a strong federal antitrust law. Nevertheless, the sudden shift in the attitude of the major parties suggests clearly that public opinion, alarmed by the growth of giant corporations, was moving rapidly in that direction.

The first federal antitrust bill was introduced in the House of Representatives in January, 1888; the first Senate proposal was submitted in May. The House measure, and fifteen similar bills, never got out of committee. In the Senate, a bill drafted by Senator John Sherman of Ohio, which declared unlawful all arrangements between persons or corporations that tended to restrict competition or increase prices, was extensively debated, but did not come to a vote.

Over the next two years both houses struggled with a large number of proposals and counterproposals dealing with the trust problem. No significant party division emerged during these debates. Some congressmen raised serious constitutional objections. . . . A number of legislators expressed genuine concern lest, as Senator George F. Hoar of Massachusetts put it, "some crude, hasty legislation which does not cure the evil" be adopted. But finally, in June, 1890, a bill known as the Sherman Antitrust Act was passed with only one dissenting vote in the entire Congress.

PROVISIONS OF THE SHERMAN ANTITRUST ACT
In sweeping terms this law declared illegal "every contract, combination in the form of trust or otherwise, or conspiracy, in restraint of trade or commerce among the several States, or with foreign nations." Persons who made such agreements or who

"monopolize or attempt to monopolize" such commerce were subject to fines of up to $1,000 and jail terms of up to one year. Furthermore, any private individual who was "injured in his business or property" by persons or corporations violating the act was authorized to sue for triple damages in the federal circuit courts. Thus the law made combinations in restraint of trade both public and private offenses.

That so broad-gauged a law attacking such powerful interests could pass in a predominantly conservative Congress by such an overwhelming vote seems on the surface difficult to explain. Some historians have concluded that a massive explosion of public wrath compelled Congress to act. Others, focusing on the vagueness of the law and seizing upon such evidence as the well-known remark of Senator Orville H. Platt of Connecticut that his colleagues were only looking for "some bill headed: 'A Bill to Punish Trusts' with which to go to the country" have concluded that Congress was engaging in the most cynical kind of politicking and had no intention of actually inhibiting the combination movement. Still others have suggested that the bill went through easily because the lawmakers, not yet greatly concerned about industrial concentration, considered it of minor importance.

Each of these explanations has a superficial plausibility. The trend toward monopoly had been widely denounced by reformers, farm organizations, and other critics. Many members of Congress were unblushing admirers of big business. The measure received much less attention than a number of trivial bills; excited no partisan divisions; was passed after being considerably revised in committee almost without discussion. Actually, these interpretations do not seriously contradict one another. The public was aroused but unclear about what should be done. Congressmen felt compelled to move against the trusts but did not want to *injure* business. Few persons expected the Sherman Act to produce drastic results.

Probably the act won such easy acceptance because it made no fundamental change in business law. Conspiracies in restraint of trade and attempts to create monopolies were already technically illegal. Under English and American common law these practices were considered against public policy and many statutes imposed punishments on those who engaged in them. Although judicial definitions of restraint and monopoly shifted from time to time, by the nineteenth century the idea that competition was desirable, monopoly dangerous, had become, it is fair to say, part of western culture. In America the additional principle that corporations could be controlled by the states which chartered them was also well established. What the Sherman Act did essentially was to empower the *federal* government (which had been concerned neither with interpreting the common law nor with the chartering of corporations) to enforce these same general principles. Senator Hoar explained the matter succinctly during the debates: "We have affirmed the old doctrine of the common law . . . and have clothed the United States courts with authority to enforce that doctrine . . . undertaking to curb by national authority an evil which under all our legislative precedents and policies, has been left to be dealt with either by the ordinary laws of trade or . . . by the States."

COMPETITION WAS WIDELY FAVORED

Some Americans feared the new industrial combinations like the plague; others thought them both inevitable and beneficial. Men disagreed about the character of individual trusts and individual business practices. However, Congress and the country were convinced that monopolies ought not to exist totally unchecked and, as we have seen, most observers still believed that competition provided the simplest and most effective method of balancing contending economic forces. Senator Sherman's first antitrust resolution defined the common objective clearly: "To preserve freedom of trade and production, the natural competition of increasing production, the lowering of prices by such competition." In the course of the debate only one congressman, Senator William Stewart of Nevada, a man of small influence, challenged this purpose; others who objected to the various bills did so on constitutional grounds or because they believed specific remedies unworkable.

The weaknesses of the law, most notably its failure to define such terms as restraint of trade and monopoly precisely and its reliance upon Congress' power to regulate interstate commerce to justify federal action, stemmed from genuine constitutional problems and from the fact that the terms were difficult to define. By leaving the interpretation of the law to the courts, Congress was only following centuries of precedent in this area. In any case, to have spelled out every undesirable business practice would have been impossible, given the complex and dynamic conditions of that day. Disturbed and baffled by the growth of trusts, Congress settled for a restatement of old principles and the mobilization of a new force, the federal judiciary, to defend them, fully conscious that it did not know what the exact result would be. "Mr. Speaker," an Arkansas congressman declared at one point, "I am willing to give my sanction to this bill . . . filled with doubts, yet compelled by a sense of the exigency and the emergency of the occasion to do whatever seems best."

Congress could have attacked the trust problem in other ways—for instance, by changing the patent laws, or by reducing tariffs, or by compelling federal incorporation of large enterprises under strict controls. The method it chose bore little immediate fruit. In the decade of the nineties, the executive branch instituted only a handful of antitrust suits and in 1895 the Supreme Court sharply limited the scope of the Sherman Act by deciding, in *U.S. v. E.C. Knight Company,* that monopolization of the manufacturing of an article by a single combine did not constitute restraint of interstate commerce *per se,* even if the goods later entered into such commerce. The inadequacy of the Sherman Act, however, resulted only partly from the way it was interpreted and executed. The competitive system it sought to buttress was at once less threatened and less effective than the framers of the law had imagined. After 1890 the trend toward industrial combination continued, but so did industrial competition. Soon a battalion of colossi bestrode the industrial world, but it was not a narrow world that these Caesars could really dominate—the expanding American economy bore the weight of the big trusts handily, if not entirely without strain.

Eventually men learned that competition worked less perfectly than they had believed. Then they found supplementary means of regulating business affairs and enforcing a modicum of economic justice. In the early 1890's, however, both understanding and adjustment, along with much travail, lay still in the future. Nevertheless, by that time the basis of the modern American industrial system had been firmly established. We must now consider some of the by-products of this development.

1850

In September, the Compromise of 1850 is established; California is admitted into the Union as a free state; a tougher Fugitive Slave Law is enacted; the slave trade is halted in the District of Columbia; and popular sovereignty, a policy that gives citizens the power to determine whether their territories will be free or slave, is declared in the territories of Utah and New Mexico.

1851

The first Fort Laramie Treaty between the U.S. government and various Great Plains Indian tribes is signed.

1852

Harriet Beecher Stowe writes *Uncle Tom's Cabin,* which indicts not only slavery but Northern complicity in it. Still, the book is an immediate popular success in the North; it causes great alarm in the South.

1854

The Kansas-Nebraska Act is passed, voiding the Missouri Compromise of 1820 and possibly extending slavery into territories north of 36°30' latitude under the doctrine of popular sovereignty.

1857

The *Dred Scott* decision is handed down; the incendiary Supreme Court decision declares that blacks are not citizens and that neither the states nor the federal government can prevent the extension of slavery.

1858

The Lincoln-Douglas debates take place in Illinois, where Democrat Stephen A. Douglas's Senate seat is at stake. Also at stake is the issue of slavery expansion; Abraham

Lincoln argues for free soil and Douglas offers popular sovereignty.

1859

White abolitionist John Brown's raid on Harpers Ferry occurs; designed to lead to a general slave uprising, it ends in failure and in Brown's execution.

The first oil well is drilled by Edwin L. Drake near Titusville, Pennsylvania; within four years, three hundred firms are competing to drill, refine, and sell petroleum.

1860

Abraham Lincoln is elected president of the United States.

South Carolina begins the South's secession from the Union, which culminates in February 1861 in the establishment of the Confederacy.

1861

The Civil War begins on April 12, when Fort Sumter is attacked by Confederate troops.

On July 21, the First Battle of Bull Run is fought at Manassas, Virginia.

1862

The Homestead Act, which grants free public land to settlers, is signed by Lincoln.

The Confederate Congress passes a conscription law that requires most able-bodied men between the ages of eighteen and thirty-five to sign up for military service.

The Union army is defeated at the Second Battle of Bull Run.

The Battle of Antietam, the single bloodiest day of the war, is fought without a conclusive victory for either side.

1863

President Lincoln signs the Emancipation Proclamation.

The U.S. Congress passes a conscription act.

Confederate soldiers celebrate a victory at Chancellorsville.

The Confederacy suffers a devastating loss at Gettysburg.

Union forces succeed at Vicksburg.

Lincoln delivers his famous Gettysburg Address.

1864

Congress passes a law providing equal pay for black and white soldiers.

General William T. Sherman captures Atlanta, Georgia.

Lincoln is reelected to the presidency.

1865

Confederate general Robert E. Lee surrenders to Union general Ulysses S. Grant at Appomattox Courthouse in Virginia.

Congress establishes the Bureau for Refugees, Freedmen, and Abandoned Lands, known as the Freedmen's Bureau.

President Lincoln is assassinated by John Wilkes Booth.

Vice President Andrew Johnson takes the oath of the presidency.

Mississippi becomes the first state to enact a Black Code; most other Southern states soon follow suit.

The Thirteenth Amendment is ratified.

The first steel rails are manufactured in Chicago.

1866

Overriding a presidential veto, Congress passes the Civil Rights Act of 1866.

Elizabeth Cady Stanton becomes the first woman candidate for Congress.

1867

Congress passes the First, Second, and Third Reconstruction Acts over presidential vetoes.

1868

On February 24, the House of Representatives votes 126-47 to impeach President Johnson.

On May 28, the Senate acquits Johnson of high crimes and misdemeanors.

The Fourteenth Amendment is ratified.

Ulysses S. Grant is elected president.

Conceding defeat to Sioux Indians under Red Cloud, the United States agrees to withdraw from forts on the Bozeman Trail.

In the Battle of Washita, U.S. troops under the command of George Armstrong Custer slaughter Chief Black Kettle and his band of Cheyenne Indians, including women and children.

The Working Woman's Association is established.

Congress mandates the eight-hour day for public works projects.

1869

The nation's first transcontinental railroad is completed.

Elizabeth Cady Stanton and Susan B. Anthony establish the National Woman Suffrage Association to work for a national suffrage amendment.

The labor organization, Knights of Labor, is founded.

1870

The Fifteenth Amendment is ratified.

John D. Rockefeller organizes the Standard Oil Company; by 1879, the corporation owns or controls more than 90 percent of the country's oil-refining capacity.

1871

The first black representatives to the U.S. Congress (Joseph H. Rainey, Robert DeLarge, Robert Brown Elliott, Benjamin S. Turner, and Josiah T. Walls) take their seats.

Congress formally votes to end treaty-making with any Indian tribe.

1872

The Freedmen's Bureau is allowed to expire, and the bureau is dissolved.

1873

The failure of a major banking firm triggers the Panic of 1873, an economic depression that lasts for five years.

Andrew Carnegie opens his steelworks in Pittsburgh, Pennsylvania.

1874

Custer leads an expedition that discovers gold in the Black Hills in territory promised to the Sioux.

1875

Congress passes the Civil Rights Act of 1875, which outlaws segregation.

1876

Custer and all of his troops are killed by Sioux and Cheyenne Indians at the Battle of Little Bighorn.

1877

The Compromise of 1877 secures Republican Rutherford B. Hayes's claim to the presidency in exchange for the return of home rule to the South.

The war against the Nez Percé ends with the surrender of Chief Joseph.

Strikes spread throughout the nation's railways as workers protest wage reductions; two-thirds of the nation's railroads are paralyzed. The strike is broken by federal troops at the cost of one hundred lives.

1882

Rockefeller reorganizes Standard Oil into the first industrial "trust."

1883

The Supreme Court declares the Civil Rights Act of 1875 unconstitutional, opening the way for the passage of numerous "Jim Crow" laws.

1886

Geronimo and his band of Apache surrender to General Nelson Miles.

On May 4, seven police officers are killed when a bomb explodes at a political gathering in Chicago's Haymarket Square. Eight anarchists are later arrested, tried, and convicted.

The American Federation of Labor is founded.

1887

The Dawes Act, designed to break up the tribal system and convert Indians into farmers, is passed.

Congress passes the Interstate Commerce Act, establishing the nation's first independent government regulatory body, which is empowered to regulate railroad rates.

1890

Sitting Bull is killed on the Standing Rock Reservation in South Dakota.

Big Foot's band of Sioux is massacred by U.S. soldiers at Wounded Knee Creek.

The U.S. Census reports that, for the first time in American history, manufacturing output is greater in dollar value than agricultural production.

Responding to growing public outcry against trusts, Congress
passes the Sherman Antitrust Act, making arrangements
"in restraint of trade" illegal.

1892

The Supreme Court orders the dissolution of the Standard Oil
trust; the corporation is reorganized in New Jersey as a
holding company.

1893

Colorado grants women the vote.
An economic depression sets in motion four years of hard
times across the country.

1895

In *U.S. v. E.C. Knight*, the Supreme Court rules that the Sherman Antitrust Act does not apply to manufacturing.

=FOR FURTHER RESEARCH=

ANTEBELLUM AMERICA

Henrietta Buckmaster, *Flight to Freedom*. New York: Crowell, 1856.

Lydia Maria Child, *The Duty of Disobedience to the Fugitive Slave Act*. Westport, CT: Negro Universities Press, 1970.

Arthur Charles Cole, *The Irrepressible Conflict, 1850–1865*. New York: Macmillan, 1934.

Avery Odelle Craven, *The Coming of the Civil War*. Chicago: University of Chicago Press, 1957.

E.N. Elliott, *Cotton Is King and Pro-Slavery Arguments*. New York: Johnson Reprint, 1968.

Don E. Fehrenbacher, *The Dred Scott Case*. New York: Oxford University Press, 1978.

Ludwell H. Johnson, *Division and Reunion*. New York: Wiley, 1978.

Samuel May, *The Fugitive Slave Law and Its Victims*. New York: American Anti-Slavery Society, 1856.

James Ford Rhodes, *History of the United States from the Compromise of 1850*. London: Macmillan, 1893.

Robert Royal Russel, *Antebellum Studies in Slavery, Politics, and the Railroads*. Kalamazoo: Western Michigan University Press, 1960.

Elbert B. Smith, *The Death of Slavery*. Chicago: University of Chicago Press, 1967.

THE CIVIL WAR

William L. Barney, *Flawed Victory*. New York: Praeger, 1975.

E. Merton Coulter, *The Confederate States of America, 1861– 1865*. Baton Rouge: Louisiana State University Press, 1950.

Richard Ernest Dupuy and Trevor N. Dupuy, *The Compact History of the Civil War*. New York: Hawthorn, 1960.

Keith Ellis, *The American Civil War*. New York: Putnam, 1971.

Jeffrey Rogers Hummel, *Emancipating Slaves, Enslaving Free Men*. Chicago: Open Court, 1996.

Reid Mitchell, *The American Civil War, 1861–1865*. New York: Longman, 2001.

John G. Nicolay, *Abraham Lincoln*. New York: Century, 1890.

Francis Winthrop Palfrey, *The Antietam and Fredericksburg*. New York: Scribner's, 1882.

Charles Pierce Roland, *An American Iliad*. Lexington: University of Kentucky Press, 1991.

Charles Royster, *The Destructive War*. New York: Random House, 1991.

Emory M. Thomas, *The American War and Peace, 1860–1877*. Englewood Cliffs, NJ: Prentice-Hall, 1973.

Charles Willis Thompson, *The Fiery Epoch, 1830–1877*. Indianapolis, IN: Bobbs-Merrill, 1931.

RECONSTRUCTION

William Ranulf Brock, *An American Crisis*. New York: St. Martin's Press, 1963.

Hodding Carter, *The Angry Scar*. Garden City, NY: Doubleday, 1959.

Eric Foner and Olivia Mahoney, *America's Reconstruction*. Baton Rouge: Louisiana State University Press, 1997.

Stanley Fitzgerald Horn, *Invisible Empire*. Cos Cob, CT: J.E. Edwards, 1969.

Milton Lomask, *Andrew Johnson: President on Trial*. New York: Farrar, Straus, 1960.

John Roy Lynch, *The Facts of Reconstruction*. New York: Arno, 1968.

Scott Reynolds Nelson, *Iron Confederacies*. Chapel Hill: University of North Carolina Press, 1999.

Paul Skeels Peirce, *The Freedmen's Bureau*. Iowa City, IA: University, 1904.

Green Berry Raum, *The Existing Conflict Between Republican Government and Southern Oligarchy*. New York: Negro Universities Press, 1969.

Jim Ruiz, *The Black Hood of the Ku Klux Klan*. San Francisco: Austin & Winfield, 1998.

Richard Taylor, *Destruction and Reconstruction*. New York: DaCapo Press, 1995.

J.T. Trowbridge, *The Desolate South, 1865–1866*. New York: Duell, Sloan, and Pearce, 1956.

NATIVE AMERICANS

Alan Axelrod, *Chronicle of the Indian Wars*. New York: Prentice-Hall, 1993.

Angie Debo, *A History of the Indians of the United States*. Norman: University of Oklahoma Press, 1970.

Arrell Morgan Gibson, *The American Indian*. Lexington, MA: D.C. Heath, 1980.

William Thomas Hagan, *The Indian in American History*. New York: Macmillan, 1963.

Charles Hamilton, *Cry of the Thunderbird*. Norman: University of Oklahoma Press, 1972.

Mark A. Lindquist and Martin Zanger, *Buried Roots and Indestructible Seeds*. Madison: University of Wisconsin Press, 1994.

William Christie McCleod, *The American Indian Frontier*. London: Dawson's, 1968.

J. Walker McSpadden, *Indian Heroes*. New York: Crowell, 1950.

Lee Miller, *From the Heart*. New York: Knopf, 1995.

Woodward B. Skinner, *The Apache Rock Crumbles*. Pensacola, FL: Skinner, 1987.

Frank Waters, *Brave Are My People*. Athens, OH: Swallow, 1998.

James Wilson, *The Earth Shall Weep*. New York: Atlantic Monthly, 1999.

THE GILDED AGE

Richard A. Bartlett, *The Gilded Age*. Reading, MA: Addison-Wesley, 1969.

Fon Wyman Boardman, *America and the Gilded Age, 1876–1900*. New York: H.Z. Walck, 1972.

H.W. Brands, *The Reckless Decade*. New York: St. Martin's Press, 1995.

Charles W. Calhoun, *The Gilded Age*. Upper Saddle River, NJ: Prentice-Hall, 1997.

John E. Findling and Frank W. Thackeray, *Events That Changed America in the Nineteenth Century*. Westport, CT: Greenwood, 1997.

John A. Garraty, *The New Commonwealth, 1877–1890*. New York: Harper & Row, 1968.

Morton Keller, *Affairs of State*. Cambridge, MA: Harvard University Press, 1977.

Randall William Peirce, *Centennial*. Philadelphia: Chilton, 1969.

Don Carlos Seitz, *The Dreadful Decade*. New York: Greenwood, 1968.

Page Smith, *The Rise of Industrial America*. New York: McGraw-Hill, 1984.

Mark Wahlgren Summers, *The Gilded Age*. Upper Saddle River, NJ: Prentice-Hall, 1997.

Alan Weinstein, *Origins of Modern America*. New York: Random House, 1970.